A Journey for Happiness

The Man Who Cycled to Bhutan

CHRISTOPHER BOYCE

Wishing you joy, peace,
and happiness of all kinds
on your own journey
Christopher
Boyce

DEKYID

First published by Dekyid 2022

ISBN: 978-1-7399990-0-1 (PBK)
ISBN: 978-1-7399990-1-8 (HBK)

Printed and bound by Bell & Bain Ltd., Glasgow.

Typeset in 10.5 point Sabon by Main Point Books, Edinburgh.

Cover design by Katie Sykes.

Contents

For Father and for Soul,
for without either there wouldn't be much of a life

PROLOGUE

A moment for all moments

It had been close to 500 days since I'd left Scotland on my bicycle and, as I sat in my tent watching the sun set over the Himalayas, the tears began their delicate flow.

I never expected it to be like this. Not even close. And I was certain that it was this way because I had let go of all expectations about how things would finally end up on this journey. Although, as I glanced back many months ago to the moment in which I took a last look at the small flat and closed the door on my unhappy life, I couldn't have hoped for this. I certainly hadn't written about it in my career researching happiness, let alone read much about this sort of thing. This had been far beyond me.

Within the mountains I was gazing at, I could feel all the mountains I had climbed to get to this moment. I could feel all the roads that had led me here – the lonely roads that had stretched out beyond horizons, and the busy roads that hadn't led anywhere I'd much wanted to go. So many wrong turns, dead ends, and plain difficult days.

Also with me were the smiles of all the strangers I'd chanced upon along the way. From quick glimpses as I passed through remote villages or enormous cities, right up to the strangers who hadn't stayed strange for long, stretching beyond themselves to help me a little further along the way. I could sense all of them in this moment. And besides the mountains, the roads and the people, there were all the challenges and all the heartaches that I had ever faced up until this point in my life. Everything was present in its own big and small way; because, like all moments, and all the things having those moments, they are all intricately linked. They have to be – and in ways that we will never have an explanation for – each moment unfolding from the one before, going right back to the start.

If any part of my journey had been just slightly different, then I wouldn't have been in this exact moment, one which I will cherish forever. A moment that has been a crucial part of everything that has taken place ever since. It has helped me maintain some peace, and some hope, when everything around me is in chaos. Perhaps the profundity of what I experienced there and then was what my journey had been building up to all along? It felt so. For a very brief moment of my very brief life, there was nothing but pure and unadulterated bliss.

On the surface, this book is about how I came to be in such a moment – the ridiculous irony that propelled me to set out to an obscure destination on a bicycle; the friends and the foes I encountered along the way; the challenges, some of which had me fearing for my life; and the sheer delight of travelling the world with nothing more than can be hauled about on a bicycle.

There is no shortage of action and adventure in what follows, but this book goes much deeper than that. It has to. Because this is about happiness – yours, mine, ours. A state of being that we all rightfully long for. Through an epic cycle journey, with a few extra stories thrown in, *A Journey for Happiness* explores what it will take for us all to be a little happier in this world of ours.

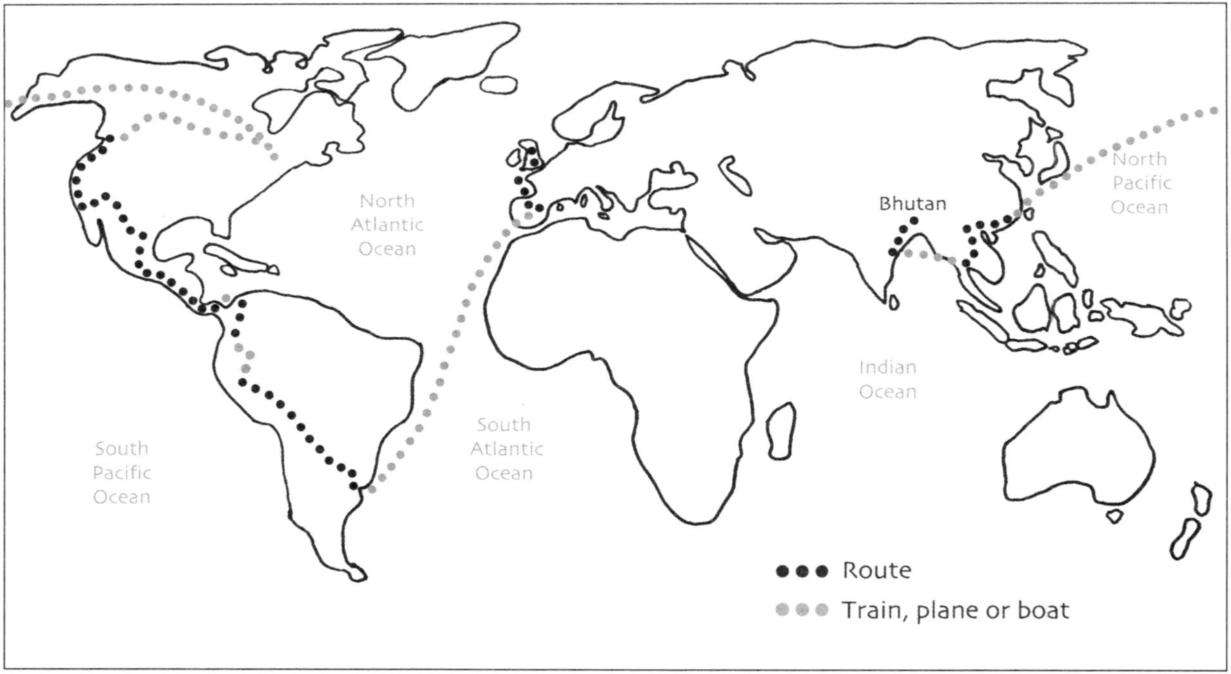

A Journey for Happiness route overview: From Scotland to Bhutan

CHAPTER 1

A journey for happiness begins…

"When I was five years old, my mother always told me that ***happiness*** *was the key to life. When I went to school, they asked me what I wanted to be when I grew up. I wrote down '****happy****'. They told me I didn't understand the assignment, and I told them they didn't understand life."*
Attributed to John Lennon

There was something about the orange carpet beneath me. I loved the way it swirled in different shades of orange from nearly brown to nearly yellow. It was mesmerising. I could gaze at it for hours at a time, especially when the sun shone directly onto it through the window. It felt soft underfoot and, despite what was happening outside, it nearly always brought a reassuring warmth to the small room that I inhabited back then. To my five-year-old self it was a very magical carpet. It would greet me as I woke up each day, and invoke within me a fascination and joy at being alive.

Back then, I would have struggled to put words around how I felt and why, because there wasn't much to compare and contrast my life with, yet I now recognise that what I was experiencing then was a special kind of happiness. Not a regular kind of happiness, only about smiles and laughter. That is an important kind of happiness, but it is impossible to hold onto. No, the kind of happiness I had back then was a deep and fulfilling kind, where just being myself seemed to be enough. Perhaps you've felt it at least at some point in your life; maybe when you were also really young, and more protected from the inexplicable musts and mustn'ts of this world. For me it is the most precious thing in the world – it always has been and always will be.

The quote with which I began this chapter has been attributed to John Lennon. It's not clear whether he actually said it or not, but it is, without doubt, my favourite quote about happiness. I imagine it being the sort of thing I could have said when I was a five-year-old. I am sure it resonates with a lot of people, and how they may have felt at some point in their lives when they were younger versions of themselves. I think it speaks to a fundamental truth about the purpose of our human existence. A truth that we may one day realise we have completely forgotten. Or, much worse, in our desperate longing for a happier life, we may realise we've been taken down a path of false hopes and broken promises.

Humble beginnings

Back when I was five, we lived in a humble three-bedroom terraced house. Maybe it was a bit of a squeeze being a family of five, plus a cat, a hamster, and some fish, but I never remember thinking there was a shortage of space. It certainly didn't bother me. It was quite the opposite. I loved it! I shared a bedroom with my younger brother, for whom I felt unwavering affection. I had the top bunk, he the bottom, and I would feel comforted to know I was not alone. If I ever woke at night, I'd only need to look below to see the swirly-orange carpet and my little brother sleeping peacefully, and I'd feel at ease. We had a back garden too. It was small but there was enough grass for us to play together upon.

We weren't poor; we weren't rich either – not that I had any conception of what those words could possibly have meant at that tender age. All I ever knew was what I encountered in my daily life, and that, for the most part, felt good. There were no comparisons, it was just life as I knew it; and I was certain that

I had all I needed.

My Mum stayed at home to look after my brother, an older sister, and me, and it was a safe and stable world that included visits to the local park or shops, as well as the odd play group. My Dad stepped out before sunrise each day to go to work as a milkman. He'd normally come back tired, with a curious milk odour about him. He'd then sit on his chair in front of the television, and I'd watch as his large and worn-out hands attended to his milkman books. These books were well-thumbed through, dirty around the edges, and bigger than my head. Dad had a long thin pencil with a distinct detachable rubber on its end. He would meticulously rub numbers out of his books and then etch in new ones, muttering things under his breath. I didn't really understand what he was doing or why, but I was captivated. He'd often fall asleep on his chair by mid-afternoon in front of the television; and that was Dad.

I would wonder what it was like being my Dad. There was always a mystery to his life. Not only because he went somewhere I didn't know about each day, but also because there seemed an unwillingness to share what was happening in his world. He must have been weighed down by the pressures of having to support a bigger than average family on a modest and sometimes unreliable income.

Bigger, better, shinier, faster

We make most of our decisions because we hope they will someday make ourselves and the people we love happier. That was probably why my Mum stayed at home, and my Dad went to work. I was fortunate in those early years that my parents could and did incubate us in time, rather than in money. It is a rare and difficult thing to have a parent able to give full-time childcare on a low to medium income. I suppose it was the desire to improve the family's wellbeing that was why, not long before I turned six, we moved to a new house. It was much bigger. When I first visited it, I remember thinking that it was the sort of house I could surely get lost in.

The house needed a lot of work, which, as it turned out, would end up keeping my Dad very busy over the years when he wasn't working. Yet, we now had four bedrooms. That meant that each of us children would be able to have our own room. It felt exciting. I remember walking from school with my Dad to this new house for the first time, wide-eyed with curiosity. I think we all felt hopeful, even expectant.

Of course, in those days, owning your own home was supposed to signify something important. It represented that you had truly arrived in the world, and were firmly on your way up in life. An esteemed member of society. Back then, borrowing large amounts of money to get onto the property ladder was quickly becoming tattled as a necessity for any self-respecting family.

Our new house was a real stretch for a family of modest means. It signified middle-class, and we weren't that; and so to afford the large mortgage repayments something had to change. Mum went to work as a cleaner at the local school where my older sister and I were now going. As for my Dad, with milk delivery slowly becoming less popular, with the rise in the use of the car and out-of-town supermarkets, he became a window cleaner. He'd clean the windows of many of the people he'd previously delivered milk to. It paid a little more, but judging from the increased arguments that I was hearing about money, it wasn't enough. It also seemed like more difficult work for him, especially in those cold and wet winter months.

There was never any question as to whether this new lifestyle would improve our lives or not: of course it would. Though it didn't; not for me. I felt really cold in that house, and lonely too, with all the space we had. I have several painful memories of sitting huddled up someplace, often hidden from others and shivering. I didn't like having my own room either. It was small and drafty, with no swirly-orange carpet, and noisy from the large volume of traffic that passed by my window night and day. There was less family time too, as everyone became busier, and we all seemed to become more possessive of space – less ours and more mines. Happiness seemed to have become something we each individually pursued, doing battle for, rather than sharing. There never seemed quite enough happiness to go around, and there was resentment when one family member had it, and another didn't.

As a tiny being, I tried to make sense of this new world I found myself in, but I could not. Part of me wonders whether I ought to have been happier, as I was so often told I should be. Apparently, I was supposed to count myself lucky – because others had it much worse than I. I felt guilty for not being grateful enough for everything my parents were trying to do. I thought that I was to blame, and that there was something wrong with me for not being happy, as others said I ought to be.

Not long after the move, as I sought to adjust to the new life we had taken on, my behaviour shifted and became less acceptable to my parents. In the face of increasing discipline, I began to conceal my real feelings – at first from others, but eventually from my own self. That's a sad thing, because I know now that to be happy, we have to be in connection with the full spectrum of our emotions – our emotions can help us, including the difficult ones. Children – in fact all of us – need help in understanding these emotions.

Something important got lost in that big house. As a family we lost our cohesion; we lost our way. We caved into the expectations of our time and culture, in terms of what someone with a good life was supposed to have. It was easy to do back then, much as it still is today. We want bigger, better, shinier, and faster, because we believe it will improve the quality of our lives and bring us happiness. That these things will complete what feels like an incomplete self. But where do those beliefs come from? I know I wasn't born with them. Yet, in hearing constantly from others that we really do need bigger, better, shinier, and faster – be it from our friends, justifying luxuries of their own, politicians making promises, stories in the news, and those trusty salespeople with their bombardment of seductive advertisements – it is no surprise that we come to adopt such beliefs.

We have our personal experiences too, whereby we finally obtain something we've longed for. We may experience something of a pleasure, but that pleasure is rarely as deep and prolonged as we were led to believe or hoped it would be – just a fleeting happiness, rather than anything deeper. It comes, and then it goes, leaving behind a craving for still more. And of course, we have to pay for these things somehow, and that often means working longer hours in jobs that are rarely fulfilling. It hardly ever seemed worth it to me. I often wonder whether it was the pain I felt as a child, when we moved from a small modest house to a big unaffordable one, that was crucial to me making an academic career for myself trying to understand the role of the economy in increasing people's happiness. As Rumi, the Sufi mystic, poet, and philosopher, said: "The wound is the place where the light enters you."

A happiness researcher in training

Whilst my home life wasn't always happy, I did well at school. Very well. My ability to learn what I was being taught met the approval of others, and I relished the attention that I received. I felt safe at school, and my teacher would smile at me each time I completed a worksheet, which was normally much quicker than anyone else. The delight I saw in my teacher's eyes spurred me on to want to learn more about the world around me. People and Mathematics interested me the most. Maths, because I was just uncannily good at it, and as for people, well, I was very curious about them. Why do we do the things we do? At that age I was already baffled by what I saw.

Why did people so often do things that seemed to achieve the very opposite of what they claimed to want from life? I felt confused as to why my Dad would bellow at me that "We aren't paying to heat the streets", whenever I left the back door open. Yet, he wouldn't scold himself at all each time he did it, which, as I carefully observed, was much more often than I. I could never understand why my Mum always said she would start a food diet on a Monday – following a weekend in which she had first indulged in all the things that she said were never to be part of her diet again – only to cave into something by Friday; and then the process would repeat the next week. I also couldn't understand how some people, with seemingly less money than us, managed to visit and have fun in hot countries every year, whereas we always ended up arguing in a caravan in Swanage.

People don't behave rationally. They don't behave as they are supposed to, at least according to the Economics that I began studying at age 14. Economics combined Maths and people, which meant that it was a perfect way to satisfy my interests back then. I was seduced by the ease with which complex human behaviour could be explained using simplistic mathematical models. Humans, I was assured, are innately selfish; desire increases in their own happiness, and they make rational decisions, such as always wanting more rather than less. At the time, given my experiences and no other alternatives to explain what I saw, I thought these principles represented humans quite well. Particularly the one about desiring more happiness.

However, I was puzzled as to why in my home, as the years went on and we acquired more things, we never got any happier. Sure, there'd be moments of pleasure, but it was more like temporary relief from a life that, on the whole, wasn't particularly fulfilling. If we kept purchasing stuff, then we'd get more temporary relief from the drudgery. Yet, once all that temporary relief had expired, we wouldn't be left with much, except another thing to tuck quietly into the corner of a house that was too big. We certainly didn't experience a sustained improvement in our state of wellbeing. There was always stress and strain, and most of that stress and strain came from a lack of money. If only we had more of it, to pay for the things we thought we needed. There were always bills to be paid. "All this," my father would say to me angrily, "has to be paid for, and money doesn't grow on trees." It was a struggle to reach the next paycheque. We were always skint. The mantra was,

"If only we had just a little more, then we'd be okay." Yet, we never were okay. There were arguments. No-one listened or tried anything different. All it came to in the end was just debts and unhappiness.

Yet, could I really compare my personal experiences with centuries of economic thinking? It had to be that my family were just odd. A rare exception to the norm. As my experience of the world increased, I realised that my family and many of my experiences in childhood were no exception. It was typical. Many of us will act as if having bigger, better, faster, shinier will bring sustained happiness, yet it rarely does. Sadly, as I now understand from the happiness career I would come to embark upon, in trying to obtain bigger, better, faster, shinier we will often make sacrifices to other areas of our lives – areas in which we are much more likely to find sustained happiness. Of course, most people know this, at least deep down.

Still, what else can we really do? It seems to be what everybody else is doing, so there has to be something in it. There must be. And we are bombarded with hundreds of messages each day, suggesting something or other will solve a problem that we have. Often it is a problem we didn't know we had until it was framed that way. Then comes a firm belief that we do really need that thing to solve whatever that 'problem' is. One day, once we've had that thing for a while, we'll begin to think we couldn't possibly live without it. (Not like we did, just as happily, before we knew this 'problem' ever entered into our heads.) It is difficult to fight the defunct economic theory that grips our daily lives.

Despite my early puzzlement with Economics, I ended up taking my economic studies very seriously. I found myself at university, being the first in my family to go, and I went on to obtain both a Bachelor's and a Master's degree in Economics. I surprised a lot of people, none more so than myself. Basically, it turned out that I was very good at it, and there was a good chance I'd have a 'successful' career. I still enjoyed trying to understand people, and I could just about do the Maths. It was when I began a PhD in Economics that things got too ridiculous. I felt so surprised that the supposedly advanced economic theory I was being taught still did not bear witness in the actions of those around me, let alone myself. I began to feel angry, like I had been cheated all these years into believing something I knew, in the depths of me, was false. What I was being forced to learn to 'tick the box' so that I would be considered an expert on the economy seemed like complete and utter nonsense. I was, by this point, also much more confident questioning existing knowledge, and I was beginning to play with my own ideas about what a life well-lived felt like.

Re-discovering happiness

I've always been much better at knowing what I don't want to do than what I need to do. Most of my life decisions have arisen because whatever I was doing at the time brought enduring unhappiness. Whether it be my struggles with alcohol (more on this later), being in a turbulent relationship, or my difficulty at home as a child, it has been my clarity around knowing these have not been bringing me happiness that has motivated my choice into doing something – anything – different. Much more so than me having any clear idea of what that 'something else' might be. Sometimes we know we just have to get out of what we're in. And hopefully we have enough support around us so that we can.

When I was just a few months into my Economics PhD, I went along to my supervisor, adamant that I wanted to quit. My PhD supervisor seemed to take my explanation as to why in his stride. He was, and still is, one of the leading scholars in what was the then burgeoning field of Happiness Economics. Much of his own research into economic growth and happiness contested established economic theory, and so he seemed to completely understand my difficulty.[1] It also seemed very apparent that he didn't want to lose me as a student so easily. I think he probably saw something important – that I didn't then value – in my willingness to take unconventional steps to question the established order of things.

He told me that there were other options besides me quitting my PhD completely. I could move to the business school, for instance, or perhaps to Psychology. At the mere mention of Psychology, I experienced a resounding surge within my body. The field had long interested me, and I'd already begun reading how psychological insights were increasingly being used in Economics. I'd also lived with a couple of psychologists back in my undergraduate days, and I was often more interested in what they were learning than my own studies. What had always interested me the most about Economics was how it helped me understand people's behaviour, and so the links to Psychology were obvious to me. I'd often quipped that Economics was truly a sub-discipline of Psychology, since Economics was fundamentally about understanding people's decisions in the financial world – a relatively small part of being a human.

So it was quickly settled; I would move to Psychology and carry out research into how the economy influenced people's happiness and wellbeing. There were a few sniggers from my fellow Economics students when I mentioned the move to a lesser discipline (in their eyes), yet I knew in my gut I was making the right choice for me.

Happiness had just gotten very serious in my life. Happiness became more than an unspoken life goal; it was officially my job. If the journey for happiness hadn't begun the day I was born, then it had certainly begun now.

Happiness in our lives

It is not just five-year-old versions of John Lennon and me that make the claim that happiness has an important role in our lives. The ancient Greek philosopher Aristotle said, "happiness is the meaning and purpose of life, the whole aim and end of human existence." The Dalai Lama, the exiled Tibetan leader, says that "the very purpose of our life is to seek happiness." It is undeniable; experiencing happiness is integral to our lives.

However, an important element of how the ancient Greeks discussed happiness is that they were careful to distinguish between the different kinds of happiness. There was the '*hedonic*' kind of happiness, which refers to the feelings of pleasure, excitement, and joy in the moment, as well as the absence of painful feelings, such as anxiety and anger. Hedonic happiness tends to come and go, our emotional state fluctuating throughout the day, which is typical for most people. And then there was what the Greeks referred to as '*eudaimonic*' happiness.

According to Aristotle, eudaimonic happiness was obtained by following the cultural ideals of excellence of his time, i.e., living a virtuous life, through being brave, temperate, and wise. It's deeper than hedonic happiness, and a modern take on eudaimonic happiness would be the ability to flourish or thrive as a human being; this includes having freedom to be ourselves, our connections with others, and living a meaningful life. It was this '*flourishing*' type of happiness that Aristotle was speaking to when he stressed that happiness was the purpose of our human lives. I am sure that my five-year-old self – were he to have understood such words – would have been in complete agreement.

There is variation in our understanding of what happiness is, and people are often talking at cross-purposes with one another when they talk about happiness. This can be confusing and can result in some people dismissing happiness as a viable human goal altogether. These differences as to what happiness is, as well as how each kind of happiness matters to our lives, will have to be unpicked as we journey (in this book this happens in Chapters 5, 7 and 16, when each kind of happiness is most relevant to what is happening at the time).

If the truth be told, I've not come across many people – other than those who are truly happy – who don't claim to want at least a little more happiness, of whatever kind, in their lives. Thanks in part to utilitarianism (an ethical theory that encourages actions that maximise happiness), the desire to increase happiness also lies at the heart of economic theory. Many economists believe that a person will always choose the things that give them the greatest personal happiness. With this line of reasoning, economists claim that we don't need to know how happy people are because their choices will reveal exactly what makes for a happy life.

It came as a surprise to many economists, however, when in 1974, people's self-reported happiness scores were first used to show that economic growth had not seemed to improve human happiness in industrialised countries.[2] Though this finding is still contested, as I will get onto later in more detail in this book, it has also long been known that humans are not the hyper-rational machines, always maximising their happiness, that economists have built most of their mathematically dense theory upon. We are far more complex. We are far more interesting.

Humans don't always choose the things that make them happier. As I will describe in more detail in a later part of this book, this is not because happiness isn't important, but because humans – all of them, both you and I included, no exceptions – are prone to making mistakes. We can't see into the future, we don't like taking risks, we don't anticipate that novelty will quickly wear off, we care about what others think, and we hate the idea of losing something. There are a whole host of other systematic errors of judgement we make that mean we struggle to get it right when it comes to choosing the things that make us happier in life. Sadly, many of these innate biases are routinely used to encourage us to do things that are not in the interests of our own long-term happiness, but instead, in the interests of sustaining an economic system which prioritises profit above anything else. It is an economic system that has long ceased to serve us.

Choosing happiness

We can learn all we want about what makes us truly happy as individuals. However, in all honesty, my research didn't tell me all that much more than what my five-year-old self sitting on that swirling-orange carpet already knew, deep in that wide-open heart of his. Most of us – if, between the busyness, we have the time to think about it – will know it too. I am talking about the sort of things that, upon our death beds, we will wish we had made more time for in our lives[3] – our relationships, doing things that are meaningful to us, taking better care of our physical and mental health, not giving ourselves and others such a hard time over our 'mistakes'...

I ended up spending more than a decade as an academic researching happiness. I tried to use my research to bring an intentional focus to happiness in my own life and the lives of others. I was very successful in a professional sense, in that I published a good number of articles in respectable academic journals, and obtained a fair bit of funding to do the research I wanted to do. However, as the years rolled on, I realised to my horror that I wasn't particularly happy, and that my research didn't seem to be helping others either. Admittedly, I'd found some happiness early in my career, through walking the talk. For example, I travelled a fair bit, I learnt to hitchhike and get about on a bicycle, meeting interesting and different people; I reduced my possessions, and I cooked a lot more. I also took time exploring my own mental health through therapy, reading, and self-reflection, as well as investing time in relationships with family and friends (which meant indirectly I may have helped others become a little happier too). I also put less energy into work as the years went on. As long as I published well and brought in research funds, which I did, most people were happy enough with what I was doing and let me get on with it.

However, improving my own happiness reached a limit. And I saw that my happiness would always be limited by the academic environment that I found myself working within. I needed to spend less time on my own in front of a screen in a fluorescently-lit office, less time chasing research funds that were few and far between, and less time writing academic articles that only a few people would ever read. I needed greater job security, to spend more time sharing insights about happiness research with people beyond the academic world, and to have more time for myself and those I loved. Many of the things that are important for happiness seemed out of reach to me, an apparent expert on happiness. That seemed beyond ridiculous. Whilst I *knew* better, I was up against it when trying to actually *live* better. And as I looked around me more widely, I knew there would be limits for my happiness in any society centred around economic efficiency and economic growth. That goes, I think, for most of us.

Fortunately, over the course of my happiness career, I'd learnt that there are some societies that have been trying to do things differently. And in the case of Bhutan – a small kingdom in the foothills of the Himalayas, that focuses all its societal decisions on happiness – very differently. I had wanted to visit Bhutan, this famed Kingdom of Happiness, ever since I first heard about the place. However, I didn't want my journey there to be conventional – no, no, no – I wanted my journey there to have happiness at its very core. Why journey otherwise? And so, before we get going on some intrepid journeying, I need to tell you a little about Bhutan, and why I needed to get there on a bicycle.

CHAPTER 2

Why Bhutan? Why a bicycle? And why me?

"Just imagine if you were to tell people you were cycling to Bhutan."
Matthew Hopwood, July 2017

I could have made it to Bhutan on a long-haul flight from Scotland in less than 30 hours – maybe via a flight connection in Delhi or Kathmandu. That thought would cross my mind whenever I had a difficult day on the bicycle. Now, given it costs $250 a day to obtain a visa to enter Bhutan, a return trip lasting just a couple of weeks would have been most of my salary for two months. At that kind of cost, I'd have had to make the most of my once-in-a-lifetime opportunity being there. Plus, when I got back, probably exhausted from all the seeing and doing, I'd have had to catch up on all the work that I'd put aside. Still, I imagine I could have told one or two stories about some of the things I would have seen and done in Bhutan. Perhaps I'd have felt rather self-satisfied at being one of the few privileged enough to have been able to enter the 'Land of the Thunder Dragon'.

For those that aren't familiar with Bhutan, it is a small kingdom in the Himalayas, and a country that rarely fails to fascinate. Quite unbelievably, Bhutan does not have one single traffic light – it is the only country in the world where this is so. Not because there aren't many cars, but because instead traffic police direct the traffic. Television was banned for many years, finally introduced to the country only in 1999. The sale and production of tobacco, however, remains completely illegal.

Bhutan lays claim to being the world's only carbon-negative country, removing more greenhouse gases from the atmosphere than it emits, through offsetting and the export of renewable energy. Furthermore, its citizens are constitutionally obliged to protect the environment and as a result, more than 70 per cent of the country is covered by forest. Bhutan is also home to the highest unclimbed mountain in the world, at 7,570 metres.

Some of this might sound severe and strict – but if you track back on any of these curious facts, and begin to question how and why Bhutan is the way it is, it will always come back to one simple thing: happiness.

A country with happiness root and centre

Bhutan focuses its entire national policy on happiness, rather than the economy. In fact, it is world famous for doing so. (It's also famous for the inordinately high cost of obtaining a visa to enter the country – which itself is a happiness policy with the goal of preserving the Bhutanese way of life). This Buddhist nation of fewer than a million people has long valued happiness. It is written in their ancient legal code that, "if the government cannot create happiness for its people, then there is no purpose for government to exist". Whilst other countries may have happiness written into their constitutions, they do not come close to the seriousness with which Bhutan considers the happiness of its citizens.

In an interview with the *Financial Times* in 1972, the fourth King of Bhutan, Jigme Singye Wangchuck, first introduced the world to the country's now famed model for sustainable development: Gross National Happiness. In an offhand comment, the king asserted that Gross National Happiness was far more important in Bhutan than the size of its economy, its Gross National Product. Though Gross National Happiness began as a guiding philosophy for making national policy decisions, in 2010 the idea was transformed into a fully measurable concept – the Gross National Happiness Index.

Happiness in Bhutan is underpinned by good governance, sustainable and equitable socio-economic development, preservation and promotion of culture, and environmental conservation. The idea is that all of these aspects must be considered by Bhutanese policy officials in order to promote and preserve happiness, now and in the future. The Gross National Happiness Index allows Bhutan to gauge local, regional, and national levels of happiness, as well as create policies that will directly improve happiness. This doesn't mean leaders of Bhutan don't pay heed to the economy. They just consider growing their economy to be a means to an end – namely, happiness – rather than being an end in itself, and one to be prioritised above anything else.

In our globalised world, where so many seem convinced that economic growth is an end in itself and a cure for all ills, it is astonishing that this tiny nation has managed to carve out such a unique model of societal progress, not to mention being geographically sandwiched between the giants of India and China, both previously having annexed large parts of this relatively peaceful Himalayan region (Sikkim and Tibet, respectively). I learnt about Bhutan very early in my happiness research career, and once I did, I was captivated. If there could be another way to live a more enriching life, then the tiny country of Bhutan offers us a lot of hope towards living it. I had long imagined going there.

That said, let's be clear – the journey we are about to embark on in this book is not about Bhutan. Nor is it really about cycling. It is a journey about a human being that had been tired, frustrated, and unhappy for much too long in their life. A human being that knew that there had to be something better, something more deeply fulfilling than what they were doing.

Bhutan was just the destination; albeit a pretty interesting destination for a journey for happiness at that. However, as we will explore in later chapters, it is a mistake to count on finding happiness at any destination, no matter how difficult or not the journey getting there.

As for the cycling, well, after careful consideration, I thought it would give me the best shot of finding happiness along the way. There are many different ways we can travel to our destination, yet if the journey there isn't one that has happiness at its heart and soul, then shouldn't we question whether it is worth going at all?

What I liked the most about my journey was its sheer absurdity. It didn't quite make sense to most people, at least not on the surface. Yet, given my life up to that point, it made complete sense to me – more sense than anything ever had before. The journey was what some people might refer to as a 'calling'. Something that, once we have become fully aware of it, can be difficult to refuse. We all have these callings, and perhaps more often than we like to recognise. To respond to them, we must listen carefully to ourselves and to the world; and most importantly, when we receive our calling, we must be ready to take a great leap of faith.

What is it that matters the most for our happiness?

For about a decade before my cycle journey began, I carried out countless statistical analyses to determine what it was that made some people happier than others. The results were illuminating, given how we have shaped our societies. Though, as I've said before and will say again, the results wouldn't have surprised the small five-year-old boy I once was, sitting on his orange-swirly carpet.

The most important factor for happiness, according to any survey data in which people are asked to report how happy they are (details on how happiness can be measured will come in later chapters), is always something involving our relationships with other people. Those who speak to neighbours regularly, or are in committed relationships, for example, tend to be happier. Next comes health. Both physical and mental health are important, yet it is mental distress that debilitates our ability to find happiness the most; much more than people expect. Then, it is having a sense of meaning and purpose in life, which is often bound up with helping others, or having a spiritual or religious path in life. A person's personality, such as their levels of conscientiousness or extraversion, is another strong predictor of happiness. Relatedly, whether a person acts in line with their beliefs and values, which is what psychologists call *authenticity*, is also an essential ingredient.[1]

Some of my best published work highlighted the role of personality in our happiness. In a key piece of research I undertook with colleagues, we showed that small changes in our personalities were more strongly linked to changes in happiness and wellbeing than changes to our social and economic circumstances. We then went on to demonstrate that personality – which most people presume to be largely fixed across life – is actually just as likely to change as how much a person earns.[2] Yet, sad as it is, most of our energy goes into obtaining increases to our income, than working intentionally on ourselves.

The trouble is that for me, and frankly for most people I know, it is difficult to put time and energy into our relationships, health, and personality. We all know they are important, but on a daily basis, we must somehow deal with encouragement and temptations to do things that have minimal benefit to our relationships, health, and personality. Sometimes what we are encouraged and tempted into doing can be plain destructive to these areas of our lives. This is not to say that there is no individual choice, and that happiness is impossible. But we have to recognise that the environment we navigate each day makes it much more difficult than it otherwise could be.

For example, unhealthy foods are placed everywhere – most often when we're at our weakest, when we are tired from excessive demands on our time. Those sugary goods in their shiny wrappers are always there when we're queueing up to buy a few things after a long day. And there are few possibilities for decent part-time work, which might give more time. We also have to navigate an online world that has been designed to distract and tempt. Whether online or during our commute to work, it is next to impossible to avoid attention-grabbing and intrusive adverts for things of questionable value to our happiness. There is so much noise and bright, often flashing lights, that we can't help but look outside of ourselves – rather than understand what is happening within us. We are obsessed with achievement, status, and power. And these obsessions take attention away from caring for ourselves and others. Some of the things we are tempted into doing are useful in their own right, but most have come to dominate our lives because they serve to enlarge the economy, rather than support our happiness.

This is not to say the economy is unimportant for happiness. When it comes to work, for instance, the statistics consistently show that whether a person is employed or not has a huge bearing on their happiness. Becoming unemployed has about the same impact as becoming physically disabled. However, most of the impact on happiness from unemployment has been attributed to the loss of purpose in life, and the loss of valuable social relationships, rather than the loss of earnings.[3]

Whether money buys happiness is a question that is as old as money itself. It is also a very tired one. The debate continues, back and forth, with little substance. The best one-sentence summary I can supply on this argument comes from the title of my last article published on the topic before I left on my bicycle for Bhutan: "Money may buy happiness, but often so little that it doesn't matter."[4] Money can sometimes bring happiness. However, unless you're struggling to put food on the table, or are overwhelmed by debt, it is nowhere near as important as many people believe it to be.

A remarkable way of illustrating the unimportance of money for happiness is by comparing the effect that it has compared to some of the things I've already mentioned as being important – such as relationships, health, and understanding ourselves. Being married, for example, has been shown to be equal in happiness terms to having an extra US$100,000.[5] Not just a one-off US$100,000 – US$100,000 *each and every year*. Imagine that! If a person increased the number of times they saw friends or relatives from less than once a month to most days, it would be the happiness equivalent of having an extra US$115,000 per year. With regards to health, to recompense a serious physical disability's effect on happiness US$200,000 would be needed each year, whilst the effect of treating someone in psychological distress with psychotherapy is about the same as US$240,000 each year – mental health outweighs serious physical debilitation. As for personality, if someone at average levels of agreeableness became moderately agreeable (i.e., increased from being more agreeable than half the population to being more agreeable than just over two-thirds of the population) this would be equal to approximately having US$105,000 more per year; if someone were to go from average levels of extroversion to moderate levels of extroversion it would be equal to about US$160,000 each year.

These numbers come from published research,[6] and they are astonishingly high. However, they are by no means causal. That is, neither the money nor the life experience would necessarily lead to this amount of increased happiness. It is notoriously difficult to get causal estimates on social and economic variables because it is not ethical to experimentally manipulate people's lives; nevertheless, these numbers are broadly indicative of the relative difference between money and these other areas of life. Yet, think about these numbers carefully for a second or two. Ask yourself, which would you rather have in each situation? Seeing friends and family regularly or US$115,000 extra each year? Being in a committed and loving relationship or US$100,000 extra each year? Of course, the question is hypothetical, and there are ifs and buts, such as what our situation is to begin with and our statistical assumptions about causality for instance... But let's assume you have a typical wage and reasonably good relationships, and that the truly causal effect were the same in relative terms. I would hazard a guess that the belief that money is important for our happiness would certainly have some of us choosing the money over our friends and family, over our physical and mental health, and over being our true self. And that is what we routinely do in our everyday lives for much less money. We are encouraged to do so. Not only by the economic system, but we convince ourselves and each other to do so too.

We have come to believe that money *is* happiness.

Even if we don't personally believe money is important to happiness – and there are many of us who are the exception to this rule – the economic theory that underpins our entire economic system is predicated on the belief that it is. The boss needs to get the company to grow, because they have shareholders who want to see financial returns, and as a result, people always end up working more than they want. This makes it difficult for any of us to act in a way that doesn't put what matters the most in life at grave risk.

Could I really create a journey for happiness?

From carrying out all this research over the years, I certainly knew what was important for happiness. However, I too was at the mercy of a wider system, and I was doing my best to cope within it. Plus, although we may know that our relationships, health, and personality are important, this doesn't always mean we know what to do if these areas of our life aren't going very well. I had often struggled with the important areas of life, and that normally meant I shied away from doing anything about my problems at all. For example, when I felt like a relationship wasn't going well, I'd avoid talking directly about the difficulties. Or if I was feeling anxious, the anxiety would overwhelm my ability to ask for the help that I desperately needed.

How do we turn awareness into practice? I felt stuck. For years I had been wondering whether I'd ever be able to create a life concretely centred around happiness. I had my doubts. But perhaps, I thought, going on a journey that had happiness at the heart and soul of it might be a good way to begin. A journey in which I would visit places where, owing to a slightly more supportive environment, choices for greater happiness might come a little easier. A journey in which a concern for happiness would form a key part of how I travelled. A journey in which I could throw myself into prioritising relationships, health, and personality. I knew that such a journey might include Bhutan. Not as a final destination – but alongside other places across our globe, where the economy does not trump all other human concerns.

I had thought about hitchhiking my way around the world. I'd started hitchhiking in my early 30s; I did it for the first time with others one day completely on the off-chance, travelling from Manchester where I then lived, to North Wales. I was fascinated so much by hitchhiking that I soon decided to make it my primary mode of long-distance travel. Wanting to liven up my academic job a little, I travelled to a few work conferences in this way. It was scary, yet there was also something enthralling about it. It was a step toward greater happiness, and it felt surreal: just me standing at the side of the road with my thumb raised in the air. Perhaps for only a few minutes, but sometimes many hours, until a perfect stranger would stop and offer a ride, for a few miles or many. It was never about saving money; though it took a long time, it was about connecting.

Those that stopped for me were from all walks of life, yet they were always kind and generous. They were humans after all, and generosity and helping others is core to who we are.[7] I remember when I once rode with a father and son team, driving their home-delivery van, and after a long ride, in which they'd bought me a cheese sandwich and a cup of tea, I got picked up the near instant they dropped me off by a man in an open top sports car. There was another time when I was picked up by two guys, best of friends, who once upon a time had shared a prison cell together. We laughed and joked with one another all the way to Sheffield.

I had also thought that my journey might involve working on boats, so that I could cross oceans in a slightly more sustainable way, as well as doing lots of overland travel. The important thing was that I wanted to travel in a way that maximised the opportunity for happiness, by prioritising what I knew to be important from my own research: travel that prioritised people, that prioritised health, and would give me the freedom to be myself. I didn't want to sacrifice these elements for the sake of comfort and convenience. Indeed, I would have sacrificed at least some of them, had I simply flown to Bhutan and luxuriated there for a couple of weeks. These sorts of comforts and conveniences are costly. And I've never found that comfort and convenience comes with much in the way of sustained happiness. I needed the real stuff.

Nature had to be a part of my journey too. A lack of access to nature growing up in South London on a busy road contributed to my family's struggle for happiness. Research shows, as I'll delve into much later, that living near green and blue spaces has mental health benefits. The effect isn't large, but when you add that up across communities, it can have enormous collective benefits.[8] When I started going for long walks and cycles in nature, much later in life, I'd always come back rejuvenated – mentally clear and physically energised. And when at 32 I started camping, my pact with nature was cemented.

Why I got on a bicycle and headed for Bhutan

In July 2017, about three months before I would leave by bicycle for Bhutan, the thought of cycling there hadn't crossed my mind. I was sharing a cup of tea with a curious soul that I'd serendipitously come to know.[9] Matthew had a fine beard, and eyes that went as deep as eyes can go. He was a journeyman himself, having journeyed about the UK on foot for some years, collecting people's love stories. Simple. Powerful. Inspiring. As I was telling him about wanting to create a journey for happiness – which I guess in a way was my own love story – he said to me, as if from nowhere, "Just imagine if you were to tell people you were cycling to Bhutan." The seed for the journey was planted.

Initially I was reluctant and dismissive – the seed needed a little germination. In fact, the idea horrified me for some weeks following that conversation. It was absolutely absurd. And yet, that was what I liked about it – and the idea began to niggle away at me. I soon became unable to stop thinking about cycling to Bhutan. When I went away on my bicycle with a tent for about five days to the Isle of Mull in Scotland, I spent most of my time there wondering whether, not only if such a journey were physically possible, but also whether it was a journey I needed to undertake. I didn't know then whether it was achievable. In honesty, I didn't believe it was. But what I did like was that this simple idea of 'cycling to Bhutan' encapsulated everything that I wanted a journey for happiness to be about – it had happiness at the heart and soul of it. It was a pilgrimage for this unhappy happiness researcher that no-one else was going to make. I *did* need to do it. I had heard my calling, and I couldn't refuse it.[10] And so, it became one of those then rare times in my life, where what I had to do to bring happiness was clearer than what I had to stop doing to prevent more unhappiness.

The bicycle is not for everyone. Nor is attempting to reach Bhutan on one. Perhaps it is only me that needed to make this specific journey. Given who I was in that time and space, and what I knew to be important for happiness, cycling seemed perfect for me, just as something else will be better for another – just so long as it fulfils those core human needs. If we listen, we will know when the seed for our journey has come along. Hopefully, circumstances will be such, as well as the accompanying courage, to let it grow.

At this point, I want to introduce two important factors to consider about my journey to Bhutan on a bicycle – race and gender. I'm a white man. As I rode, I would often wonder how different this journey would be if I were not a white man. (If you identify with being a white man, that might not seem so important.) However, were I not a white man, although this particular journey might still be 'possible', like all things, I am certain that were I not both white and a man, things would have been different. I admit that I am blind to the discrimination that others face in their daily lives concerning aspects of themselves over which they have no control. As a man, I had fewer physical safety concerns, and far more freedom as to where I camped at night. And in being white, I undoubtedly got a different reaction from people I met than if I were a person of colour. Held in greater reverence, perhaps? And quite probably by people of all ethnicities. As one non-white cyclist told me, who put me up for a couple of nights in his Peruvian city, his fellow citizens would brandish him a fool for being on a bicycle, yet consider me a hero. I didn't fully appreciate how others saw my white-ness until a famous Thai happiness economist challenged me on this point (which I shall describe later).

Statistically speaking, however, women tend to be a little bit happier than men in most parts of the world. Added to that, men have far higher suicide rates, and on average live shorter lives. It is not all it's cracked up to be, being a man. We have our suffering. However, the view I've come to hold is that many men aren't very good at taking responsibility for their own suffering. In being blind to our own troubles, and by virtue of the power we men have and want to hold onto in this world, we end up dumping our suffering on others rather than owning it.

In the UK, the happiness levels across ethnicities have become remarkably similar over the last decade,[11] although this is not to imply that the UK is in anyway post-racialised. However, in other parts of the world such as the US, although the happiness inequality between racial groups has diminished substantially since the 1970s, the happiness of Black people is still lower than white people.

Quite simply race and gender do matter. How exactly? I don't know. But I won't deny that they do, and in ways I can't fully appreciate by virtue of my own identity. It is telling that I did not encounter many cyclists who weren't white, or many solo female cyclists. This doesn't mean that this journey on a bicycle isn't relevant to those that are not white and not men, because as humans, most of the things that really matter for happiness are at root the same. And we *are* going to get deep into what really matters – even though your own journey may not need to involve a bicycle, nor going anywhere near Bhutan.

I'll come back to race and gender as we journey. Placing them aside for now, it was clear that travelling on a bicycle would be good for my physical health. Also, because cycling can be cathartic and enables a lot of time for reflection, I knew it would have important benefits for my mental health too. Psychologists often talk about the importance of having *flow* when it comes to happiness.[12] Being engaged in a challenging activity and being fully absorbed by it, such that we temporarily suspend our sense of self and of time, can bring a lot of pleasure to our lives. Though I had experienced flow often in the early days of my academic career, because I used to really like what I did, it had long since waned. Instead of work being absorbing and enjoyable, it had become wearisome. A long-distance journey on a bicycle would shake things up, and be an opportunity to get flow back in my life. I would be out in the world and able to fully engage with whatever was before me.

From a few experiences I'd had cycling in western Europe, I knew that, like hitchhiking, a bicycle can bring connections with all sorts of different people. People can be curious when they see a cyclist with lots of baggage in tow – where are they going, where have they come from? – and it is easier to stop and talk to a cyclist than those who travel much faster. A cyclist will stop often, exactly when and where they want to, and sometimes people will offer help. Perhaps I would learn something from the people I met to improve the relationships across my life. As will be revealed later in this book, I did.

Without a doubt, cycling to Bhutan would also bring challenge in all manner of shapes and sizes. We may not think it, but challenge is also an important part of happiness.[13] By definition, challenge is not easy, but it is our encounters with a range of challenges and how we manage to deal with them that provide an important source of happiness from travel.[14] This is not to say we should force ourselves and others into things that are far out of our depth. Yet, those unplanned and unexpected encounters are often the basis for the stories that we share upon return. These are the experiences that shape us.

I was excited about cycling through lands of all different kinds and ending my days by setting up camp with a beautiful view of those places. Due to the camping and reliance on my own leg-power, this journey would be cost-effective and low impact – meaning I would be able to travel for longer than if I had to think about travel fares and accommodation. Perhaps the most crucial component of my journey was the meaning and purpose behind it. It was the absence of purpose in my day-to-day work that was weighing the heaviest upon me. I needed purpose back in my life, and the journey for happiness that I was about to embark on – as would become clear somewhere on the west coast of the Americas – was bigger than I.

Scotland to Bhutan: The people and places in between

It is a very long way from Scotland to Bhutan: 4,813 miles (7,754km) to be precise – if one goes west to east and can fly like a crow. Yet, there is also so much in between that ought to be part of a journey for happiness. This journey wouldn't be direct. In fact, a fair number of people have laughed when I reveal the route I ended up taking to reach Bhutan. And at the start of my journey, I received a fair few comments from people saying I seemed to be going in the opposite direction from my stated destination. I had intended it to be this way, more or less, as it is not just Bhutan paving the way forward when it comes to happiness. There were other places that I wanted to include, as well as all those people I was set to meet in between.

And so, I began by warming up both my language skills and my sat-at-a-desk-too-long body, on a journey down to Barcelona in Spain. From there I flew to Buenos Aires in Argentina and cycled up through Latin America, spending time in some of the happiest countries in the world, most notably Costa Rica, which in 1948 abolished its military and decided to instead invest in public health and education, and now boasts a life expectancy of 79.6 years and an adult literacy rate of 97.6%. I continued on through North America, including Mexico and the United States, finally reaching Canada, a country that could claim to have the world's most progressive national index of wellbeing. On account of its citizen participation, ability to pin-point regional differences, and direct links to policy Canada surpasses Bhutan's own national happiness index. Then, it was over to Asia. I finally found my way through to Bhutan via South East Asia, including Vietnam, a country that comes the closest to meeting its population's needs without completely busting the earth's bio systems, and lastly India.

Of course, I didn't pass through everywhere in the world that is doing something interesting with happiness – I missed out New Zealand, with its pioneering approach to wellbeing policy, and those supposedly 'happiest in the world' Scandinavian countries, for example. A central tenet for any happiness journey needs to be letting go of going everywhere and doing every-thing – only travelling where we really need to go, and that might mean going nowhere at all. Second, and most importantly, a journey for happiness must leave a lot of room for the unexpected. To encounter happiness where we don't expect to find it, and where happiness can be at its rawest – those places in between the big destinations, where most people will not go. Whether that be the small villages up in the mountains, where people live simply and have an unfailing capacity to share whatever they have; a small community set up in the jungle with happiness at its core; or an encounter with a curious soul in a local store in a remote part of the desert.

Had I flown to Bhutan, those people and landscapes would have passed by in a flash. There is no doubt that I'd have reached the famed happy land of Bhutan more easily. Yet, I needed a journey focused on connecting with those kind and generous people, those beautiful landscapes, and just as importantly, my rather lost self. It would be all these people and places in between where the deepest understandings about happiness would come. Bhutan would shine elusively, yet brightly, in the distance.

So I quit my job, and I was gone. Well, it wasn't like that at all, but bear with me.

CHAPTER 3

Out beyond the front door

"Be bold, and mighty forces will come to your aid."
Goethe

There were about ten of them. And I was completely surrounded.

At first, they bombarded me with questions in a language I was still trying to get to grips with. *¿Quién eres? ¿De dónde eres? ¿Por qué estás aquí en nuestro pueblo?* I struggled to answer them. There was no space. And in any case, by this stage of the journey, answering questions about who I was and what I was doing wasn't easy.

It was the end of June 2018, and by this time I'd been on the road for nine months. It was to be my last night in Guatemala. I intended to cross the border into Mexico the following morning.

The day had been typical. I'd glided through mountains – some ups, some downs; nothing too strenuous. I'd eaten mysterious fruits bought at the side of the road, and there'd been the odd conversation here and there, as there always was in this part of the world. I felt content. But the day was coming to its end, and it was time to look for a spot to camp for the night. Somewhere hidden, away from houses, not too far from the road, close to water, and – if I was lucky – a beautiful view. Those simple things I had come to know would enable me to create a happy home for the night. Though, on this occasion, I couldn't find a camp spot that had enough of those things to feel comfortable. It was becoming more densely populated too, as I rolled onwards, and I knew I'd have to ask someone local if they could help. I still often feel a bit anxious about asking for help. There is a vulnerability in doing so.

I had to push my bicycle up a steep hill to get into the village. It was tiring to do after a day's cycling, and there was no guarantee it would be worth it. I could already see them on the other side of the track as I pushed my bike. They were boisterous, frenzied even, and fully immersed in whatever it was they were doing. None of them had yet seen me. As I leaned my bicycle up against the wall mid-way up the hill, I watched them carefully. That was when their attention shifted entirely toward me; first one, then the others.

The oldest was perhaps nine or ten years old, and the youngest a little more than four. And these children wanted to know just about everything about me. Their joy of playing, and excitement at meeting me, made my whole body surge with warmth. They began asking more questions than I could possibly answer. When I found a little gap in their wonder, I managed a few words: "*Me llamo Cristóbal. Soy de Escocia. Estoy buscando un lugar para poner mi tienda por la noche.*" They went quiet. Mouths wide open; they seemed amazed by what was before them. This strange-looking being with a bicycle, in his ripped and dirty shorts, yet speaking their language with an odd accent. They were eager to hear more, and their faces gleamed. I pointed to the church just up the hill and asked whether that might be a good place to put up a tent. Probably, they seemed to say, though they didn't know for sure. They thought it best if I ask the church pastor first.

That evening I didn't stay in my tent, but instead I slept in the pastor's home. The children had taken me directly to him, and without hesitation, he had invited me to stay with him and his family for the night – I suspect he did it more for the sake of the children than for me. They were fascinated by the curious cyclist that had happened to chance on their remote village and squealed with delight when the pastor said I could stay. I spent most of that evening outside, immersed in their world and child-wonder. I carried each one of them on my shoulders at least once, some several times, each insisting on their turn. There was a big water fight in which I was unquestionably the main target, which soothed my body after a long day riding in the heat. We picked and ate some mangoes together, and I was led by hand to all corners of their small and basic village. Anyone that crossed our path was introduced to me. These children related authentically with the stranger that was before them. They reminded me of something I had once been – happy and unafraid to be. They didn't have much, but they had each other, and they certainly had me for the rest of that night too. This was more than I could ever have hoped I would experience when I first set out on my journey.

Before I left Scotland many months before, I never expected to have an experience even close to the one I had in that Guatemalan village. What was more surprising was that I would go on to have countless more like it. They're the sort of experiences I thought only happened to other people – people with real courage, a serendipity about them, or perhaps a touch of magic. I didn't think I could ever have very much of any of those.

Back to my front door

Hell, being in Guatemala was about as far from my thoughts as it could be before I left. It was more a case of focusing on getting out of the front door and beginning. I had many mundane yet scary tasks to attend to. First, I had to hand my notice in at work and leave my flat. Both were sources of safety and stability. I had to figure out what to pack onto a bicycle, and then *actually leave*. There were all those people to say goodbye to, and for who knows how long. I began to doubt whether this was going to be the journey for happiness that I had first imagined it would be. Still, all the thoughts of what I was leaving behind did help me feel grateful for the life I'd been able to lead up until then. Maybe my life wasn't so bad. No, it wasn't so bad – but I was done with letting a not-so-bad life stop me from living a more fulfilling one.

When I set off, I'd have put the odds of actually arriving in

Bhutan at perhaps one in five, at best. But it didn't help to think like that. The important thing was to just begin, and then take it one step at a time – that must be the way with any journey for happiness. Yet, I couldn't help but think of all the things that could go wrong along the way. Maybe I'd be robbed. Perhaps I'd have a serious accident. Or I'd get stranded in the middle of nowhere with no food or water, etc... Like most people, I've read many stories and I've heard many tales.

What was also heavy on my mind was the prospect of returning. What would I do with myself when I came back? Would I ever come back? Would my academic career be in tatters? Would the person that I would go on to become care about that? Such thoughts terrified me! Yet that didn't stop me tormenting myself with endless possibilities. My mind can be a very useful tool, but its tendency to think about all eventualities, including the most unlikely ones, has been debilitating. It had been that way with my mind for such a long time that I'd begun to believe that thinking as much as I do was just part of who I was, at my core. I had also developed a very strange belief that if I thought about something happening enough, then it would lessen the chance of it actually happening, as if I had special powers – but really it was just a way of coping.

Growing up, it was always things that I least expected to happen that would have the largest effect on me emotionally. That was how it was for the good stuff, and the bad stuff. As such, the more I expected something horrible to take place, the less likely it could harm me emotionally when it did happen. I'd be prepared. I'd gotten into the habit of thinking as much as I could about all the things I didn't want to happen, and trying my best to not think about all the things I did want to happen, even though I knew there's not much happiness in thinking that way. It is a limiting belief system. There was a lot to overcome on this journey.

Fortunately, I've been able to step beyond many of my fears in life, and my journey demanded I come to terms with my anxiety-prone mind. I wouldn't have called myself courageous: what may look like courage from the outside has often been propelled by the fear of not doing something. And, in the end, not attempting to cycle to Bhutan was far scarier than not attempting to. I had a chance of fulfilment on this journey. Not stepping towards that at this moment in my life seemed like a recipe for life-long regret and, as far as I was concerned, that was a whole lot worse than most of the things that might happen to me.

Preparation for getting from the front door and onwards to Bhutan

I didn't plan my route in much detail. I decided I would be better off planning minimally and getting on with it. It was faith I needed – I knew I could do this. Yet, I do still smile to think that when I set off, I guessed that the whole trip wouldn't take more than a year, maybe ten months (it took nearly double that). I had imagined I might make it back in time for the next academic year, giving me the chance to slip back into the academic world without too many people noticing I'd been away.

I looked at the map of the world – vaguely noted the distances – and hoped that I'd make it to Cusco in Peru for Christmas that year. I'd then get through South America by the end of February, pedal across central America by April, and then be up in Canada by June. Once I reached Asia (by boat, I had hoped), I'd only need a couple of months before I finally arrived in Bhutan. On a map it looked so straightforward. Yes, I was naïve. It takes much longer to cycle a distance than to run your finger along a map. Given my experiences cycling up to then, I believed I could do it in that timeframe; I still think I could have. But if I had, I wouldn't have had very much happiness to write about in this book.

I didn't prepare myself physically at all. I didn't think I needed to. My main transport in life had long been the bicycle, and I was reasonably fit. I was confident that my body would be able to handle cycling most of the day on most days. In any case I'd build into the cycling slowly. If I did struggle physically, then I could stop and rest.

I did, however, take my time figuring out how I was going to get all that I needed into the few bags that would be attached to my bicycle. What I chose would be my only possessions for many months. I hadn't thought that four pairs of underwear would be nearly enough for my journey. Yet they were, and easily. I'd mostly be in one of my two pairs of cycling shorts during the day (worn under a tatty pair of shorts to keep me looking not too serious), and whenever I was fortunate enough to get a shower, those cycling shorts, along with the odd t-shirt, would get a wash too. They'd normally be dry and ready to wear again by the morning. Sometimes I'd just jump into a pond at lunch time with whatever I was wearing, and it would have much the same effect.

I didn't quite have enough space to bring my beard trimmer or my thermos flask. I could have added an extra bag or two, but then what would be my stopping point? I knew that whatever space I had, I would fill it all. And whatever I did bring would have to be carried up every mountain, and ultimately, halfway around the globe.

The bulk of the things I brought were for camping. I wanted enough so that I'd be reasonably self-reliant, and be able to set up a happy little home almost anywhere I liked. I knew that whatever I chose to bring or not bring, I would – in the end – become accustomed to having or not having. On the bicycle, much like in life, we get used to what we have rapidly. And the research that I and others have done confirms this is so.[1] Much of the stuff we cart around in life brings us little in the way of sustained happiness.

Before I left, I gawked at all the things I'd amassed in my flat over the years. I had nowhere to store it all, and I needed to rid myself of most of it before I departed. In the end I gave a large part of my stuff away – either to friends or free shops. It was a relief. Plus, the giving felt good. I wondered why I had ever bought some of these things in the first place. They hadn't enriched my life as I thought they might. Rather they had ended up in a cupboard some place, gathering dust.

On a journey like this it is tempting to buy new kit, but I mostly made do with what I already had. I had most of the camping gear already. I patched up the pannier-cycling bags that

I'd bought to journey by bicycle through England and France, five years earlier. Both pairs of cycling shorts I took with me were at least eight years old when I left, and had done many thousands of miles already. I'm both proud and embarrassed to say that those shorts lasted the whole of the journey, and I still wear them when I cycle now.

The tent only made it halfway. It lasted until I was caught in a desert in Arizona, with a tent-door that no longer zipped up and a really large hairy spider (and goodness knows what else) crawling around outside. The panniers turned out to be too old and leaky; they didn't make it out of Buenos Aires, my landing point in South America. I bought new ones there.

And then there was my dear, sweet, gorgeous bicycle. My bike was only a couple of years old and didn't have a name or a gender back then. Nor was it quite the soul mate that it was to go on to become. Yet with a sturdy steel frame, 37mm tyres, 2x10 speed gearing, it did feel reliable. Gulliver, as I came to call him, would be capable of getting me most of the way round the world – although I'd need to know a bit more about bicycles to have a chance of that. Sure, I could fix a puncture, but other stuff I felt less confident about. I signed up for a couple of bicycle workshops to learn how to change disc brake pads, the cable wires for both brakes and gears, and replace a chain. I also learnt how to change a wheel spoke and true a wheel. Some of it I never had to do, and I would have struggled to remember how to have done it had something gone wrong. But it was enough to build my confidence before leaving.

Saying goodbye

I didn't grow up in Scotland. However, I've never felt more at home in a place. I'd been doing my happiness research at the University of Stirling for five years, and over the years since getting out of South London, I'd lived in many different places. Too many. This was mostly because my career demanded I move, which is a major happiness concern in itself, since it makes it more difficult to establish supportive and caring relationships with people. For me, there was always a sense of running away in it too – in the hope that I'd find more happiness somewhere else. I'm not ashamed to admit that there was at least a little bit of that going on as I embarked on this journey.

I had no family in Scotland, yet I made plenty of friends. I became involved in activities that were more about coming together than the actual activity. The reason I felt so at home in Scotland was because it was here where I first began to lean into those around me. Rather than rely on myself as much as possible to deal with (or more accurately suppress) my emotions, as I had learnt to do habitually since early in life, here I had begun to spend time developing relationships that were compassionate rather than blameful. And so, the two weeks before I left were a conveyor-belt of sad and joyful goodbyes. Part of me didn't want to go, as I wondered what would happen to these relationships I was leaving behind, and whether I'd see Scotland or the people I loved there again in my life.

One might say it is about the specific land and people. And it is. But it also isn't. Scotland is a special place, full of special people. But where isn't? All humans need a sense of belonging,[2] and it was the time I spent in Scotland where I first began to appreciate that. That is the sort of learning we can take anywhere. And once learnt, as my journey was about to show me, the necessity of feeling at home takes priority before almost anything else. And then we'll find home wherever we are – even for one night in a remote village in Guatemala. As Maya Angelou once expressed: "You are only free when you realise you belong no place – you belong every place – no place at all. The price is high. The reward is great."[3]

I also had to say farewell to ties that had not been healthy. That was more difficult. Relationships with others can be painful when we don't get the love and acceptance we need,[4] and I can root many of my harmful habits in believing myself to be deeply unlovable. When I was younger I found more solace in a new possession, or the bottom of a pint glass, than from those that I thought were supposed to love me. It had felt easier and more immediate to consume something than to take a look at my relationship troubles. If only I'd known earlier in my life that relationships could be different than those that I had been presented with – seemingly fixed, rigid unchangeable ones. If only I'd known earlier that with commitment to share, understand, and empathise, we can, in time, change and grow together.

There were some people in my life for whom I thought our relationship was too far gone. That it was beyond salvation. I wasn't hopeful about any future relationship with my Dad when I finally left. We were barely talking. And yet, as I'll describe how and why later, the change and growth that my Dad and I experienced together as I journeyed would easily be the most important thing to come from my journey. (I'd say the same if I were to wake up tomorrow to hear the UK prime minister announce the government's primary goal was to prioritise wellbeing over economic growth on account of my journey!) As for my grandfather on my mother's side, I suspected when I waved goodbye to him just before I left the UK, that it would be the last time that I saw him. And, bless his soul, it was.

And finally there was the embarrassment

Humans are social animals, and one thing we are biologically programmed to do is compare and contrast with one another.[5] There may be struggle in our own lives, yet it can be reassuring to know that, at least, others think we have it good. Some of my research highlighted that one of the reasons money doesn't bring as much happiness as we believe it will is because once we have enough income to cover our basic needs, we think less in absolute terms. Instead, we care more about whether we are doing better than others or not.[6] Such innate comparison has benefits evolutionarily, in that it helps people learn from others and make improvements to their lives. Yet, comparison can, as Theodore Roosevelt said, "be the thief of joy".

In our distant past, emulating others could sometimes be

the difference between life and death – for example, in growing enough food for your family. For many throughout the world, physical survival is not much of a threat, yet our existential survival is. We all want to be seen, valued, and respected. And we try and do that these days by having things. Being esteemed within our community does matter to us, and our need for esteem could be used for the betterment of humankind. Sadly, though, it is too often used to sell more cars and gadgets – despite the effect of this consumerism being at best marginal, if not damaging, for our individual and collective happiness.

The academic world is a bit different in expression, but at root it is the same. The esteem of an academic doesn't rest so much on material goods, but instead on publications. It is important to publish more than others, and in better journals. I'd spent years evaluating my performance, and ultimately my self-worth, based on how much I'd published compared to others. There was, of course, always someone publishing more and in better places than me. Judgement and criticism are an essential ingredient to a typical academic's mind-set, and what other academics thought about my cycling journey to Bhutan weighed heavily upon me. My journey was an odd one. No academic in their right mind would do it. None indeed had.

And so, before my journey began, whenever I had a spare moment between feeling anxious, sad, and fearful, I would feel embarrassed. Once I got going on my journey, and after I'd seen that the world is in fact not even a sliver as scary as I had believed it to be, and in between feeling contentment, happiness, and elation – feelings of embarrassment would still rise up. It is difficult to step out of your community and try something different. People judge. So, at the start I didn't share much about my journey; I just got on with it and cycled. Sometimes I'd display the hashtag for my journey, #AdventureInHappiness, on the back of my bicycle, but I would imagine people being disapproving or offended when they came up behind me in their cars as I rode. I had spent hours making that sign, seated at my grandfather's kitchen table just before I left the UK.

With time, my embarrassment subsided. I began to write regularly for my blog, and share my reflections about happiness from the journey. Non-academic folk, most notably my Dad, at last began to engage with the ideas I had spent a decade developing as an academic. Many of the academics I had worked with have since surprised me with their admiration for what I was trying to do. The more I opened up, the more interested people became. When, later along the road, I found myself on Mexican television speaking in (fairly okay) Spanish about my humble journey to Bhutan, I realised I felt proud of what I was doing, and I wasn't worried about the viewer's opinion of me.

I had let go of what others may or may not have been thinking of me. Ultimately, that was more about letting go of what I thought about myself. I had always felt encouraged by society to judge others, and therefore myself. To find happiness I would need to let go of that judgement. And with time I did.

With all this going on inside of me – the fear, the sadness, and the embarrassment – it was difficult to get out of the front door; but I managed to do it on the day I intended. I had to be bold and have faith. A few days into the journey on my way down to Barcelona, I wrote in my journal: "It's an odd feeling to realise that I am present in something I had only previously imagined – my dream has come to pass and I can scarcely believe it. I'm without a job and without a home – perhaps really interesting things can now happen."

And really interesting things, like the experience in Guatemala, would go on to happen all of the time. It took a while though, because there were quite a few things to let go of that have long held me back in my happiness. The next half a dozen or so chapters will describe how I got past blocks to my happiness, many of them culturally conditioned, and stepped into being one of those people who seem to have a touch of happy magic about them. But before we get into that, let's talk about money, and how much a journey like this ought to cost.

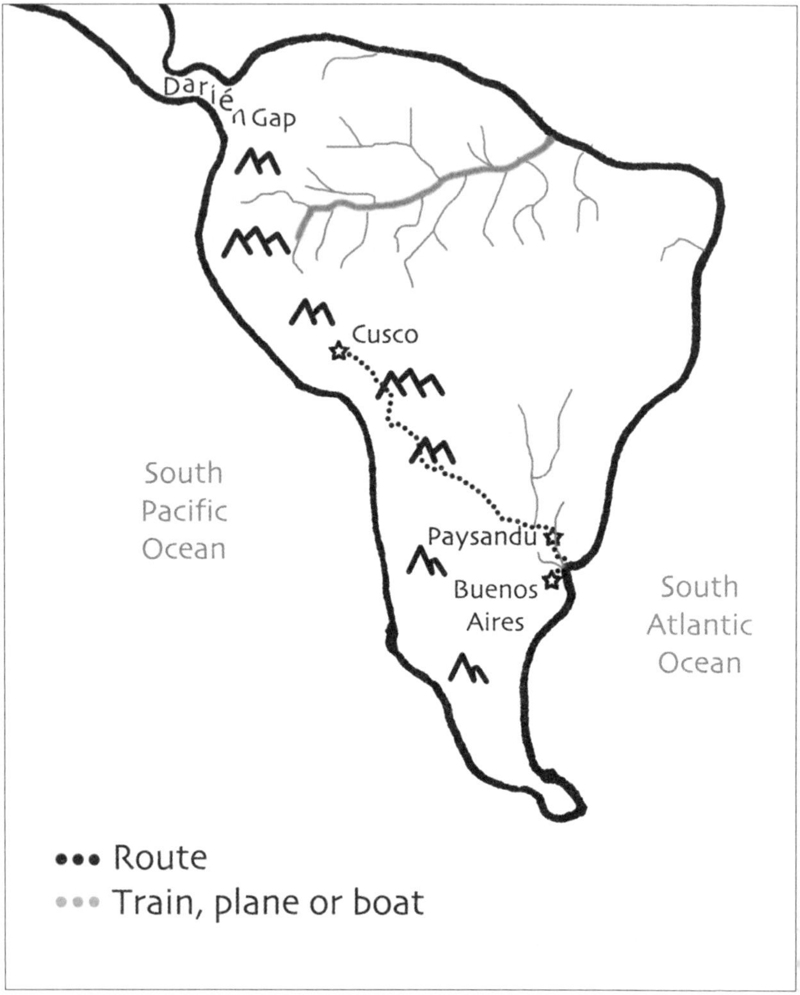

From Buenos Aires to Cusco

CHAPTER 4

Paying with freedom

"We invented a mountain of superfluous needs. You have to keep buying, throwing things away. It's our lives we are squandering. When I buy something or when you buy it, we're not paying with money. We're paying with the time from our lives we had to spend to earn that money. The difference is that you can't buy life. Life just goes by. And it's terrible to waste your life losing your freedom."
José Mujica (Pepe), 40th President of Uruguay

What I got paid when I was a PhD student – £12,000 (US$16,000)[1] each year – was plenty for me to live well. I had money left over each month to save too. I have never needed more than I received as a PhD student, yet as the years rolled by, and I became a well-published and respected academic, they paid me more anyway. And so, rather than develop expensive habits that wouldn't do much for my happiness, as my research kept showing, I kept my pleasures simple.

In fact, I got round to ditching some habits that had long ago stopped bringing much happiness. I also began shedding some of life's necessities so I could see how I felt without them. I wanted to understand what was essential for me to live well. I still did exhilarating things that were sometimes expensive, but I began to fritter less away on needless things, and saw that I could find exhilaration in less expensive ways. I became more mindful of how I spent money. Sometimes it was difficult, especially at first, as I weaned myself off needing to look a certain way or have certain things to meet the expectations of those around me. After some time though, I relaxed, and a few people showed up who thought I was groovy just as I was.

Since I had saved quite a bit from living a minimal lifestyle, and because I needed so little to live day-to-day on a bicycle, when I quit my job as an academic happiness researcher I estimated I would be able to go several years without needing to work for money. That's an immense privilege and I consider myself fortunate. Yes, there was choice and commitment involved in making it happen, but I am not deluded into thinking that everyone has the same choices.

The many possible routes on a journey for happiness – choice, circumstance, and chance

As I cycled through Spain in the first weeks of my journey, camping out every night for the sake of both cost and happiness, I would spread out my map of Argentina in my tent at night before I slept. The sight would awaken within me a child-like wonder and awe that there were real lives being lived at each and every point I was looking at; lives that were probably more frugal than the one I had lived up to the point. What would each point on a map smell and look like? And, as I ran my finger along different possible routes, I marvelled at how those smells and sights might change from one point to the next.

With whom would I cross paths? What would happen? Would I dare to lose myself in those smells and sights? Would I find some happiness? And at what cost?

And so, as I stared wide-eyed in my tent at the lines connecting all the dots to villages, towns, and cities that I yet knew nothing of, I wondered which ones I'd come to know. How exactly would I make my way northward up to Bolivia once my bicycle and I had set out from Argentina's capital, Buenos Aires? I needed to make some choices from the options that my circumstances provided.

To gain entry to Argentina via an air border on my passport

(a British passport allows far more freedom to move about our planet than most passports), I needed to have proof, with confirmed onward travel, that I would be leaving the country within 90 days of arriving. That was going to be difficult to do, when in all likelihood I would end up passing through a nondescript border town whenever my legs decided they wanted to get me there. Showing border officials my map, running my finger along some of the lines of roads, and giving them an earnest smile wouldn't have been enough. One of the least expensive options that I could find before boarding the flight from Barcelona was to take a short ferry ride from Buenos Aires over to Uruguay. I booked the ferry for a few days after landing – and that, out of the many thousands of different possibilities, was how I chose which way to set off into that vast continent.

Still now, I often wonder what this journey for happiness would have looked like had I set off in any other way. Different roads and different people; different smells and different sights; different costs and different happiness. Though as much as we celebrate choice in modern market economies as being crucial for happiness, it can also be overwhelming, and paradoxically can lead to less happiness.[2] With too much choice there can be worry about regret and indecision. The fear of missing out can diminish our ability to be present with what we finally end up choosing. Besides, having the choice between a multitude of similar looking goods is not really freedom, is it? Nor is being able to buy up all the possible choices. True freedom is having the time to know who we are, and then to be able to act, based on that clear knowledge.

As it turned out, I have no hang ups or regrets about my journey. There were plenty of things I'm grateful I experienced, and other things I really wish I hadn't, but had these things happened or not happened, then it might have been a very different journey for happiness.

Or perhaps not?

What has become clear to me is that all the insights I had about happiness, as I rode to Bhutan, would have probably come out the same had I taken a different route. That is because they go beyond specific chance incidences, they go beyond choice, and beyond circumstance. Some of what I learnt about happiness may have come quicker than other things had I proceeded a different way or had a different set of circumstances, but I'd have worked with whatever happened to cross my path, and I am sure I would have got to those insights in the end. I'm certain that, regardless of who we are or where we go, most of the insights about happiness contained in this book will have to be contended with in some shape or form. There are the things to be chosen – the where, the how, and the when; the circumstances – what we have, what we look like, and where our passport permits us to roam; and then there is pure chance. Happiness in all its guises comes in acknowledging the dance between these three.

Uruguay – starting as I ought to have continued

Before setting off from Scotland, I had never expected to pass through Uruguay. However, I was glad that a chance ferry ride had me doing so. Uruguay's 40th president is an unusual character, and it was the inspiration I found in thinking of him that made Uruguay (out of all 25 countries I would come to pass through) the country where I spent the third lowest amount of money per day.

José Mujica, affectionately named Pepe by Uruguayans, led the country from 2010 to 2015. He was dubbed by the BBC as the "world's poorest president".[3] An ex-freedom fighter and political prisoner for 13 years, his wealth lies within the integrity of his words and deeds. Throughout his presidency, rather than live in the luxurious house that the state would ordinarily provide, he opted to stay in his wife's farmhouse, on a dirt road just outside the capital of Montevideo. He also donated 90 per cent of his salary to charity, such that his wage was in line with the average Uruguayan income. He was adamant he could live well with that.

I was only in Uruguay for five days, and I kept reminding myself of José Mujica's words. One of my favourite ideas of his, which is an extension of the quote with which we began this chapter, is that when we weigh up whether to buy something or not, we should think not in terms of the monetary cost, but instead how many hours we would need to work to buy that thing. It is not a question of whether it is worth the money, but whether it is worth the time we have to give from our lives to get the money to buy it? Sometimes it is a thing we desperately need – yet so often it might not be. It can be what José would consider another 'superfluous need', and the time spent working to obtain it can get in the way of actually living our lives, and spending time with one another.

It was José and others like him[4] that inspired me to get together enough savings to make this journey possible (though let's not forget that I had a decently paid job, no dependents, and, in being a white man, I would have statistically earnt more than if I were not a man nor white through being covertly, though probably unconsciously, favoured in the job market. Discrimination is real).[5] My circumstance, as much as my choices, made it easier to have money left over at the end of the month. However, thinking in terms of lost hours of life needed to buy things, at higher levels of income, items generally cost less of our time. That makes for greater temptation to fritter money away on relatively unneeded things. Money can be a curse if we're not careful, since there is a lot to tempt us away from what is important. Yet ultimately, I had my eyes fixed on buying myself some freedom from working, rather than having many things I didn't need.

In Uruguay, I managed to spend close to £10 (less than US$15) per day. That was a target I wish I'd been rigid with throughout my journey. Although it was helpful to have more money for this journey than I needed, if I had been more mindful about my spending, I suspect I would have found greater happiness. It meant options that didn't serve my happiness were alluring to me. The possibility of checking into a hotel was nearly always available to me; I bought far too much Gatorade, developing something of an addiction; and I left restaurants bloated full of pizza far too often. With a tighter budget these wouldn't have been possibilities open to me, and I'd have been happier without them.

I faced many of my early journey anxieties around language and safety head on in Uruguay. I camped every single night whilst I was there, and on the second night, after being directed to the banks of the River Uruguay by a local man, I camped in a spot that is etched in my mind as being one of the most beautiful places I've ever slept. Given how much I've camped out under the stars, that is some statement. What makes it more beautiful in my mind now than others is that I didn't take a photo of it. Not because I didn't want to, but I couldn't. I was in possession of a very old smart phone that my brother had given me before I'd left, and it had stopped working (temporarily, because it came back to life a week or so later). I'd never had a smart phone before on account of my explorations around what I needed to live well, so it didn't feel like a great loss at the time. Still, no photo would have done that moment justice, and the memory wouldn't have been quite the same either. But trust me, it was – like countless spots I would camp in over the following months – divine. Lacking a photo seems to heighten its magic. My memory savours the place in a completely different way than the many camping spots I experienced for which I do have photos. I feel the charm of the spot more intensely than others, and sometimes I like to wonder whether this one was real, or whether I was only dreaming.

I was in Uruguay for only four nights before I crossed the border back into Argentina, zipping straight on through. I met some very kind people there. At the time I thought I'd just gotten very lucky. However, as I'll describe later, it wasn't because I'd gotten lucky at all; that is just how people tend to be in this part of the world. And they are happier for it too. I had a lot to learn about humanity.

Since I was without a camera, I asked a few of the people I

met to take some photos and send them on to me. A popular photo from my journey (which would one day appear in *The Times* and elsewhere), is one taken by a road worker called Carlos. He was in a bulldozer repairing an old road that was dusty and very difficult to ride a bicycle upon. As soon as he saw me, he quickly stopped his work and beckoned me to stop too. At that point I was still somewhat distrustful of others, with a "what does this guy really want?" kind of mindset, and though I stopped, I was cautious. As it turned out he just wanted to offer me some of his ice-cool orange fizzy drink on a hot day, and have a chat. He also took that very beautiful photo of me and emailed it to me a few days later: a photo that catches me wide-eyed with early-journey energy – lots of anxiety behind those eyes, yet lots of excitement too.

Ratcheting up the costs of a journey for happiness

On my final night in Uruguay, I tested my fear by camping in a local park at the Uruguayan-Argentinian border town of Paysandú. Some of the locals I met said I would be absolutely fine to spend the night there. I wasn't so sure. There were quite a few people about the place. Nevertheless, I faced my fears and, though I didn't sleep well that night, I was fine.

Once I crossed the border back into Argentina, I lost focus on challenging myself to step beyond my fears, and for various reasons, including a life-threatening crisis in Peru, I would pay little mind to thrift for most of South and Central America. My costs ballooned. One general reason for my lack of care around what I was spending is that the British Pound goes a long way in this part of the world. This meant that partaking in a little bit of this and that – with no sustained benefit to my happiness –wasn't as expensive as it ordinarily would have been compared to back home. The little costs added up. Once I arrived in the considerably more expensive USA, I had to buck up my ideas, and become a lot more mindful of my spending. The consequence of that mindfulness with money, as I'll explain more later, was that I got to experience a lot more happiness.

So how much did my journey cost overall? I'm a bit embarrassed about revealing this figure to be honest, especially given that a major premise of the book is that greater happiness comes from looking beyond money. However, I value honesty, and I know others do too, so to stop your wondering, let's get this out of the way now. All told, I spent roughly £15,000 (US$20,000) on my journey. It was entirely self-financed – no sponsor, no debt, no bullshit. I don't know if that is high or low for a journey of this type, that lasted close to 18 months. I know it is certainly an amount of money that most people, even if they were to save every penny and not spend on non-essential items, would not have spare to travel the world with. And it is certainly higher than the two months' salary it would have cost had I simply taken a fortnight round-trip by plane to Bhutan. However, some will spend more than this on a new car, and this journey cost less money than my earnings over a similar 18-month time-period as a PhD student, way back when. Some would spend a lot less, others a lot more – a product of choice, circumstance, and chance, as ever.

What I spent overall was certainly higher than I had anticipated. I had no concrete target to begin with – I had thought that I had become so mindful over the years about money that I wouldn't need a target and it would be naturally low. I was wrong.

The journey turned out to be twice as long as I had anticipated, and there were many costs that I hadn't considered. For all the general bike maintenance, spare parts, and camping equipment that I needed to replenish along the way, I spent around £1,500 (US$2,000); ten per cent of the overall cost. Among some of the major items were the new pannier-cycling bags in Buenos Aires (after it became clear that the old ones wouldn't make it very far), a complete bicycle drive chain re-build in Nevada, and a new tent in California, as well as the odd new chain, brake pads, pedals, and tyres here and there.

Boats, trains, planes, and a taxi set me back about £3,000

(US$4,000), a fifth of the overall cost. That included boats to take me along the Amazon river and getting past the impassable-by-land Darién gap linking South and Central America, a mammoth four-day train journey in Canada, which I boarded certain I was returning home, a madly expensive taxi run to get my badly sprained-ankled-self and my bicycle away from mounting civil unrest in Nicaragua, and flights that – in an effort to limit my environmental impact – were direct and therefore more expensive than otherwise. I spent £300 (US$400) on ATM withdrawal fees alone! Minus these general journey expenditures, my day-to-day living costs across the whole journey were about £20 (US$27) per day.

What does this say about money on a journey for happiness? This particular journey to Bhutan on a bicycle needed some financing to make it happen, and I was able to live in a way prior to this journey which not only helped me get the money together, but also accustomed me to fairly minimal living. If I did it again, I'd do it on much less – half as much per day, at least. Though, I'd probably take twice as long about it as I think there'd be more happiness that way, so it might add up to the same! Now that I'm confident in what a journey for happiness like mine can offer others, as illustrated by the crowdfund that enabled this book to find its way into your hands (thank you), perhaps I'd try and get some outside finance to make the journey happen.

Certainly, a journey of this magnitude requires some resources. However, what I now know having done it is that a journey for happiness can be embarked upon without going far away at all. Rather than cycle to Bhutan again – which I don't regret for a second – I'd have my happiness journey right where I am. In fact, I've been struck that exactly the same happiness insights I learnt on my journey apply to writing this book, getting through the covid-pandemic, and so many of the things I've done since, which have cost very little. What I would come to learn about happiness on this journey goes beyond the journey itself. So let's not get hung up on money – doing so has been limiting us as a species for far too long. A truth which I'll come back to again in this book is that money is a *strategy* that we can use to meet needs (often very inefficiently), but it is not a need in itself. Other strategies are available.

However, lest anyone with enough money forget, when it comes to money and happiness, there is also poverty. And, unless personally experienced, it is difficult to appreciate the challenge of getting through day-to-day poverty. I have no personal experience of this. Money may have been tight growing up, but it wasn't poverty. Instead, I've taken to reading the research, listening to people's stories, and being compassionate. We might look and judge other people's life outcomes, yet how they arrived there will often have been because they had a lot less choice than others. It might just be where they happen to have been born or what they look like. Perhaps it is a minimum-wage job with mouths to feed, or heavy debt because pay cheques aren't enough. If there is no job and a visible addiction, then often at root there is a painful trauma that isn't visible. Money is not one of the keys to happiness, yet poverty is certainly one of the keys to misery.[6] It can be difficult to find a way out of it – let alone gather the resources to feel confident enough to get on a bicycle and ride to an obscure destination.

Poverty aside, it was those travellers who spent much less than me that I found myself envying the most, as I journeyed to Bhutan. Not simply *because* they spent less, but because of the experiences they had. Unlike me, who could quell the fear of vulnerability by staying in a cheap hotel rather than camping out, they faced their fears head on. Actually, they seemed to be entirely fear*less,* and had boundary-pushing experiences all of the time, just like the sublime one I would go on to encounter with those Guatemalan children in their village I described at beginning of the last chapter. Much of the time it was because their financial resources were strained. They had little option but to be wide open to the gifts of this world. And it wasn't just taking, because they gave a lot to the people they met. They were beyond money.

Then, there were those who spent a lot more than I did. They travelled quickly from place to place, wanting to see and do everything while they had the chance. They barely stopped, and yet – though they saw and did many things that I didn't see and do – they never could see and do it all in the way they had hoped and expected. There was always something they'd left unseen or undone, something they would have to come back for, not quite fully satisfied. Because I snaked slowly, and sometimes painstakingly, through unfamiliar lands on my bicycle, I saw and did different things. It is difficult to say whether it was any better or worse to journey the way I did. However, it was a lot less expensive each day, and ultimately, a lower daily expense allows for a longer, and a potentially deeper journey.

What was clear, however, was that having more than enough money can get in the way of experiencing some of life's sweeter blessings.[7] Just as not having at least some money can get in the way of options, having too much rules out others. Circumstances, including seemingly favourable ones, are always a limiting factor to what we can experience and achieve. This makes it all the more important to ask ourselves: what we are trying to achieve and why?

CHAPTER 5

Letting go of Bhutan

"Here I am guiding my own life – living my own way. It's not all happiness – sometimes it is downright painful – but this journey is taking me to places of complete joy. I am not sure what and who will come back but I don't care at this point."
Journal entry, 13th January 2017

It had been exactly 80 days since I'd left Scotland and here I was, settled down into my sleeping bag for the night, set against the most incredible scene. Never before had I seen such a sight.

To the right of my little green tent sat an enormous cactus, the illustrious Huachuma. The spot next to this impressive specimen was the flattest I could find on my route to the top of the highest point I'd reach by bicycle on my journey (4,260 metres/13,976ft). I had already cooked and eaten dinner on my small stove, and as I lay there wrapped up warm, I gazed in awe at the majestic mountains that stretched out into the distance. Those mountains had been there for time immemorial, and for many days now, feeling like little more than an ant next to them, I had been traversing my way through. There were a few clouds in the sky, beginning to glow fire-red from the setting sun's rays. The day was coming to its end, and despite not reaching the summit as I had expected and aimed to do earlier in the day, I was feeling more than satisfied with where I was. This moment had a touch of the sacred.

Night fell, the stars came out, and I lay there thinking about the experiences leading up to the moment I was in now. Since leaving Cusco, Peru, seven days earlier, I had surmounted four mountain passes only slightly lower in altitude than the one I had spent most of this day climbing. On some days I'd climbed relentlessly upward, ever fixated on reaching the top. Pain would build up in my legs, and there would be hardly any let up for most of the day. Sometimes the road just kept rising up and up, ever higher into the sky. Meanwhile the heat pounded down upon me. Occasionally there was a heavy downpour that would revitalise my body a little; other times it only added to my struggle. There had been times when I wondered whether the pain or joy I was experiencing would ever end. Until it did, as it always does.

Twice when I reached the top of one of those mountain passes – or at least what I thought was the top – I hadn't been able see a thing through the clouds when I looked around me. I didn't know whether to laugh or cry, given I had spent the day hoping to see something spectacular – and how, in my desire to reach the top, I had left much better views behind. Views much like the one I was gazing out toward now from my tent.

I was glad I'd decided to let go of reaching the top that day. After all, this was supposed to be a journey about happiness, not achievement. Too often the two get confused. And here I was in the mountains of Peru, revisiting a lifelong habit of expecting happiness to come once I'd achieved something difficult and even painful. It wasn't just getting to the top of a mountain where this focus on achievement rather than happiness was playing out in me – it was the entire damn journey. I was under the impression that I'd find personal happiness, if and when I succeeded in arriving in Bhutan. Maybe I would, but maybe I wouldn't. Maybe if and when I finally reached Bhutan, it would be cloudy both inside and out.

As I lay there, watching the stars and the silhouetted mountains, I began to think further back than a few days, to when I was a successful academic happiness researcher… Back then, and certainly most of my life before that, I had been very far away from being in a permanent state of satisfaction…

A satisfying kind of happiness

One question a happiness researcher like me will ask people is: "Overall, how satisfied are you with your life nowadays?" People are asked to score their answer to this life satisfaction question on a scale from 0 to 10, where 0 is "Not at all" and 10 is "Completely". Yes, it's simple, but remarkably informative.

There are other ways of understanding a person's happiness that are more objective, such as scanning the brain to see if certain areas have been stimulated, or watching someone and recording how much they smile and laugh. However, how a person reports themselves to feel about their life strongly relates to these more objective measures, and so asking people directly saves a lot of time and resources.[1] It also means that the person responding to that question gets to decide what happiness is for themselves, rather than relying on someone they don't know to tell them how happy they are, based on which parts of their brain light up and how much they are seen to smile.

And yet, can – and should – someone's happiness be reduced to a number between 0 and 10? I worked with this question throughout my happiness career, and in my opinion, such a question trivialises happiness immensely. The idea of boiling happiness down to a mere number turns some people off the subject completely. Happiness must be surely more than a number. However, we have to accept that some people like numbers a lot, especially those economists. In fact, numbers can be really helpful, and something which has become clear in the realm of politics over recent decades is that "if we don't measure something, it becomes neglected".[2] Many aspects of the economy are routinely measured, and as a result, the *size of the economy* has come to dominate our lives and our political dialogue. It seems fair to say that in the process of adding up how much is bought and sold in an economy, we have neglected happiness – as well as many other important things that can't be counted in a straightforward way. Therefore, putting numbers on happiness ought to bring more attention to happiness in our societies. And it has... a little.

We might also dispute whether knowing how satisfied someone is with their life gets to the nub of the nature of happiness. There are, of course, other kinds of happiness than life satisfaction, some of which better reflect what happiness means to most people, and I'll get onto those kinds later, when they become more relevant to this journey. In this chapter, however, I'm focusing on the *life satisfaction* question. What causes people to answer with high levels of life satisfaction is relevant to what I was caught up thinking about that night, as I gazed out from my tent halfway up a mountain. And what's more, it's the question most commonly asked relating to happiness in the research – before I set out to Bhutan on a bicycle, I had published many academic research articles using the satisfaction question myself.

You may even have answered the life satisfaction question in the past, perhaps asked in a survey, or because you've seen it somewhere and wondered about your own happiness. If you haven't answered it before, it is worth asking yourself now. How satisfied with life are you nowadays from 0 to 10? Are you a "Not at all" satisfied 0, a "Completely" satisfied 10, or somewhere in between? I've certainly asked myself this same question at various points in my life. (Given how much of my own career researching happiness relied on understanding people's answers to this question, it would be odd if I hadn't!)

I couldn't get no… Or, how my levels of satisfaction have changed over time

My life satisfaction has varied a lot over the years, much as it will do for most people. For example, about three months before I left on my bicycle for Bhutan I gave myself a 6 out of 10. That's not the lowest it's ever been, nor is it the highest. I had a rough time toward the end of my PhD: a seven-year relationship had come to an end, and I was questioning whether to keep going with my studies. At the time I couldn't see the point of much in life. These things were inter-related with other things going on around me, and overall I wouldn't have given myself much more than a 4. However, this wasn't as bad as it was when I was 20. Then, things were really bad.

Though I didn't ask myself when I was 20 how satisfied I was with my life – because I wasn't a happiness researcher then – I was experiencing severe distress. My life was very far away from how it was 'supposed' to be. I was depressed and chronically anxious. Not that I knew that at the time, as it just seemed like a somewhat worse version of my teenage years. Instead of general unhappiness punctuated with occasional and fleeting happiness, as life had generally been growing up, at 20 it was just one big block of sadness, that I could see no way out of. I thought there was something wrong with me. This is how I remember it looking back.

By the time I was 33, however, I was giving myself an 8 out of 10 on life satisfaction. That's quite high; the average for people living in the UK is around 7.5.[3] At that point, I was progressing in my career by publishing lots of academic articles in some of the most reputable journals, and obtaining a decent amount of money to fund my research. By then I was also spending a lot of time outdoors, and I had some supportive relationships around me. I was even in love again. However, after some time, although my career objectively improved, my desire to write more academic articles or seek research funds waned. I lost interest in what I was doing at work, which felt pointless. After a while, my satisfaction with life dropped to how it was before I left on my bicycle for Bhutan: an okay – but below average for someone living in the UK – 6.

Despite being a happiness researcher, I've never scored a perfect 10 on life satisfaction – and that includes immediately after completing this bicycle journey to Bhutan. I have often wondered how my five-year-old self, sitting on his swirly-orange carpet, might have answered this question about how satisfied he was. To tell you the truth, I think my younger self might have been more than a little perplexed as to what it would have meant to be satisfied. Being satisfied has always seemed a somewhat strange concept to me. The popularity of 'life satisfaction' as a happiness gauge stems in part from its wide usage in customer satisfaction surveys. Yet, being satisfied with a product is one thing, being satisfied with a life quite another. We might think that satisfaction is closely related to contentment, but as I'll describe, what people do when they answer questions about how satisfied they are with their life suggests that it doesn't have that much to do with gauging contentment.

Personally, I've wanted to live a life that is better than just satisfying, and I seem to recall that my five-year-old self was better than satisfied. He was off the charts. He was on a completely different scale – quite literally, because the kind of happiness he was experiencing (just as I would later go on to find in abundance on this journey, and will describe in a much later chapter, when I realised I had it) was far richer than merely 'satisfying'.

That doesn't mean it is not useful to ask people how satisfied they are with their life. It may be an imperfect metric, but the question has helped us get much closer to understanding what matters to people. One clear limit is that our answers to the life satisfaction question depend on a number of things, some of which we might think shouldn't matter at all. For example, our life satisfaction has been shown to depend on what has been happening throughout our day, whether a loved one is present or not when we answer the question, and whether we're asked the question over the telephone or in a face-to-face interview. It also depends on the question we were asked immediately beforehand, and what the weather was like at the time. Tomorrow we might answer the same question differently – even though our response is supposed to be about our life overall, and the conditions of our life overall will probably be much the same today as they will be tomorrow.

Once researchers account for these factors in their studies – and they can to a reasonable degree – our answer depends to some extent on what we have in our lives. However, life satisfaction also depends upon what we expect or would like to have. It takes a person about five seconds to answer a life satisfaction question. In that time, we go into our minds and ask ourselves whether we have all the things that we *believe* we need to be happy. If our life situation doesn't meet our most basic needs – a roof over our head, food on the table, a fit and healthy body, someone to talk to, feeling safe – then this is a real problem that results in people expressing dissatisfaction with their life that no amount of reconfiguring what they wish they had will be able to get around. However, if we more or less have all of our physical needs met, yet for whatever reason we expect or would like something different, then we may also report feeling dissatisfied. For example, if we want a higher income than we currently have,[4] or a bigger house – or perhaps if we are only halfway up a very high mountain, rather than being already at the top.

Forever dissatisfied

Most of us have expectations around what constitutes a good life. We may have certain goals we want to achieve so that we can live that good life; some of those goals might already be realised. Some, however, have not yet been realised, and it may be that they never are. For example, maybe we expect to get a good job, earn a lot of money, get married, buy a house, have kids, and travel around the world. If we *believe* these things are important and we haven't achieved them, most likely we'll feel dissatisfied. However, if we have achieved them, what is often the case is that they are not as satisfying as we had *believed* they would be. In part, because they could always be better – a better job, more money, a better partner, a bigger house, quieter kids, and more places to visit. However, also because they might not have actually been the best way for us to meet our core human needs, and what we've been doing all along is simply conforming to social narratives, to the stories we have been told about what a good life ought to entail.[5]

Essentially, what we *believe* will bring satisfaction is often the result of what others who know us well and our culture have conveyed to us *should* make for a 'good life'. That doesn't mean that the so-called good life actually will satisfy us, if we ever achieve it. As I'll describe later, when considering happiness in Latin America, being completely satisfied in life also doesn't necessarily equate to a person smiling and laughing more throughout their day. As Daniel Kahneman, psychologist winner of the Nobel Prize in Economics in 2002, puts it, "Life satisfaction is connected to a large degree to social yardsticks – achieving goals, meeting expectations."

With our desire for continual striving, it is a wonder we could ever consider ourselves fully satisfied. And it is why we might look at some people, including our own present and past selves, and think, "They have it all, how could they not be happy?" I know I've done it; I've done it a lot, and it is a hard habit to break.

Early in my happiness career, what I really wanted was to publish my first academic article. When I finally achieved that, I felt really satisfied. Perhaps I increased by one whole point for a short while. Yet soon, that satisfaction subsided, and I wanted to publish another article. And when I achieved that I was very satisfied too, but not quite as satisfied when I published that first article, and also it was for a much shorter time. I quickly went on to wanting to publish another one. Soon I started to *expect* to obtain academic publications, and others expected them of me also. It was part of my job, and if I wasn't publishing, my career was at risk. So what I did was keep striving – and on and on and on. After a while, it stopped satisfying me altogether.

Publishing academic articles is very much like getting paid more and generally having more. We want more, and we rarely seem to have quite enough to be fully satisfied. Just a little more, we may say to ourselves. And we'll say just a little more, even when we finally have what we once upon a time thought would be more than enough.[6] Quickly, what was once more than enough can seem like it isn't. We keep pushing on – until one day, we believe, we'll really make it.

This need for better and more is one explanation why larger economies haven't brought about commensurately more satisfaction to people's lives. And, of course, always wanting to do better was one of the reasons why I couldn't find much in the way of sustained happiness in my research career. The curious thing in cultures which are dominated by growing the economy and needing to perform ever better is that being at least a little bit dissatisfied serves that notion of progress. If we are dissatisfied, then we might strive to do and buy the things that are claimed to satisfy. Yet, we'll rarely be satisfied that way. None of this is to say that an emphasis on growth or performance has to be a bad thing. But is it a means to an end, or the end itself? It used to be the case that when huge swathes of the population were unable to meet their most basic material needs, a larger economy was essential for improving the quality of people's lives. In some parts of the world this is still very much the case. As a result, way back in the 1930s, we began measuring the size of our economies – the Gross Domestic Product – and we hear about whether it is growing or falling all the time. Yet, we should be measuring other things with as much gusto, and be considering what ultimate end we want to achieve.

Finding satisfaction by cycling to Bhutan

What I witnessed in my family when I was growing up was this permanent state of dissatisfaction: the state of never having quite enough. We've all seen it to some extent in ourselves and others. In my family there was occasionally real struggle with having enough; though I think our biggest issue was being indebted, and the insecurity that went with that. A lot of my family's energy went into paying for the things that we had bought because we *believed* they were part of the 'good life' and would bring us sustained happiness.

I'd gone on to publish research articles on the link between money, indebtedness, and happiness. I had become a leading expert on the subject, taking great care to live the research, and not act the way my family had with money. What I did instead – and at first, I didn't realise how similar this was to my family's behaviour – was to aspire after more of those academic publications. I'd always want another, and I'd 'run into the red' emotionally in order to obtain them. That is sometimes okay, if it brings sustained fulfilment and the goal feels intrinsically worthwhile, but it did not. And that process of continual striving is very difficult for anyone to get away from.

What I noticed, as I was going up and down those mountains – nearly three months into my journey, aiming to reach summit after summit, with my eyes set on some day arriving in Bhutan on my bicycle – was that I was at it once again. There I was, with an emphasis on the achievement of a goal: the next mountain pass, the next country, and finally arriving in Bhutan on my bicycle. I would often imagine myself arriving one day in that far-off land. I'd picture in my mind getting my first glimpse of Bhutanese mountains rising up in the distance, and see myself feeling triumphant. I'd be successful, satisfied, and everlastingly happy. It is nigh on impossible to shake the notion that achieving goals will bring happiness, particularly if that goal-focused mentality has been there for most of our lives.

And these goals that we have, they are not always *our* goals. They are often built around someone else's expectations as to how we ought to be – perhaps what our family expect of us, our teachers, our friends, our community, and so on. Sometimes those goals might have intrinsic value beyond our needs for social approval, and they often are for some people, some of the time, but this is not the case for everybody. If they were truly important, then achieving these things would be far more strongly linked to life satisfaction than the research shows. Life satisfaction tends to depend on whether we are living the life we *think* we should be living. If we are not living that life, then we suffer psychologically. If we are living it, then so long as we don't quickly adopt a still higher bar, then we'll get at least some satisfying kind of happiness out of it.

On a bicycle in the middle of the mountains, camping more or less where I liked, there was no-one I had to please, no one to answer to. It was just me and my potential to be satisfied (or not) by what I had set out to try and do. I didn't expect myself to actually arrive in Bhutan. In those early days I knew it was an absurd, almost impossible, journey. However, I did think that because I had *said* I was going to cycle to Bhutan, not doing it would, in the eyes of others and therefore myself, be a failure. These were *my* thoughts and *my* expectations. Completely unfounded, but also recognisably a product of being goal-focused for much of my life, and something I was going to need to let go of on this journey for happiness. Most will have heard the old adage that 'happiness is a journey, not a destination', yet the belief in the opposite runs deep within us. How do we actually get beyond that belief?

Entering the liminal space

A liminal space is a term that the anthropologist Victor Turner used to describe a situation in which the normal rules that guide our daily lives are temporarily suspended. It is a space that is between cultural realms; an unknown, where it is possible to explore new territory and experiment with being a different person. We might find ourselves in a liminal space by taking a short break, away from our habits and the environments that create those habits. It can be a challenging space; however, it is in such a space that profound breakthroughs can happen. Most of us might benefit from being in a liminal space once in a while. Sadly, by virtue of how we've constructed our societies, being in a liminal space is all too rare for many. And it is also a very scary place to be in. Or at least it may sound scary until we're actually in such a space, and then we may see – as I did half way up that mountain – that we deserve much more than a satisfied life.

I had never heard of the idea of a liminal space until some months after I returned.[7] Yet, it describes pretty accurately where I was throughout most of my journey. It was up in the Andes that I first entered into such a space. Up until then I had been recreating the same impediments to my happiness that I was trying to break free from. The first months were a period of me coming to terms with myself – working through my fears, sadness, and shame – but once things had begun to settle, a space for transformation opened up. This was my journey, and it was down to me to define my own parameters of success and failure.

It was down to me to figure out what expectations I wanted to hold. And after a little deliberation, I opted for no expectations. There was no benchmark for this journey. It would go where it needed to go, and for as long as was necessary. It is why I decided to camp halfway up the side of that mountain, rather than push onto the top that day. It was at that point that ideas of success and failure became outlandish to me.

At the time, I wrote on Twitter that: "The idea of failure keeps me following rules, fearful, subjugated, and doing things that do not serve me. But where did the concept of failure come from? It certainly did not begin inside me. I was always encouraged to put off following what was right for me because if I did not, I would miss out – miss out on a successful life. Somebody else's idea of a successful life."

Sure, I still hoped to arrive in Bhutan, because the goal was meaningful beyond personal satisfaction – as I'll come back to later, but I did let go of the expectation that achieving that goal would bring me happiness much beyond a short-lived satisfaction. And with that letting go, a tension began to release within me – a tension that has always prevented me from being as present in the world as I would like to be. A tension which imagines me somewhere in the future, wondering whether doing something will bring me the happiness I crave. And if I'm not in the future, then I'm somewhere in the past, thinking about all the things I might otherwise have tried to achieve in life – having regrets, or wondering whether I'd missed out on something. I didn't feel lost, I just felt a little bit freer. I knew where I was, and that was high up in the mountains on a bicycle, with just a few worldly possessions, watching the stars twinkle over those mountains.

And as I looked in the other direction, at all the mountains that were still to come, I smiled at the thought that if this journey were to take its natural happy course – not too fast, not too slow – then I might still be on a bicycle in a year's time. Much longer than I would have ordinarily allowed myself. This wasn't an ordinary space. And this wasn't an ordinary journey.

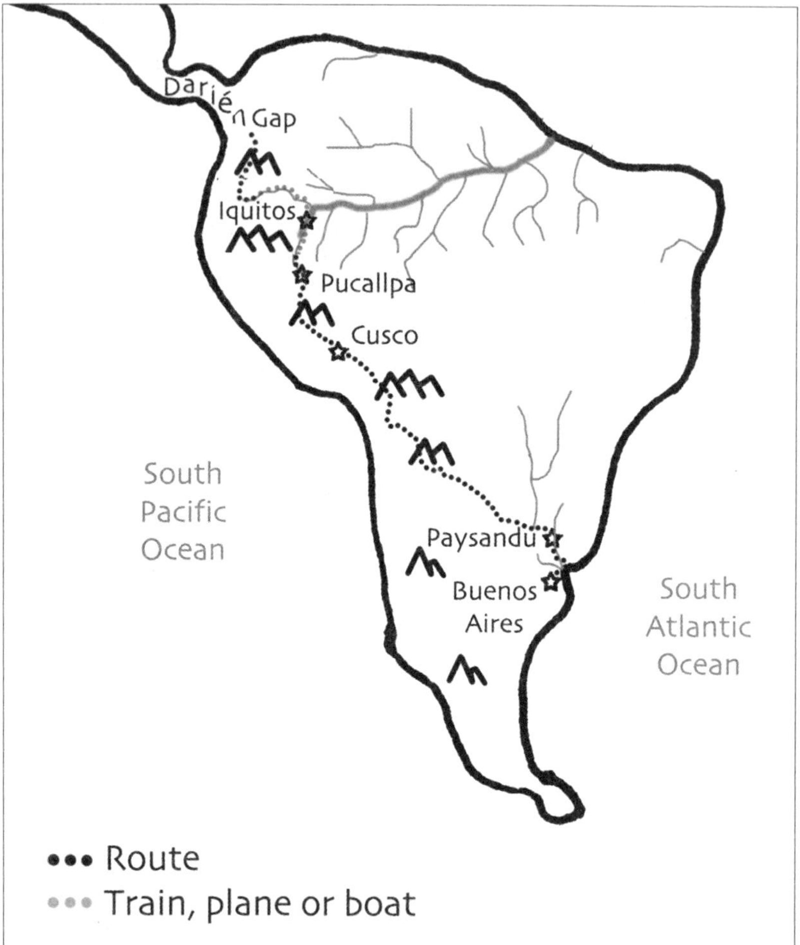

Getting from Cusco and out of crisis

CHAPTER 6

Along comes a crisis

"I'm scared, I'm alone, and I'm sad. I don't like this – I don't like any of it. Until I get the magic of deep connection, I'm on my own. I don't know where it will come from, but it will come. Something on the world outside will light a fire inside of me. And then several experiences will roll from that. Until that time, I am where I am – I try to accept that."
Journal entry, 24th January 2018

How do we get through a crisis? Sometimes we just don't. And even if we do, the whole process can feel senseless and isolating. Many of us have been close to the edge, to some extent or another, and it is never easy to find our way through. As I sat there by the side of the road, blood pouring, no-one in sight, wondering why me and why now, I doubted whether I'd get through this one. My journey – perhaps my life – seemed over.

It had been another spectacular start to the day. I'd slept peacefully in the fresh mountain air, having bathed in a nearby stream and eaten heartily the evening before. In the morning, I unzipped my tent to watch the sun come up on the mountains and cooked my breakfast. It was my usual porridge, soaked overnight with a rich assortment of fruit and nuts; always delicious and full of energy to feed my lightly aching muscles, and get the creaking bones going for the day. With my happiness no longer bound up in one day arriving in Bhutan, and the sense that nothing was lacking in my life, I felt an ease like never before.

I packed up my things to get moving, took a final long look

at the spot where I had slept, offered my thanks for being looked after for the night, and smiled to myself at just how good I had become at finding such stunning camp spots. I'd gotten more confident with how I was travelling, and I was far less fearful. I couldn't know that after what was to happen just a couple of hours later, it would be longer than a month before I would have the strength to set up my tent in a random spot like this again.

The trauma

I was focused on the children playing in the street. They'd seen me approaching on my bicycle, and a small boy no more than eight years old had skirted across the road to attempt to block my path. There was nothing untoward about his movement. He was smiling, giggling actually, and so was I. I knew he only wanted me to stop for a minute and connect with him. I'd been riding for a couple of hours already that day, and I was eager for connection too. I began to slow down. However, being so captivated by this boy's excitement, I wasn't aware of the stray dog that loomed somewhere over to the left.

For anyone riding a bicycle, dogs are a routine but major hazard. In some countries, typically those in which there are many dogs roaming free, and bicycles are less common, dogs chase bikes. Sometimes it is an ineffectual hunt. However, just as likely, it will be more menacing, and a vicious snarling pursuit will ensue. It is plain scary at times. I'm not exactly sure why dogs chase bicycles the way they do, but that doesn't matter. What is important is to have some way of dealing with them when they come. Some cyclists carry a big stick, and wield it if a dog gets too menacing. Others carry a few stones and throw them in warning. One person I met on my journey told me that he brandished a machete at any dogs that bothered him. "They get the message", he told me. I bet they did. So did I, as I backed away a tiny bit and smiled politely.

Some people just stop and get off the bicycle. The moment a person stops cycling, the dog normally stops too – perhaps seeing that after all you are human, and not something that they might expect to chase and kill. I'd come across countless dogs already on my journey: Europe was never a problem, Argentina fairly gnarly, but both Bolivia and Peru had been testing. However, I'd always been confident that if I kept focused on the road, I could cycle faster than the dogs could run. That is what I'd become accustomed to doing, and so far it had worked without any trouble.

As I approached this little boy in the street I was going about as fast as a snail, although I hadn't quite stopped. I wasn't at all aware of the dog. Normally, I would hear it coming – this one was quiet and sneaky, such that I didn't see it until the last second. By then my leg was already in its mouth, and its teeth were sinking into my calf. It was a surreal experience. At the precise moment it happened, I found it hard to believe that it was my leg that the dog was getting its teeth into. The searing pain that followed made me certain it was definitely my leg. Fuck. This was bad. Really bad. Well, at least in the moment, and for roughly the next month or so, it was bad; sometimes it was downright awful. And yet, in that moment, I managed to stay sufficiently composed to deal with the immediate practicalities.

At first I wailed in agony. Then followed a pure rage, bellowing from deep in my belly. I raged at the dog. And I raged at the children that I had slowed down for. Then I raged at the mountains, and at the rivers too. Everyone, including the dog, scattered from sight, into the few buildings that made up this tiny village.

For a moment, I found myself watching the scene detachedly from the outside – there was a man screaming at the world in a language that was incomprehensible to anyone else around him. He was certainly crazy looking. Not least because I wasn't sure who or what I was, in any of this. I was in what psychologists would call a disassociated state, a common coping mechanism for dealing with a traumatic situation. Sometimes we will disconnect from the here and now to cope with feelings of helplessness, fear, or pain. It is quite normal to do this. Most people will have experience with some sort of disassociation in their lives, even if it is just very mild, through daydreaming or spacing out. Disassociation is a way of dealing with painful feelings in the moment. It's an avoidant coping strategy, which sometimes our minds find necessary.

The composure

The wound looked bad and there was a lot of blood. I was in the middle of the mountains and there was definitely no way I could cycle. The next city was over 50 miles away, and I'd need help getting there. Before thinking too much about that, first I needed to get myself patched up. When I had cleaned things a little, I could see that most of the wound was superficial. However, one of the teeth had gone deep into my calf, and that was the source of most of the pain. I did what I could to plug the wound and bandage myself up. While I was doing this, a man about my age emerged from one of the buildings and tentatively approached the scene. He was sympathetic and wanted to help, but there seemed little he could do to help my medical needs. What I really wanted help with was finding out about the chances that the dog had rabies.

The adrenaline was pumping through my body, and my Spanish-speaking skills crumbled. I couldn't find the word I needed in my overloaded and scattered brain. All I could think of asking was whether the dog was crazy – "*¿Está loco el perro?*" "*Si, el perro esta loco.*" If it had bitten me, then it had to be a crazy dog was his thinking, I suppose. But that didn't mean it had rabies. I think he said that the dog was crazy more as a way of reassuring and empathising with me. I certainly needed that, and the reassuring presence of another in the moment helped. I just couldn't grasp the word for rabies in Spanish. I'd never had to use it.

Pain from the wound aside, if there is a chance of rabies then fast action is absolutely necessary. Rabies transmits through the saliva of infected animals, and if this dog had it, then I certainly would have been infected. Without medical attention rabies is 100% lethal. One hundred per cent! I'd been vaccinated before

I left, but a rabies vaccination before receiving a rabies-infected animal bite is not enough to prevent infection, although it does mean that you need just two post-exposure shots, rather than the more complicated and protracted four to avoid death. Regardless, the first post-exposure shot needs to come within 24 hours.

I managed to hitch a ride on a passing truck. My bicycle and I were helped into the back, and those mountains, amidst which I had previously dissolved many of my expectations about this journey, zipped by me. The roads were potted, and the truck had to make a few stops, so it took about three hours to get to the city of Huancayo in Peru. Yes, I was still in Peru. This had happened just one week after that divine spot on the side of the mountains, with the lit-up red sky and the cactus to my right. I thought about rabies most of the way to the city. What could I do? What did I need to do?

The priority was to get medical attention. I got dropped in the busy city centre, and I was on my own. There was far too much going on around me – many cars and trucks, noise, heat, and lots of people, many of them shouting to make themselves heard in a standard Peruvian city centre scene – and I felt overwhelmed and disorientated. I pulled myself together, as there was no-one else to do it for me, and asked some locals for directions to a hospital. They pointed me in the direction of the first medical establishment of the day. It was a small clinic. Other than being a calm place and pointing me onwards to a local hospital, they couldn't help. Wheeling my bicycle and limping badly, I made my way to the hospital. It was a bigger place, but they were also unable to help me. As far as I could understand things, this was because I wasn't a local resident.

I realised that my bicycle was a burden in my trekking about the city, so I found a room in a hotel and dumped everything there. As much as I wanted to collapse on the bed there and then, there were urgent things to attend to first. With the help of people working at my hotel, I took a taxi to a hospital further away. It was a busy place and there was a long queue. I'd have to wait a while, but they told me that I'd definitely be seen. They cleaned the wound thoroughly – digging down deep into it, as I winced in pain, and bandaged it properly. I began talking about rabies (*rabia* was the word for it – I'd been so strung out earlier I'd not thought to try the English word with a Spanish flair). But I didn't understand a lot of what was being said. It wasn't clear whether they would be able to give me the rabies vaccination or not – they seemed to be saying that they might not have it. They told me I'd need to go to another treatment centre later in the evening.

I went back to the hotel and sat on the bed: my first moment to breathe, and take stock of what had happened. I was amazed at how composed I'd stayed dealing with practicalities up to that point. I then thought about what I still needed to do. First and foremost, I had to maintain this composure. I hadn't contacted anybody for support, nor did I think it wise to do so. There was, I thought, a fair chance I wasn't going to get a rabies shot. I wanted to reflect carefully on what I would do in that case. I was worried that other people's reactions and opinions, probably with their own fears mixed in, might get in the way of helping me remain collected enough to make the right choice in that event.

The dog that bit me was a street dog, with no particular owner. That's common in Peru. There was always some chance it would have rabies. However, I was beginning to think, with some certainty, that it wasn't infected. It hadn't looked rabid to me. I couldn't be sure; how much risk was I willing to take? I would have to wait until I went back to the hospital that evening to know whether I would have to make a decision, if no vaccine was available. I felt alone and scared. Watching online videos of people dying from rabies didn't help.

In the end when I went back, I did get the post-exposure vaccine, and thankfully it was a smooth process. I needed another shot three days later, so I'd have to stick around the city to get it – but I wasn't going anywhere fast, because I also had some physical healing to do. I gave a deep sigh of relief. It was time to go and collapse onto that bed. There was pain, but more of a throbbing by then. I could walk, but I had to take it easy, and I was confident I would be able to cycle again one day. However, would I want to?

The fear

There was no way I would ever reach Bhutan without facing a crisis or two. In fact, getting to Bhutan was only going to happen if I overcame whatever challenges that crossed my path – some would be of my own making, others not. It was inevitable that something would come along that would seem insurmountable. And that was okay, especially since I had, by the time this particularly ferocious crisis came along, let go of binding my up happiness with one day arriving in Bhutan. That said, I never thought something like this would happen so early on in my journey. Things had been going so well.

The day I was bitten by that dog was unquestionably difficult. Whilst I was at peace with myself at the start of day, after the bite I was mostly up in my head, feeling anxious. After all that tension I needed a release. In my own time, just as it is with any trauma no matter how great or small, I would need to process what had happened, let it go, and move on. And that's never easy.

The next day was peculiar. I'd slept well and I woke up energised. The dull pain in my leg aside, for which I now had strong painkillers, it was as if the day before hadn't happened. After a small breakfast I hobbled out onto the street and observed the hectic scene of a regular Peruvian city. There were car horns sounding every few seconds. Uneven pavements prompted many to walk on the road. There were vibrant colours, lots of smiling people, and rows of small shops selling all manner of things. The radiant sun beat down upon us all. I breathed it all in. I was alive.

I made my way across the city in some pain, yet I was feeling curiously joyful. I went to a local market, not at all phased by the hustle and bustle, and met some kind people there. I also found some pleasant local restaurants and ate a mountain of food. Later, I spoke to some of my family, and conversations with them seemed unusually good. I felt enriched and present; everything about the world seemed so beautiful. This is how it can often be with a near loss.[1] We see how some of those everyday things we might normally take for granted are vital for our happiness.

Gratitude is an essential personality trait for happiness and we can cultivate it,[2] although in the daily run of things it is easy to be pre-occupied, in the battle against focusing on what we *don't* have, rather than what we do.

The next day was similar to the first, and by the third I was walking without much struggle. I began thinking about when I should try and get back on the bicycle. On the fourth day, however, everything came apart. I had been sitting in a small city square watching colours and shapes go by, and suddenly nothing seemed quite real anymore. It was all so noisy and busy. I looked at the faces of people walking past me, and everything felt unfamiliar and perverse. I retreated to the hotel as quickly as I was able, feeling overwhelmed, but in every direction I saw dogs, slowing my retreat, and filling it with terror. Before I'd been bitten, I had barely noticed dogs roaming the streets. I'd been wary whenever I'd seen one across this city since the bite, but suddenly I was absolutely terrified at the sight of them. It wasn't just the dogs. The world that I had felt at peace with over the last few days suddenly seemed threatening and hostile. I believed everything was out to get me.

When I got back to the hotel, I locked the door and tried to regain the composure that I had witnessed in myself since the dog's attack. I could not regain it. It felt like the ground was falling away from underneath me. There was nothing to hold onto as I looked into the fearful abyss of myself. Who was I? And what the hell was I actually doing with my life? I was desperate; I needed help.

The support

Up until this point in my journey, I hadn't reached out much to people back home. I'd been sharing little bits about my progress on my blog about happiness, and occasionally sharing things through social media feeds. I'd mostly been keeping a low profile – still trying to work through all the fear and embarrassment I described earlier. At the very start of this journey, I had been so head-down and focused on getting to Bhutan, I hadn't made much time to speak with the people I'd left behind. This dog bite experience would change something fundamental about the way I related to people back home, not only on my journey, but when I returned, too. I would ask for help – articulating the need clearly – and I'd receive it in abundance. My relationships have deepened immeasurably since.

I knew I needed support to get through the dog-bite trauma, and I had quite a few people who would be able to hold onto their own emotional reactions, and focus on what was taking place for me, being an active listener to my struggle. When crisis strikes, it is important to have people who are willing and able to put things aside to support you. But I would first have to reach out, and overcome my reluctance to ask for help. I had always thought that I need to be strong and self-reliant – or at least appear to be that way. Perhaps, given what I've done with my life, that's how many people would be inclined to see someone like me. Yet, way deep down, there is still that little boy, orange-swirly carpet or not, who sometimes wants to cry and needs a reassuring hug. And that same little boy wants to be there for others when they need help too.

Over the coming months following the dog bite I received a lot of support. What I've found is that when a person asks for help with clarity and consciousness as to what is needed, others are often glad to help. There are boundaries to consider – there is a need to be considerate of what we're asking for. Others must be able to say no, and without us taking that 'no' personally. That 'no' is about them, and their capacity to support, not about us. And because of the pressure we are all under, due in part to our cultural focus on work and the economy, most people won't have much capacity. It's not personal, it's cultural.

That evening I spoke to a friend I'd known for some years.

We spent hours talking about what I was going through. They helped to ground me, listening with care to what was going on. We then hatched a plan to get me back on my bicycle and away from the busy city. I suspected that otherwise I would sink deeper into my fears and have an ever-harder time leaving. It didn't matter where I went and how far. It wasn't about whether or not I continued on to Bhutan or not. I just had to move.

The next day I checked my wound and – whilst still not great – I knew I was sufficiently healed that I could cycle for a bit. I packed up my things and got out of the hotel. I was tense, and had a couple of moments of major panic about leaving, but I regained my composure each time, and got out of the busy city and onto the open road. I was heading for the next town, Jauja, about 30 miles away on mostly flat roads.

It was a rough ride. The leg held up fine, but I was anxious the whole way there. I spent most of the ride scanning for dogs and I'd see them before they could smell me. When one dog got aggressive, I freaked a little and venomously threw a stick I was now carrying with me at it. It became more aggressive, and I sped out of there as quick as I was able. At the next town I took a hotel. I was relieved to have made it, and sat in the sun in a quiet plaza, checking in with myself. I was still anxious, but it was nothing like the day before.

Although the town was okay, and certainly more peaceful than the city, I didn't feel like staying for long. I wanted to keep moving. The next reasonable stopping place was 40 miles away, and I thought I'd try for that the following morning. On the road the next day, I re-found my connection with the mountains, and there was some deep joy. The road was again mostly flat, but the landscape either side astounded me – and there were no problems with dogs, either. With this good experience behind me and the next town being pleasant, I stayed in a hotel for a couple of nights. I began to think about the longer term. Bhutan was far from my thoughts. However, finding a place where I could relax for a while and get local support was at the forefront of my mind.

The resilience

Iquitos is the largest city in the world inaccessible by road. Once a thriving mini-metropolis during a 30-year rubber boom in the late 19th and early 20th century, it is nestled deep in the Amazon rainforest. With affluence long in its past, this abnormally large city in the middle of nowhere is, to a large extent, sustained economically through international tourism. It is a popular place to visit for those seeking adventure, wildlife, and mysticism. I knew I'd find some support there.

Realistically, there are two ways a person might reach Iquitos – one is via the air, the other via a cargo boat floating down the Amazon basin. I had no appetite for speed, and the idea of swinging in a hammock for several days drifting along the world's biggest river (with respect to water volume, not length, for any Nile-ists out there) seemed perfect for a recuperating dog-bitten cyclist. It is also a very affordable transport option, and how most local people travel.

It had been just over two weeks since I'd been bitten when I arrived at the port in Pucallpa. Once I'd come down from the Andes, it was a tough and humid climate for cycling, but I had begun to regain some confidence and feel happy again. And, by the time I was on the boat relaxing in my newly purchased hammock, watching the lush vegetation of the Amazon rainforest pass by in front of me, my thoughts finally turned to the wider journey. In the first moments after I was bitten by the dog, I was certain that my journey was over. Unquestionably. It was indeed terrible, but as I gently swung, I recognised that it could have been much worse. Of course, it could have also not happened at all – but at some point, something else would have happened that might have been wholly unpleasant. Something that may equally have put my journey and life at risk. To be sure, the dog bite wasn't to be my only potentially-journey-ending crisis. It would have been odd if there hadn't been such experiences. Life – the journey – doesn't work like that. Nor should it. Rather than asking why this crises had happened, the question I needed to ask myself, was how would I meet this crisis, and the others that came my way? This was after all a journey for happiness, and part of any journey for happiness is to deal with crisis when it arises, as naturally it always does.

No-one is exempt from losing a loved one. Random natural occurrences affect our lives. Sometimes horrendous things are done to us by others. How do we cope? Whilst some may experience a long and protracted level of distress and never really recover, others may have periods of difficulty and go on to find some sort of restoration. Others still, though experiencing negative emotions and disturbances, otherwise exhibit relatively stable, healthy levels of psychological and physical adaptation. Not only do they recover, but they seem to come out functioning competently. Such people may be able to see something positive in the whole process – they emerge strengthened and resourceful. This is what psychologists refer to as *resilience*.[3] What is it that determines whether someone will find resilience to what they are experiencing?

There are a number of key factors that contribute to a person's capacity to be resilient.[4] The first is having support from others. I had managed to tap into some of the support that I had back home, and I was also just about to arrive in the Amazon jungle-city Iquitos, where there was a good chance I'd find people that could help. Just the thought of having conversations in my native language soothed me. I also knew that there would be plenty of places where I could sit and relax, eating familiar foods in familiar-looking places, whilst I made some sense of what had happened.

Another key factor for resilience is what is known as *emotional regulation*.[5] This is the tendency for our emotions to adapt to meet the demands of the situation. Stressful and traumatic situations are inherently highly emotional. It helps to be able to manage the intensity of our unpleasant emotions through changing our evaluation of how and why something happened. For example, in my case, was it only a particularly nasty dog that I encountered, or did it represent something more harmful about the world to which I previously had been oblivious? Perhaps that dog was just as scared as I was, and had either been protecting its territory, or was simply triggered into action by an evolutionary need to chase. Did I now need to attack all dogs before they attacked me? Curiously, a couple of weeks after the bite, I felt a strong hatred towards dogs, to the extent that this comprehensively aggressive thought crossed my mind. Unresolved trauma can sometimes find its form in indiscriminate hatred. What we believe about the world influences how we feel, and also how we behave.

Having what psychologists call *grit* is also recognised as being helpful for resilience.[6] Grit is the tendency for a person to persevere, despite setbacks. I can see in my own life that there have been times when I could have been said to have grit; for example, overcoming substance dependency issues (there will be more on that in relation to this journey for happiness in a later, rather raw and gritty chapter), or getting through my PhD. Grit comprises believing three things: that what we do can influence our surroundings and our outcomes; that we can learn and grow during setbacks; and that what we are doing is purposeful. All these factors are important. For me, the first two elements have been unquestionably present throughout my life. I do think I have some influence on my surroundings, and I have experienced some personal growth through setbacks.

However, what motivates me the most to keep going with something is whether it feels purposeful to do so. Is there a greater meaning to what I'm doing (regardless of how much pleasure I may or may not be receiving through the process)? My academic job lost purpose for me, and that was a key reason I quit. My substance abuse, though at the end marginally pleasurable, had long been damaging relationships that were important to me, and so that helped me quit. But what about this journey I was on?

Regardless of expectations to continue or not, I could have gone home. I was struggling emotionally, and if the meaning of the journey was solely about how I felt, there is no way that I could have continued. My saving grace after this dog-bite crisis was in believing that what I was doing had some deeper meaning to it; it had a wider purpose beyond myself.

The positive

I would go on to find something personally purposeful in the experience. With time, my fear of the world diminished – in fact, to lower levels than I had ever experienced in my life. I was no longer in the psychology text books, but enacting experientially what I knew I had to do and be to overcome adversity. With support from those that loved me, the belief that what I do matters, and the capacity to find some sense in what I was going through, I could rebound back – and more. I was also amazed at how calm and present I remained when the actual dog bite was taking place. This was never how I had imagined I might react to such a difficulty. This gave me confidence for all the other things that might arise later in my journey. (This is not to say that, since it is possible that people *can* find purpose and happiness from adversity, that adversity *should* be endured. Possible purpose and growth from hardship does not justify the hardship we place on ourselves and others. What doesn't kill us doesn't necessarily make us stronger. For all the stories that are told of struggle and growth, there are countless that will never be told. Not everyone has the social support, the belief that what they do matters, nor the capacity to make sense of something. I was fortunate that I had all of those things. I feel eternally grateful that in that moment I was so equipped, and able to roll on.)

I spent almost a month in Iquitos. When I felt ready, I made my way by boat along the river Napo into country number eight: Ecuador. I then got stuck back into some serious happiness, journeying up into the Andes, passing the Equator and coming back into the northern hemisphere. I was on my way again. By the time I arrived in Colombia in mid-March 2018, close to five months into my journey, the dog bite was fast receding into the past. I was on my bicycle almost every day, and my confidence was bouncing back.

I was also less expectant than ever before. There was no way to predict what would be round the corner – although, in Latin America, there is more than a fair chance there'll be a smile and some laughter; as we'll explore in the next chapter, in Latin America, they do more smiling and laughing than in any other part of the world.

CHAPTER 7

The happiest people on Earth

"It is enough to be, nothing more is needed."
Epicurus

With the debilitating dog bite receding into the past, it was time to find a way to enjoy where I was. I had long been fascinated by this part of the world. Latin American countries have levels of happiness that are unrivalled, although, the kind of happiness they have is not the satisfying kind I described earlier, but a different kind. Here we find the kind of happiness that most people will recognise as such – the laughing and smiling kind. I wanted some. I wanted to not only learn why it is Latin Americans seem to have so much of it, but also how much they would be willing to share with a passing cyclist.

How happy are Latin Americans?

According to the 2018 Gallup World Poll,[1] the country where more people are likely to experience enjoyment than anywhere else is Paraguay. 91 per cent of Paraguayans report experiencing a lot of enjoyment in the previous day. Closely behind them it is those that live in Mexico at 88 per cent, followed by Panama (87 per cent), and Costa Rica (87 per cent). As many as 89 per cent of Paraguayans also say they smiled and laughed a lot during the previous day. When you consider positive daily experiences like these, it is the countries of Latin America that record the highest proportions than any other part of the world.[2]

Table1: Highest positive experiences worldwide based on the 2018 Gallup World Poll

Country position	Country	Positive Experience Index
1	Paraguay	85
2	Panama	85
3	Guatemala	84
4	Mexico	84
5	El Salvador	83
6	Indonesia	83
7	Honduras	83
8	Ecuador	82
9	Costa Rica	81
10	Colombia	81

Source: 2018 Gallup World Poll

Latin American countries make up nine of the ten countries with the highest positive experiences (Table 1). They all have rates at which their citizens experience enjoyment and how much they smile and laugh each day that outstrip other parts of the world. Countries in Western Europe score reasonably high too. For example, in the Netherlands they obtain a 78 on the Positive Experience Index. There, most people experience a lot of enjoyment throughout their days (87 per cent) and they smile and laugh a lot too (85 per cent). Countries like the United States and the United Kingdom are a little lower scoring 77 and 75 respectively on the index. In the United States the proportion of people who say they enjoyed themselves the previous day is 82 per cent, with those saying the smiled and laughed a lot being 80 per cent. In the United Kingdom these figures are 83 per cent and 73 per cent respectively. Countries where having positive daily experiences would be expected to be lower, for example, due to high rates of poverty (e.g., Sierra Leone – 61) or being war-torn (e.g., Afghanistan – 43), are indeed low.

These numbers will, of course, depend on the day in question, and what might be happening nationally around that time. However, a sufficiently large number of people are asked across a long enough period for these numbers to be statistically reliable. There is room for some error and doubt, due to cultural and linguistic differences in interpreting the question.[3] For example, what constitutes 'a lot'? Does 'enjoyment' mean different things for different people? Nevertheless, these figures are illuminating.

However, can the people of Latin America really be happier than elsewhere in the world? For many, the assertion that Latin America is home to the happiest people on Earth will come as a surprise. Perhaps it'll be outright dismissed. Surely, it is the affluent Nordic countries, such as Denmark, Finland, or Norway, that are the happiest? And by some accounts, as we're regularly told,[4] they are.

Happiness – an economic success story

As I made my way from Ecuador into Colombia on my bicycle, the United Nations-established International Day of Happiness, held each year on 20th March, was fast approaching. I was feeling despondent about the day. Since it was first celebrated in 2013, it's been pretty much the same deal every year. The news is awash with articles about happiness, and there are plenty of tips shared about how we can find more happiness in our lives as individuals. These ideas are all very useful, yet the next day it is back to business as usual. Many people will recognise that all those inspiring things – things they probably already knew they should try to do more of in their lives – are practically impossible in the everyday run of things. This frustration echoes through my reasons for leaving the career I had as an academic happiness researcher, if I wanted ever to find happiness myself.

What's more, quite possibly because it doesn't support the dominant social and economic story, we don't hear very much about the kind of happiness that is found in Latin America. An important part of the International Day of Happiness is the release of the annual 'World Happiness Report'. The report is full of thought-provoking articles on happiness, but what always captures by far the most attention is which country will be unveiled as the happiest that year. In 2017 it was Norway. However, in 2018, when I was on my bicycle in Colombia, Finland took the number one spot. The Finns also managed to maintain this for 2019 and again in 2020 and 2021 – four years in a row! The Nordic countries always do well on happiness according, to the UN's report, and nearly every year all the Nordic countries (Denmark, Finland, Iceland, Norway, and Sweden) appear somewhere in the list of the ten happiest countries.

This assessment is again based on asking people questions about happiness. The report uses answers from the Gallup World Poll; curiously, the same survey as the one I reported on earlier, that also asks how much people smile, laugh and experience enjoyment throughout their days. But why the difference in the conclusion as to which countries are happier, and does it matter? The 'World Happiness Report' list of happiest countries is compiled using answers to a *different* question in the survey that relates to happiness. In this other question, known as Cantril's ladder, people are asked to, "Imagine a ladder with steps numbered from zero at the bottom to ten at the top, where the top of the ladder represents the best possible life and the bottom of the ladder represents the worst possible life?" They are then asked to choose, "Which step of the ladder you personally feel you are on at this time of your life."

The average scores given to this Cantril's ladder question, answered by a large number of those living in each country, are then calculated. These average scores are used to position countries with respect to the happiness tables contained with the 'World Happiness Report' that we hear about in the news each year. Table 2 shows the ten countries scoring the highest, alongside some other notable countries (note, I've not included Bhutan's scores at this point – I'll get into how they do on happiness when we arrive in

Table 2: Average Cantril's ladder score by country in the 2018 World Happiness Report

Country position	Country	Average ladder score (out of 10)
1	Finland	7.6
2	Denmark	7.6
3	Norway	7.6
4	Iceland	7.5
5	Switzerland	7.5
6	Netherlands	7.5
7	Canada	7.3
8	New Zealand	7.3
9	Sweden	7.3
10	Australia	7.3
13	Costa Rica	7.1
18	US	6.9
19	UK	6.8
24	Mexico	6.5
30	Guatemala	6.4
34	Singapore	6.3
36	Spain	6.3
34	Singapore	6.3
64	Paraguay	5.7
96	Indonesia	5.1
113	Sierra Leone	4.5
145	Afghanistan	3.6

Source: 2018 World Happiness Report

Bhutan). Typically, those that score well using Cantril's ladder are small, high-income industrialised countries.

Happiness in the head and happiness in the heart

What is immediately obvious is that the Cantril's ladder question doesn't mention smiling or enjoyment at all, let alone happiness. That aside, researchers have shown that people answer it in the same way that they answer, "Overall, how *satisfied* are you with your life nowadays?", which was the question from Chapter 5. That is, happiness by this metric depends largely on achieving 'social yardsticks'; on whether we've achieved the things in life we think we ought to have achieved. It is much easier to see this when we consider the Cantril's ladder question. This is an important aspect of happiness, because it is important to believe we are doing well – yet isn't it also important to enjoy ourselves, and laugh and smile during our days? Both kinds of happiness are important when it comes to understanding and discussing happiness.

The Cantril's ladder question is what is called '*evaluative happiness*'. The life satisfaction question in Chapter 5 is also evaluative happiness. This measure entails evaluating our lives in an overall sense. An answer requires people to reflect on their entire life. The process is one whereby we think about what we would consider a good life, and whether we are close to living that good life. Expectations, typically culturally determined, matter. As I described when discussing life satisfaction earlier in the book, people typically spend about five seconds thinking about their answer to this kind of question – therefore, how much deeper reflection is going on is unclear. The questions about joy, smiling, and laughing throughout the day are known as hedonic happiness. Hedonic happiness is more about feeling good and experiencing pleasure – it equates to happiness in the moment. Our answer depends quite simply on how we feel now.

What most people understand as happiness in the first instance is probably hedonic happiness. When we read in the news about the very happy Finns, we may imagine lots of people always smiling, laughing, and looking happy. And this conception of happiness is often aided through the images that accompany those news reports. Accordingly, some Finns are themselves surprised that they are considered the happiest people on earth.[6] Whilst Finnish countrymen and women may sit around looking smugly satisfied as they read this report, there are 40 other countries where people smile and enjoy themselves more according to the Gallup World Poll in 2018.

Whilst our life satisfaction – or the answer to the Cantril's ladder question – depends to a large extent on achieving expectations and goals (such as having a high-status job, having a high income, being married, being healthy, and being financially stable and secure), the happiness we feel in the moment depends on how we spend our time (such as doing pleasurable activities, and whether we spend time with others).[7]

A person may have a high-status job that brings with it a high income, yet day-to-day they may work alone, and find that job fairly unpleasant. Conversely, a person with a low-status job might experience a great deal of pleasure and social interaction in their day-to-day life. This is not to say a person can't and won't have both – often the two do come together – yet what we *think* makes for a happier life isn't always what actually makes us *feel* happier. Though that doesn't mean there aren't other reasons we do the things we do. Certain things may bring a sense of purpose to our lives, and I'll tap into this purposeful kind of happiness on this journey in more detail later – whenever I came very close to giving up on my journey to Bhutan because I was feeling very little happiness in the moment, such as from the dog bite and all the other challenges to come, it was having a wider purpose to what I was doing that spurred me on.

The countries where people both think and feel happier

At the country level, the countries where people tend to be doing better in relation to these goals and expectations about what makes a good life tend to do well on Cantril's ladder. Those countries that do the very best also tend to have less economic inequality, which means there is less of a discord between the haves and have-nots. In countries with lower economic inequality, greater numbers of people are able to achieve goals and meet expectations.[8]

However, when Paraguayans, Panamanians, or Mexicans – who enjoy their lives more than other countries – are asked whether they think they are happy, the answer will depend on how their lives measure up to their perceptions of what a good life is supposed to look like. A person's perceptions will have been informed by a whole range of things: from national and international standards of living they've heard about, what they look like in comparison to those they see in the media, marketing they see each day, conversations with their neighbours, or happiness research they might have read about.[9] Countries with lower material standards of living don't tend to do well on evaluative happiness, because they are less likely to meet general perceptions of what a good life should entail.

It is disappointing that the 'World Happiness Report' does not report on more diverse aspects of happiness. My suspicion is that it is because the report is written largely by economists. Not only do economists have a narrower definition of what happiness is than other social-scientists (for example, they focus near exclusively on evaluative happiness, as indeed I needed to do when I researched happiness through an economic lens), they tend to disregard other kinds of happiness in the belief that they are loosely all the same thing.[10] Importantly, the conclusion as to who is the happiest from an evaluative happiness sense doesn't do too much to challenge the role of the economist in our society. Economists have come to dominate government policy, and whilst they've got some useful ideas, not many of them seem to like hearing that for a good life we only need a medium-sized economy, rather than a really big one that gets bigger every year.[11]

Nevertheless, Latin American countries tend to do quite well on the evaluative kind of happiness too. What seems to surprise many people about Latin American countries is that in the 'World Happiness Report', their happiness levels are often comparable to those of countries with much higher material living standards.[12] For example, in the 2018 World Happiness Report, Costa Rica ranked five places higher with respect to evaluative happiness than the United States (7.1 out of 10, versus 6.9). This is despite having an average income that year three times smaller (US$20,672 versus US$61,585). Similarly, Mexicans are happier than citizens in both France and Spain (6.5, versus 6.5 and 6.3) despite an average income of at least half (US$19,928 versus US$45,284 and US$40,257).

There is a link between a country's average income level and their evaluative happiness. There is an upward sloping trend that is statistically robust, yet the link between average income is much stronger at lower levels of income. At higher income levels, the relationship diminishes considerably. Above US$20,000, which is comparable to how much I got paid as a PhD student, extra income effects are marginal.[13] The link is non-existent above US$30,000. Some rich countries do very badly for their level of income. For example, Qatar has a per-person income of US$90,970 and scores only a 6.4 on evaluative happiness, whereas Singapore has an even higher per person income US$98,223 yet only a 6.3 on evaluative happiness.

There are many countries that have higher evaluative happiness than you might predict from the size of their economy. Latin American countries, like Costa Rica, Guatemala, and Mexico do particularly well. Similarly, so do the Nordic countries who do much better in evaluative happiness than countries with similarly sized economies. The reason these sets of countries do so well is because there are factors other than income that contribute to national happiness – such as health, freedom, social support, the absence of corruption, and generosity – and that helps make some countries happier than others.[14] There is some evidence that as a country's economy grows over time, then this evaluative kind of happiness is likely to improve. However, this is not always the case (most notably in the economic powerhouses of the USA and China) and the benefits of economic growth at higher income levels are marginal at best.[15] For a country to obtain greater happiness it is better to concentrate on these other aspects as some countries like Costa Rica have done (I'll describe how they've managed to do this when we arrive in Costa Rica in the next chapter).

If we consider how country average income relates to hedonic happiness, or how people say they *feel* day to day, then although there is a slight positive relationship between average country income and happiness, it is extremely weak. The medium income countries of Latin America outperform countries in other regions of the world.

If we were to consider evaluative and hedonic happiness to be equally important, then it is the Netherlands where the people are the happiest based on both the Cantril's ladder question and whether people enjoy themselves and laugh and smile a lot each day. The Dutch have high levels of both evaluative and hedonic happiness. Other countries that do well with this combination of happiness indicators include Norway, Denmark, New Zealand, and Costa Rica. In fact Costa Rica, who are outside the top ten on evaluative happiness, do much better when we consider both kinds of happiness. They would be considered the fifth happiest place in the world if we factor in their hedonic happiness levels to their evaluative happiness score.

Under this combined assessment, Finland, though still doing remarkably well, wouldn't be considered the happiest place on earth because the people don't experience as much happiness in the moment as in other places. In Mexico, on the other hand, where evaluative happiness is only moderately high, people experience a high level of joy and laughter throughout their days. When we consider hedonic and evaluative happiness on an equal footing, Mexico raises up from 23rd to 10th happiest, Panama rises from 27th to 11th, Guatemala rises from 30th to 12th, and a country like Spain drops from 36th to 59th.

Now it's my turn – how was my journey for happiness making me feel?

A simple question that can be used to determine someone's hedonic happiness is, "Overall, how happy did you feel yesterday?" Like the life satisfaction question people are asked to respond on a scale from 0 to 10, where 0 is "Not at all happy" and 10 is "Completely happy". This is more than just a yes or no question, in terms of whether a person experienced joy and laughter, but it captures the same basic idea and is similar in structure to the life satisfaction question discussed previously. However, instead of asking for an overall evaluation of a person's life, this is aimed at establishing how a person felt on a given day.

Of course, it will depend on the day in question. We might just happen to catch someone on a particularly bad day. However, averaged out over a large enough number of people (or for the same person on an epic cycling journey over a number of days), catching someone on a bad day is made up for through the good days that others had (or the good days the cyclist has). There is also likely to be some memory bias in people's answers, and again there may be some cultural and linguistic differences in interpreting the question. However, like the life satisfaction question, it has been demonstrated by psychologists to be reasonably reliable.[16] Questions that focus on emotions in the moment have helped our understanding of what makes someone feel happy throughout their day.

The research is clear that we generally experience the most happiness when we are with others – particularly when we're with people that we're close to and when we're being intimate. Generally doing something relaxing, engaging in a spiritual or religious practice, or eating (preferably with others) are all very important for feeling happy too. Commuting, working, and housework bring the least happiness.[17]

Like the life satisfaction question, I have asked myself this question in the past from time to time. However, it wasn't until I began this journey that I started asking myself this question

Figure 1: Hedonic happiness during the first six months of the journey

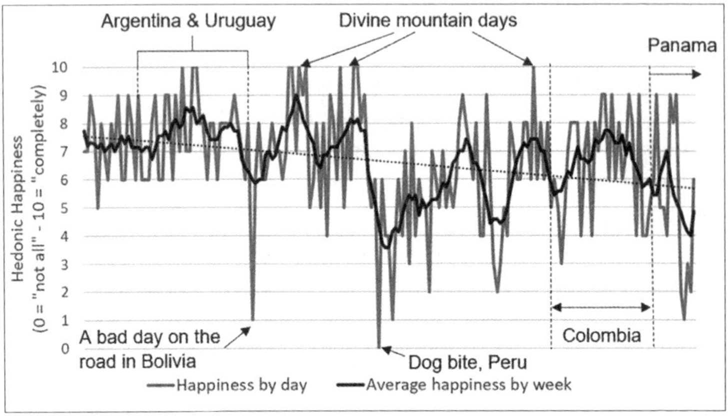

every single day. Though I claim no rigour to my personal daily assessments, my happiness scores will help illuminate the role that this kind of happiness plays in our lives.

Figure 1 shows my happiness scores for the first six months of my journey up until Panama – by day, as well as a weekly average, to highlight periods which were generally low or high in happiness.

It will come as no surprise that I didn't score a perfect 10 every day. The graph shows that day-by-day, my hedonic happiness was up and down. In the first six months I had only eleven days in which I felt a '10' kind of happy. Some days had been simply sublime, like, for example, some of those days high up in the mountains. I couldn't really have put it into a number, but 10 will have to do. Sometimes the joy I felt seemed inexplicable, and it couldn't be attached to any one specific thing, I just felt a warmth resonating from deep within me that had me smiling at the world and everyone that crossed my path. When there was no-one around to smile at, I still smiled. On other days I met lots of people, and the smiles and laughter were infectious. Then there were days that were truly horrendous – and explicably so. Like that day I got bitten by a dog: I gave that day a zero on this type of happiness. I was at a low, and worse than unhappy; I was terrified and anxious. Yet, as I processed the experience, I did rebound back somewhat.

Sometimes, as will be the case for anyone, I just had unhappy days. In the first six months I gave just over a quarter of my days a score of 5 or less. This kind of happiness naturally fluctuates. And so it should. It would be odd if a person were to meet a tragedy, an inevitability of life, with smiles and laughter. The point of considering hedonic happiness is not to make sure we feel this kind of happy all the time. The point, as I'll get into more in the next chapter, is mainly to listen and pay attention to it.

The up and down nature of my feelings is pretty much how I would have expected my daily happiness to have been. On a bicycle there are a fair amount of ups and downs. It was tough cycling in the Andes. Long before I was bitten by that dog, I had some tough days. Scaling a mountain, although there is sometimes both happiness and satisfaction once at the top, does not always feel amazing on the way up. One mountain I climbed in Bolivia, for example, was so rough on the way up I was a walking ghost by the time I reached the town at the summit. Also, laughing and smiling does not come as easily when alone. There weren't many days that I cackled heartily to myself as I rode to Bhutan.

Had I stayed at home and never set out on my bicycle to Bhutan, I'd have expected a similar up and down pattern. The average across my entire journey turned out to be 7.0. On the face of it, 7.0 doesn't seem to be very high. In fact, this is slightly lower than average, if we ask the same question to a random sample of people in the UK.[18] Whether my happiness would have been higher overall had I never left, I cannot be sure, because I'd never recorded how I felt daily like this in the past. I suspect that there wouldn't have been as many 10s back then, but then in the years just before I left there probably wouldn't have been as many really low scores either.

Ups and downs throughout life are natural. We wouldn't expect life satisfaction to vary much from day-to-day (though that is not to say it doesn't) because our life conditions are normally the same. Before I left for Bhutan, I registered a 6 on life satisfaction, and this would have been fairly consistent each day. Over the years I would have rated it slightly higher or lower if something changed how I saw myself, i.e., if I got some research funds that meant I had secure employment for several years, or if a research article I'd written that I thought was a really important piece of knowledge got rejected from a journal for a fifth time, as is quite typical in the academic world. Yet overall, my life satisfaction had been diminishing fairly steadily from the 8 I'd have given myself several years before.

How we feel each day, however, varies a lot. Sometimes there is little we can do about it. How we feel could be part of our biological process. For example, people typically report themselves to be happier in the afternoon than early in the morning or late at night;[19] this is often the body's natural rhythm at play. Similarly, females tend to have pronounced hormonal changes throughout their ovulation period that can have effects on happiness.[20] Other times we may intentionally do something to raise our happiness, like call a friend, playing a sport, or eating our favourite ice cream. Yet, many activities that can bring us happiness in the moment have their limits. Soon we have had enough of doing those things, and it is time to stop because they aren't bringing happiness in the moment anymore. Perhaps we may go way beyond the point where we should have stopped. In fact, maybe we can't stop, and we feel pain. Maybe we feel some unhappiness in the following moments because we didn't take care of other things, such as drinking enough water, or we are experiencing the slump following a large intake of sugar. Perhaps the friend had to tell us some unpleasant news which we felt sad about.

Hedonic happiness responds to the changing environment outside of us. It is not realistic to be this type of happy all the time – difficult things happen to everyone at some point. This doesn't mean we can't do things to increase our happiness in the moment, or that we shouldn't try to avoid feeling unhappiness sometimes. But we must be aware that wanting to experience more hedonic happiness – both in trying to avoid unhappiness and seeking happiness all the time – might sometimes itself be a source or consequence of a deeper suffering. In fact, the pursuit of happiness in the hedonic sense can actually limit our ability to experience this kind of happiness.[21] The best way to get this kind of happiness is often to just let it flow.

Learning from Latin America

Yet, 'feeling good now' is clearly an important aspect of happiness. Whilst there will be ups and downs, we'd probably like to know ways we can improve it, so that on average it is higher. But of the million things we can think of that would bring us happiness now, some may jeopardise our happiness at a later date. It is clear from the numbers that in Latin America people do consistently well in this type of happiness. Having travelled through on my bicycle for many months, I can personally attest that Latin Americans do seem to be happy in this way. I observed a lot of joy and laughter around me. Happiness in Latin America is largely relational rather than materialistic. Despite many Latin American countries having weak political institutions, high corruption, high crime rates, unequal income distributions, and high rates of poverty, people tend to have an abundance of close and warm relationships. Conceptions of the good life, often with roots in indigenous culture via concepts like '*buen vivir*' (to live well) or '*pachamama*' (reverence for Mother Earth)[22] are linked to community and greater care for the environment.

People tend to spend more time with one another in Latin America. They do things together. And from research carried out in all cultures, it is clear that this brings the greatest happiness in the moment – *hedonic happiness*;[23] with the quality of our relationships being the single most important factor that leads people to report greater overall life satisfaction – *evaluative happiness*.[24] And happiness can be contagious. When we spend enough time with people who feel happy, it rubs off on us too.[25] The question I asked myself was whether being around Latin Americans would bring me more happiness in my daily life on a bicycle. Eventually, it did. But first I had to learn to slow down and be present with the emotions I was experiencing. You may have noticed in Figure 1 that on the whole, my daily happiness seemed to be getting gradually lower as the journey progressed. I hadn't been letting this kind of happiness flow, and accepting my hedonic experience for what it was. Despite all my happiness knowledge, I'd still been chasing after feeling good somewhere other than in the sometimes-painful present. Things couldn't go on like this for much longer. And they did not…

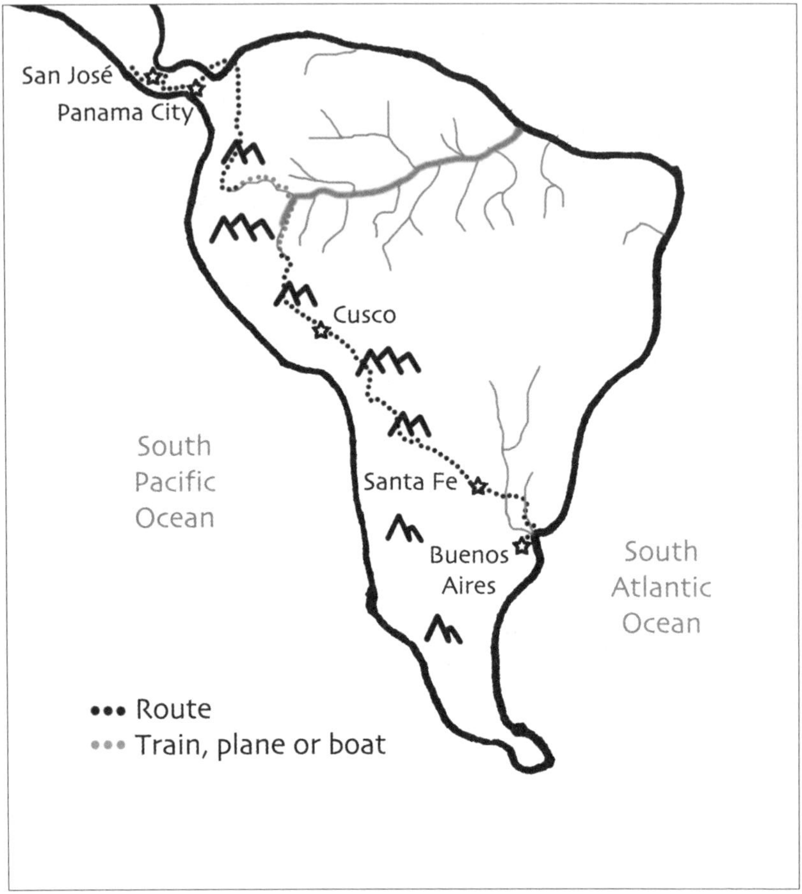

Mindfully into Costa Rica

CHAPTER 8

Life in the here and now

"I can't keep on like this. My mind wants to do things that my body is unable to do. I do not have the resources. This is unsustainable. I am suffering. Some… thing… has to… change."
Journal entry, 22nd April 2018

And there I was, once again, lying by the side of the road with my head in my hands. I sobbed.

This was in Panama. I was now six months into my journey, and nowhere near as far along as I had thought I would be when I first set out. Although I'd let go of expecting to find permanent satisfaction upon arrival in Bhutan, I wasn't getting very much of the in-the-moment Latin American kind of happiness either. I struggled to be present in the moment, and I would often ignore how my body felt and push on regardless, in search of happiness somewhere else other than where I was – in the future, or in the past. Normally it would turn out okay: when my sore body finally arrived where my ruthless mind had been demanding it be by the end of the day, I'd reflect back, and at least feel satisfied about what I'd achieved.

On other days, however, I'd get caught out – sometimes severely. Perhaps I'd push on in the heat of the day when I really should have sat in the shade and watched the world go by. Or maybe I'd misjudge the route and end up on a difficult track road that was much longer than I thought it would be. I didn't always take enough care to ensure I had at least a little bit more than I needed – often the most basic things, such as food and water, became short in supply, driving on that need to push ahead – and I made mistakes. When things became difficult, there were always other choices I could have made. However, most of the time I didn't notice those other choices, let alone consider them, because I was so tangled up inside a mind that has long ruled tyrannically over the rest of me. I was often thinking about where I 'had to' be by the end of the day, and I was barely present. Certainly not as present as I needed to be to catch some of those Latin American smiles.

What happened in Panama was the final straw. I'd made the same mistake for three cycling days in a row. It wasn't like I'd cycled that far on any of those days, it was just hot – really hot, and humid too. The first night, after a day cycling out some 60 miles from Panama City, I'd taken refuge in my tent under a road bridge that a river might have once run beneath. It was a hellish, sleepless night. Other than a stagnant pool of water close by, it was barren and dry. And although that water didn't look or smell great, the heat was unbearable, and I took to regularly dipping my body into it throughout the night to cool me down for a few minutes.

At the end of the next day's cycling, I staggered into the first hotel I'd seen in a while. It was expensive and dirty, but I was on the verge of collapse and scarcely able to speak. There'd been a hotel 30 miles earlier, a lot nicer and less expensive, but back then I thought there'd be another in ten miles or so in the next town. There wasn't, so I kept going expecting the next town to have something reasonable. In total I drank five litres of fluids that day, and that wasn't enough to quench my thirst. I ate two dinners at a local place. That wasn't enough to bring me back to life either. Only one full rest day later, and after a tonne of self-recrimination, I got back on my bicycle, feeling the need to get on with the journey.

Although I began riding before daybreak, the heat caught up with me before I'd made much progress. There was a climb that went on for way too long, and my shoes became sodden with sweat. I kicked them off and attempted for the first time on my journey to cycle in flip-flops instead. But it was too late and of little use. And that's when I found myself by the side of that road, sobbing. Those tears were mostly anger and frustration. I'd abused myself again – I'd not listened to my body, pressed on to get somewhere I thought I had to be that day, and found myself in yet another tough situation. It was only going to get hotter as the day pressed on, and I couldn't face another sleepless night by the side of the road in my tent with not enough drinking water. I needed to get to a place where I could recover. This time, I *really did have to*.

It was after I got to my recovery place that everything changed. From the outside, it probably just looked like I slowed down, but what was really happening was that I began to listen more carefully to how I felt in the moment – not just physically, but emotionally. I started to make some different choices, and it was then that the kind of happiness that people most often understand as happiness, the smiling and laughing kind, began showing up on this journey. There was much less physical pain as a result too. Personally, I see it as a process of overturning years of what was mostly a learnt behaviour of not being anywhere near fully present with what is. I'm not the only one who has learnt not to listen to how he is feeling – it's built into our 'go get 'em' culture.

It was in Panama where I relearnt how to connect with my needs of the moment, and be responsive to how I'm feeling. Just as I did as a little boy. Back then, sadness would bring tears, and joy would bring a smile. Just as they ought to. The trouble was that I never learnt what to do with those in-the-moment feelings. I didn't learn to see them as indicators of something; no-one else seemed attuned either, and I lost touch with the moment-to-moment feedback of my heart.

There is a lot of value in being goal focused

When I began my journey, I found it helpful to have small goals. Goals helped me deal with those early journey anxieties, and build confidence in what I was now doing with my life. They provided an anchor for me to hold onto when I was really worried about what lay ahead. It was helpful to break the journey down into small manageable chunks. For example, for the first part of the journey, my focus was only on reaching Barcelona. That was scary, yet doable. It was western Europe, and I was familiar with the ways and customs of that part of the world. Plus, I would have the support of a cycling buddy when I arrived in Barcelona. Then it would be a flight to Buenos Aires, the capital of Argentina, where I had another friend who I could stay with for a few days until I was ready to leave. I knew the goal after that – getting from Buenos Aires to Cusco in Peru – was always going to be a big stretch. From Buenos Aires to Cusco there were so many (too many?) unknowns, and from the outset I felt daunted. This part of the world was completely new to me, yet it was only Cusco, and not the really-far-away land of Bhutan. Plus, I'd have my map to figure out where I next needed to be. I predicted Buenos Aires to Cusco would take me about six weeks, and it did. The idea was that I'd take things one step at a time, and stay focused on these short-term goals. That way I might one day reach Bhutan on my bicycle.

Argentina was one of my favourite countries to have journeyed through. My average on the daily happiness question from the previous chapter, "Overall, how happy did you feel yesterday?", was 7.7 out of 10 in Argentina, making it the second highest on that kind of happiness of all 25 countries I ended up passing through. Maybe it was because it was the start of my journey, and I was fresh out of a job that I hadn't found fulfilling. Though, equally likely, it was because the people of Argentina were warm and welcoming. Wherever I looked, people would smile at me. Whenever I stopped, people would talk to me. Only I didn't look that much, and if I did stop, it wasn't for long.

I did a 100+-mile ride back in Argentina. That day I wrote in my journal and later posted on social media: "After cycling 165km (my first 100-miler of this trip) what I would have liked was a nice warm shower and to get into some clean clothes before slumbering down for the night. Instead, I found myself camping in a ditch by the side of the road with less than half a litre of water to wash myself. There was nevertheless a lot of love and acceptance toward my miserable self."

Despite the miserable self I had been the night before, the next day I still rode another 80 miles. I was trying to make it to the home of an Argentinian cycling family in a town near Santa Fe who'd agreed to host me for a night or two. I felt I 'had to' be there when I said I would be. In fact, I've often tended to use 'getting *there*, by *then*', as a way of motivating myself to get moving. Yet, as experienced cyclists themselves, I'm sure they'd have understood if I'd showed up a day later. They were a sweet family, and they took care of me for a few days when I arrived with my miserable self.

When I began my journey, I thought I'd do many 100-milers. I'd start off easy and build up strength. That one in Argentina, however, was to be my only 100-mile ride. It became obvious that the days when I spent most of the day on my bicycle were rarely my happiest. I suspect that I would have been much happier in Argentina had I listened more carefully to myself physically and emotionally, as I started doing after Panama. But then, if I already knew how to do this, much as with many of the things I learnt on this journey, I wouldn't have needed to go on the journey in the first place! I'd have had plenty more happiness back home – the capacity to be in the present is an essential ingredient for happiness.

The more nature there is around me, the easier I find it is to be present – nature has rich benefits to our happiness, as I'll delve into further, later on. In Panama, now six months into my journey, I was on the Pan-American Highway. This highway, except for the break between Panama and Colombia known as the Darién Gap which I boated around, runs the length of the Americas. It is best avoided as much as possible on a bicycle, owing to how busy it can be in parts. Sadly, in Panama there aren't many alternatives, and so I had my head down and was just trying to get through it. It was a far cry from being up in the Andes in South America. Up there, as well as letting go of finding personal happiness from reaching Bhutan, I found myself more in the present. Even when it was physically painful, it was where I wanted to be: the present was so beautiful there. Three months into the journey, high up in the mountains of Peru, I had been learning to be with both the pleasure and the pain, whenever they arose. Neither grasping, nor avoiding, just being.

It was a huge setback to being more fully in the present when I was bitten by the street dog in Peru. I'd like to think I would have learnt and assimilated what I needed to learn about being present from my journey sooner, had that crisis not happened. But then who's to know what may have otherwise happened? Or perhaps that crisis was crucial for a deeper learning about being present? What is clear is that the dog-bite situation took the journey on a detour; perhaps a necessary one, because we must confront crisis at some point. That detour was unpleasant initially, and certainly some presence was needed to deal with the immediate situation at hand. However, I had a hard time sitting with the emotional fallout from it, and it is one explanation as to why my day-by-day hedonic happiness seems to have steadily declined from Argentina to Panama (see Figure 1 from the previous chapter).

Although I gave myself plenty of time to recuperate after the dog bite, when I got back into cycling, I felt as anxious and time-pressured as ever. I reverted back to short-term goals – be *there* by *then*. These goals served a purpose in getting me moving again after a horrendous experience. And yet, I didn't really need to be anywhere, nor by any point – and believing that I did was not serving this journey for happiness. What took place in Panama had happened all too often in the early days of my journey. I had lost sight of an important part of happiness – being in the here and now. Not being fully present is a near lifelong habit that may have been useful once upon a time when the present was often harsh, but has ever since gotten in the way of being happy.

Getting back into the present

Sometimes I would scarcely notice, let alone appreciate the things keeping me alive and powering me forward on this journey. My rising and falling chest, expanding as the lungs within took in oxygen-rich fresh air and expelled what it didn't need. Little trembles that would reverberate throughout my body from a solid beating heart nestled between those lungs. The legs spinning around and around near-constantly, muscles tensing and contracting. It boggles me to think about all that is happening within me that I am not aware of consciously.

Many people will have come across mindfulness. It's talked about a lot these days, and there are many mindfulness techniques that can be used to get into the present. Essentially, practicing mindfulness relies on focusing on some aspect of the present moment. We just observe without judgement. It is what it is. Our focus might be on the breath, and we can observe air passing through our nostrils and going down into our expanding lungs. We observe that air, now slightly warmer, passing back through the same route. We note the sensations, the tickles. Then there is a slight pause, just before the process repeats again. And again. And again. The idea is only to keep watching, or at least that's what we try to do. Inevitably a thought comes into the mind, maybe after just one or two breaths; it might be fairly trivial stuff: "What will I have for dinner tonight?" "What will I do tomorrow?" "I wonder if my partner is upset with me after our minor disagreement this morning?" Maybe at first, we don't notice we are not focusing on our breath anymore. Maybe we do. It doesn't matter, because at some point, we will notice, and when that happens, we return our attention to the breath. It's simple – in theory!

Anyone who has tried some sort of mindfulness practice will know that it is far from simple. It sounds like it ought to be. However, a person doesn't just suddenly get it. It is instead a constant practice of seeing that our attention has slipped, and to keep bringing it back to focus in the here and now. I'm always slipping and that is normal. I'll get lost in thoughts for most of the time as I sit and focus on my breath. Our minds can be very busy places, and I've found it difficult to counteract a chaotic tendency in my head, flipping from one thought to another. Trying to be mindful can be frustrating: the inability to do something that sounds simple can be maddening (making me at times less mindful). However, the happiness benefits to mindfulness, if there is the time to sit down and try in the first place, are substantial. For example, a mindfulness course will typically improve happiness by at least as much as being in a committed relationship.[1] The main ways by which mindfulness helps in daily life is through reducing emotional reactivity and negative thinking patterns, as well as reducing rumination and worry.[2]

Over the years I've done a few mindfulness courses. Before I left for Bhutan, I had a regular morning practice, whereby first thing after getting up I'd try to do some conscious body movement and then sit attempting to observe my breath for 30 minutes. These things are helpful. When I do them, I am not so easily caught up in thoughts as I otherwise would be later in the day. I see that the thoughts are just thoughts, rather than identifying with those thoughts. The thoughts come, and then they go. Some thoughts are useful and interesting, others less so. I try not to judge; I just remain watchful. However, it still is easy to get stuck inside certain thought patterns, and I sometimes wonder if the mindfulness practice is really helping.

I've also put a lot of effort into being more present with what is taking place elsewhere in my body – physically as well as emotionally, for example, through stopping for a second or two just to check in with my feelings. Am I happy or sad now? Am I anxious or irritated? Am I hydrated or dehydrated? Do I need to get up from the screen and move my body a little bit? I've done a few workshops that have helped my awareness and acceptance of emotions. I've taken movement classes, for example, yoga or dance, where there is an emphasis on paying attention to the body. I write in a journal often. And sometimes I have written long lists of things I am grateful for. There is evidence that these sorts of practices also help with happiness, and they have helped me be more appreciative of the present.

Where did the habit of not being present come from?

However, with all the effort I put into being more present, and often failing to do so, I've often asked myself why it is *so* difficult to be mindful. Whilst mindfulness is great in getting us individually back in connection with ourselves, why am I so often disconnected to the present in the first place? This is something that doesn't get talked about enough; in fact, hardly at all. Outside of a meditation class, or once I've done my daily morning mindfulness practice, I still have to function back inside circumstances that don't encourage mindfulness. Mindfulness practice seems to me to be more like a sticking plaster for a problem that runs much deeper than simply one individual's inability to concentrate.

I was present-moment-focused when I was a small boy. I was sometimes at one with that orange-swirly carpet, for example. Yet, as I've said before, I didn't have much of an outlet for my emotions growing up, especially the difficult ones. At first, of course, there was acceptance and support for this. As a small child, even as a boy, it is expected. We all screamed and wailed in those early years. When it comes to expressing ourselves at that age, it is all we know how to do, and it is accepted behaviour. It lets others know how we feel and what we need. Yet, after a while, it became much less acceptable for me to scream and wail in the presence of others. And occasionally such expression would come with a tough punishment. What is a little boy to do?

With nobody role-modelling any other way to manage my difficult emotions and allow them a desperately needed outlet, I did what a lot of people in my culture do: I learnt to push them aside. Later, I came to see displaying my emotions as a sign of weakness. My emotions made me vulnerable, and that vulnerability was sometimes used against me – for other's entertainment or to manipulate my behaviour, for example. When there is a risk that our emotions might be penalised, it is much safer to keep them hidden. I learnt to do just that. And I learnt, like many others do as a way to navigate life, how to use other's emotions to entertain and to manipulate.

When something unpleasant is happening in my life, I learnt to cope by pushing my emotions away; to pretend that whatever was happening wasn't happening. What I came to believe is that it is somehow wrong to feel certain things, and that I am better off acting as if unpleasant feelings didn't exist. As a young boy, and for much of my adult life, I did this mostly by distracting myself, thinking of something else. Perhaps I'd think of something better to come, rather than the miserable present, which I felt altogether helpless within. With all the struggle I faced in my environment, it seemed like I had more control of my life through thinking rather than feeling. Perhaps that's a reasonable recipe for some satisfaction, but it hasn't been much of a recipe for joy in the moment, nor for sadness either.

Emotions were scary, and I pushed them away rather than feel them. My mind came to dominate how I functioned in the world, and gave me the surest way I knew to cope. It was through my thoughts, rather than through my feelings, that I tried to find my happiness. I've often wondered whether this tendency to be up in my mind might explain why I ended up as an academic, thinking so much about happiness – and being successful at it – rather than living and feeling much happiness. It is my sense that this different way of being reflects how happiness is pursued culturally throughout different parts of the world – in some cultures people tend to try and think themselves to more happiness, whereas in other cultures they are better at enjoying themselves in the moment. As I described in the last chapter, both approaches play their part.

When the time I spend in my head is concentrated toward something in the here and now, such as thinking of complex ideas or problem solving, it is a powerful and spectacular tool. I can achieve so much. However, I found I couldn't always switch my thoughts off, and it could get so intense in my head that I might have little idea what is going on in the rest of me. That was the point of the exercise – I'm protected from pain. And it became a habit, a habit that also cut me off from the more pleasant things in life. Rather than feeling present and joyful with a sunset or the new person I'd met, I might be thinking about how this sunset or person compares to other ones I've encountered. I might be thinking of something else entirely. I'd long sought to satisfy my mind, rather than feel in the present.

Therefore, for all the mindfulness practice I tried to do each morning, I'd first got a deeply ingrained habit to overcome. Back home, when the morning mindfulness practice was complete, I'd then step back into a culture where those around me tended to push away the present too – being encouraged to do so through threat of punishment or the promise of pleasure elsewhere – I was inclined to do the same as those around me. That was me trying to survive and cope. Lots of us do that.

And so, as I sobbed by the side of the road in Panama, finally in full awareness of all those lost years of not listening to myself, it was time to change.

Nowhere to go, nothing to do, nobody to be

Panama was still very far away from Bhutan, but after I'd made it to a small hostel and recovered from my self-inflicted anguish, I made a commitment to myself to slow down, and let go of needing to be anywhere other than where I was. The next country after Panama would be Costa Rica, and I was getting close to being seven months on the road when I finally arrived. Yet, regardless of where the pre-journey-self had wanted me to be by now, Costa Rica had been an important part of my journey from the outset, and I really wanted to be there as fully as possible. And so, I set myself boundaries to support me really being there – I put a limit on how much I would cycle – no more than 30 miles a day and/or to not cycle beyond 11am. They were reverse goals if you like, but I wasn't rigid on these. I didn't need to be, because the intention was clear: respect my bodily needs and check in with how I was feeling. These boundaries were there to help support that intention, and I remained flexible to the moment. It was about giving myself space, slowing down, allowing myself room to feel. And with nowhere to be, other than some 30 miles down the road – which in itself I knew wasn't at all important – I came more into the present, and that's when a whole different journey for happiness opened up before me. My journal entries illustrate this well:

> 1st May 2018: "Body not depleted. Not in survival mode. This is a huge shift. Huge."
> 4th May 2018: "Once again I sit contentedly. These days I am riding in flip-flops and stopping a lot. Things are so different to before – I will continue this way."
> 20th May 2018: "If this is my last moment, then I really need to be in it. Life is precious. Each and every moment. For one day there will be no more moments. I am alive now."
> 31st May 2018: "The sound of the rain is beautiful."

It was a major change. One that brought more happiness throughout the remainder of my journey, and my happiness scores confirmed it so. Before and after that moment in Panama, there was a step change in my daily happiness. In the 179 days before, my daily happiness was on average 6.6 out of 10 and, as described in the last chapter, although up and down as should be expected, it had on the whole been declining, including after accounting for the dog bite (if I subtract the dog bite, and the whole month after when I was still struggling from its repercussions, it was 6.9 on average). Afterwards my happiness average was 7.3, and on the whole, trended upwards from the Panamanian moment. This can be seen in Figure 2.

Although these differences in averages might not seem very large, it is important to remember that me becoming present was not the only thing happening on this journey, and there

Figure 2: Hedonic happiness across the entire journey

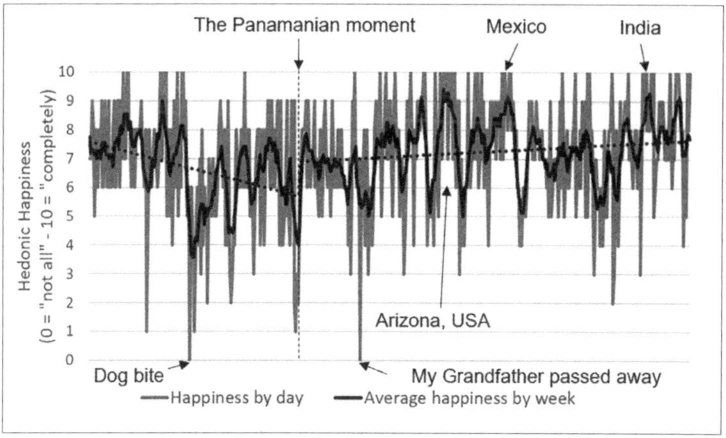

would be still more happiness challenges to come. Nevertheless, given how these kinds of questions are normally answered, it would be considered a moderate increase. Plus, if we were to account for the trends downward and upward in my happiness, before and after the Panamanian moment respectively, the shift at this inflection point was an approximate 1.2 change in daily-rated happiness. That's about the same size as undertaking either mindfulness-based stress reduction, or meditation. It is also clear that I got to experience far more '10' happiness days after this point (13 per cent of the days afterwards, versus 6 per cent before), and on the whole I had fewer low scores too (16 per cent of the days were lower than 5 afterwards, versus 25 per cent before).

Given the way of life in Costa Rica, I was surrounded by a culture that helped me make this shift. As I showed in the previous chapter, Costa Rica is a country that does well on both evaluative happiness (whether we think we're happy) and hedonic happiness (how happy we feel). What further fascinates me about Costa Rica is that it is regarded as the most successful country at producing sustainable happiness. That is, people are happy, but their ecological footprint is much lower than other countries where happiness is just as high.[3]

Costa Rica illustrates on a national scale that it is possible to be happy with less. It is a prime example of what can be achieved if a country does not fixate on the economy. There are other factors besides the economy which contribute to happiness: they include health, freedom, social support, the absence of corruption, and generosity, and what Costa Rica shows is that it is possible to have these things despite lower material standards of living than elsewhere.[4] They can be improved upon, irrespective of whether the economy is growing or not. It just needs political will.

In Costa Rica there is a full democracy, high-quality health care, lower crime than elsewhere in Latin America, forests that cover 51 per cent of the land mass, and a relative absence of corruption. In fact, Costa Rica outperforms the United States on life expectancy (80.3 versus 78.9 years, according to the United Nations Development Programme in 2019[5]) and democracy (scoring 8.13 on the 2019 Democracy Index by the Economist Intelligence Unit[6] and considered a full democracy, versus 7.96 on that index and considered a flawed democracy in the US). This has come about because Costa Rica made crucial policy decisions. These include high investments in both health and education way back in the 50s/60s, and environmental protections throughout the 80s. These changes, among others, have enabled people to live happy and healthy lives. It's no accident Costa Ricans are happy.

Costa Rica embodies a different notion of a successful life. There they celebrate the '*pura vida*': having a simple, happy, time for one another, lifestyle, and they have a national pride in finding happiness this way. It's a going-slow mentality – no rush, just be. It was being immersed in that *pura vida*, along with the boundaries I put in place to slow me down, that supported me with my own presence. People in Costa Rica were generally more present with the moment and available to connect. Less in their heads, more in their hearts.

I began to sit and watch the world go by, and it turned out to be a lot easier in that culture. Nature was vibrant and beautiful, which helped. I spent many nights camping on beaches. People would come and talk from time to time, but mostly, after my mornings spent cycling, I'd sit and watch the waves, listening to them crash wildly on the shore. I was just being. There was nowhere I needed to go, nothing I needed to do, and nobody I needed to be. I just needed to be where I was, and everything felt perfect as it was. I had finally found the time to appreciate how beautiful life had become, seven months since quitting my happiness research job. I marvelled at how easy it was to live happily with so little. Sincerely, it was a *pura vida*. Even my time in San José, Costa Rica's busy capital, felt easy.

And once I slowed down, unexpected and – dare I say – magical things began to happen. I had more time for people, and it was through being more present that I ended up with those infectiously happy children in that Guatemalan village. I had the occasional experience like the Guatemalan one at the start of my journey, but it was in Costa Rica that such experiences started happening all the time. Everyone had something to share, and I was at long last becoming present enough to see that.

CHAPTER 9

Beyond belief

"Me llamo Cristóbal, soy de Escocia, soy escritor."
The random utterances of a cyclist,
dates unknown

As I uttered these words to the people I met in Latin America, I knew that it wasn't the whole truth of things. Yet, no-one had any reason to question what I was telling them. There was no deceit. *Cristóbal* is my namesake in Spanish, and Scotland, *Escocia*, was where I was travelling from, and I had been an *escritor*, putting words down on paper, for many years. I was just playing with the story that I tell myself and others each day – who and what I believe myself to be. And in telling this new story again and again, and having strangers accept what were then only my nearly-truths, I began to whole-heartedly become what I said I was.

Throughout my journey, this new story brought me far more happiness than the one I had told about the academic researcher that felt scattered and unrooted. It was a story that placed fewer constraints on what I am. It was also a story that invited more curiosity and connection from the people I encountered, who were neither academics nor scattered.

Stories shape what happens in our world, and we need to think carefully about which ones we want to believe. I've long cherished a good story – but it took me many thousands of kilometres to appreciate that some stories have scarcely any truth or happiness behind them.

The story of the bleeding obvious

"I could have told you that!" I would often hear my Dad yell, when he read about the latest scientific discovery in the news, eating his Sunday breakfast of sausages and eggs. To him, proud of me as he was, with a career that exceeded my family's station, I was researching what he would have then called 'the bleeding obvious'. He has always been man resolute in his knowledge of many things of the world, one of which was that having more money would be an essential component to making him happier with his life. And he has lived his life accordingly – mostly in debt, always playing the lottery, and none too happy. He is a firm subscriber to the notion that just a little bit more money could go a long way, and that a lot more money would mean never having to worry again. Ever.

He has never won big on the lottery. Despite telling my Dad that studies on lottery winners show that improvements to happiness are much smaller than people expect them to be,[1] and that money doesn't suddenly make our relationship troubles easier to deal with, our bodies and minds healthier, nor our personalities more likeable, he'd still like to have the money and see for himself. He believes he'd be able to prove the scientists wrong. There has to be something wrong with the people they asked in all those studies, he thinks.

He believes the story – the one that's in the interests of those that run the lottery to tell – that a win is not only more likely than it really is, but will enable all his dreams to come true, and he will finally have his promised happiness. The lottery people depend on that story for their survival. They are not the only ones that depend on the money-buying-happiness story for their survival. Marketers and salespeople use that story to keep us buying things so that they can maximise their profits. Our employers benefit from it, through our desire to work long hours and keep striving to outdo one another for promotions. It is a politician's claims about the economy that will get them elected.

The money-being-key-to-happiness story is a difficult one to contest, with so many people having a vested interest in maintaining it. We've constructed our entire society around that story being true, and it is difficult to believe anything else. People can get quite angry and defensive when someone suggests it might *not* be true. It took me a long time to shift my own beliefs on the topic, and it took longer still for the 'money doesn't buy much happiness' belief to exert much influence on my life decisions. I've come to the conclusion that scientific evidence won't be enough when it comes to overcoming the money=happiness belief we have ingrained in our social fabric. We have to first acknowledge the power of story, and then perhaps we can start telling a different one.

We see what we believe

Whenever my research on money and happiness appeared in the news, and it often did, there would be lots of comments from the general public. Some welcomed the research. "I always knew money wasn't the key to happiness," they happily chirped. Others, however, angrily disagreed, with some suggesting that, rather than wasting research funds on pointless research – 'the bleeding obvious' – I ought to instead turn over all that research funding directly to them, so they could demonstrate how that money could, in fact, buy them plenty of personal happiness.

There was one occasion, several months before I left for Bhutan, when a new piece of research turned up in the news, claiming that money could buy a person happiness after all.[2] The assertion was that a person only needed to buy things that matched their personality in order to find happiness through spending money. What was really frustrating was that, two months previously, I had issued a press release for my own money and happiness research, in which I had again highlighted that more money would buy relatively little in the way of happiness. What I found really disturbing to see, however, was that this new research had gained far more attention than mine. It wasn't better research – in fact the research was fundamentally flawed, as we demonstrated in a journal comment to which no one paid attention, when it was finally published three months later[3] – but it had a far more compelling reason to garner attention: it conformed to the story that many people have a vested interest in maintaining.

What I found most striking were the public comments in response to this new 'money buys happiness' research – they mirrored the comments that my own research on money and happiness received. There were those that happily chirped in agreement to have their beliefs confirmed in a scientific study; those that vehemently disagreed; and lots and lots of cynicism. People weren't changing their minds as a result of the research. No, people already knew for themselves what the answer to the money and happiness question was, and they interacted with the evidence according to those beliefs.

Confirmation bias is a well-known phenomenon in the field of Psychology.[4] We lap up evidence that confirms what we believe to be true about the world, yet find every reason under the sun to dismiss evidence that challenges our deeply-held beliefs. It is easy to point to something that justifies what we believe. Perhaps someone we deem respectable will have said it, or we may have witnessed what looks like cause and effect with our own eyes. These days, social media algorithms have become very good at directing us to all the things we 'like', which often supports evidence for what we already believe rather than challenges us. Some of the evidence we come across might be published in scientific journals and written in books we've read – which, when it supports our view of the world, counts for a lot. There is nothing wrong with confirmation bias per se – it is a natural process that we humans, you and me both, use to navigate a complex world. It is one of many biases that I'll speak about in a few chapters' time, that are part of our evolutionary make-up. There are tonnes of them, and as I'll explain later, such biases easily have us making mistakes that don't serve our longer-term happiness.

I got a stark taste of this confirmation bias early on in my academic career, in the place I had least expected to see it. When I first arrived in a Psychology department to begin my PhD, having studied Economics for years, I had little idea as to what confirmation bias was, so I didn't realise that this was what I was witnessing at the time. I remember enthusiastically telling every psychologist who I met that I was going to be researching money and happiness. "That's very interesting", many of them would politely say. However, as I got to know the psychologists, some were more honest in their responses, and behind those polite smiles was an inability to understand why I would want to waste any time on researching such a topic. There had apparently been decades of psychological research showing that money, though important for happiness up to a point (which had long been reached in many industrialised economies), was on the whole not a very strong contributor to a person's happiness. I read most of this psychological research and I felt deflated, already my PhD was in tatters.

But something didn't add up, because over in Economics, where I had only just finished my studies, they were getting very excited about the question of money and happiness. Research into the topic was positively booming over there. Economists were showing, with scarcely any reference to the work in Psychology, that money had a major role to play in making people happy. At least, that was what I was reading about, in the most celebrated academic journals in the field. It would take me several frustrated years in academia to understand that it is next to impossible to publish in Economics if the subtext of the research is that money isn't very important for happiness. That doesn't fit the story over there.

We don't weigh up evidence and come to our conclusions that way. Largely we take on board the stories that we're told. As an Economics student, I had the story that more money always equates to more happiness told to me again and again, and when I repeated that story accurately in the exams, I was rewarded. The belief that money buys happiness underpins every single economic model that I encountered from the age of 14 to 24. It is the cornerstone of the subject. And to say that money isn't an important contributor to happiness in Economics is close to heresy.

Further still, outside of the classroom, I – like everyone – experienced a similar story. If I were to have or do this or that thing which costs money, I would be lastingly happier. That story began weaving itself within most of us long before we could walk or talk; at an age when we soak things up like a sponge. There was rarely any solid evidence for it (although on television the bed sheets washed using the laundry powder Daz did look 'whiter than white', and everyone seemed far happier for it to me), yet it seemed convincing to my impressionable young mind, and I was ripe for taking it on board in my studies of Economics. I heard the story that money buys happiness so many times from bigger and smoother looking people that I just assumed, as many of us end up doing, that it must be true. Plus, I matched what I'd been told with the personal experience of having that short-lived buzz that often comes from acquiring something new. It was self-evident, bleeding obvious, in fact – and like anyone, I just needed ever more amounts of the stuff. I wanted to keep on buzzing.

Academics are as prone to confirmation bias as anyone. Those that don't have some awareness of confirmation bias and are unwilling to question where their beliefs about the world have come from, perhaps more so. If we happen on a piece of evidence that implies money *can* buy happiness, then we leap on it as a society. It's a very fitting story, matching the one we most often hear.

I don't dispute that if we spend money in line with our personality, then we may be able to buy more happiness, as that research I mentioned earlier suggested. I mean it *is* bleeding obvious really. However, as the psychologists in those early years would often remind me as I carried out my research, doubling nothing is still nothing. The effect of money on happiness is not nothing, but money's effect, whether we spend it on things that align with our personality or not, is trivial, relative to other things that are just as obtainable, if not more so – including healthier relationships or meaningful shifts in personality. Remember, for example, the monetary values I presented back in Chapter 2 – marriage, for example, being worth the equivalent in happiness terms to around US$100,000 each and every year. And a shift in a personality trait like extroversion (itself being surprisingly much more likely to change than a change in how much we earn) to be equivalent to about US$160,000 each year. Even if the amount of happiness that money would ordinarily buy were doubled, then our relationships, our personality, and a whole host of other things, are still far more important. We're just not encouraged to find our happiness in these ways. It's not good for business, it's not good for the economy, and it's certainly not a story that will sell newspapers!

What story would you prefer to believe?

I have long been fascinated with the work of psychologist Carol Dweck. Her work focused on how intelligence develops throughout life.[5] There are two main competing views of how intelligence forms. On the one hand, there is the view that intelligence is something that is fixed. The amount of intelligence a person has is a fixed entity and that's that: the idea here is that you can't improve your innate intelligence. In the opposite vein, there is the idea that intelligence is malleable. That is, intelligence changes incrementally across time, and can be improved through effort.

Curiously, Carol Dweck and her colleagues demonstrated that a person's own intelligence behaved in a way that depended on their general beliefs about how intelligence forms. Someone with a 'fixed entity' belief about intelligence would tend to

Wide-eyed with early journey energy in Uruguay – November 2017

Day 42: In Argentina and the first serious encounter with mountains

Above: Happy amidst the Andes – January 2018
Below: Tired and frustrated amidst the Andes – March 2018

Curious encounters with people along the way

These characters were recording a music video up in the mountains of Peru

On a beach in Costa Rica with two God-loving rappers

In a family's home in Mexico – 'full belly, happy heart'

One misty morning high up in the mountains, having slept with the cows on a family farm after I tapped on their door in search of a place to stay

Who? Me! Crossing the equator in Ecuador and back into the Northern Hemisphere – March 2018

That most incredible scene described in 'Letting Go of Bhutan', Chapter 5 – January 2018

Mighty forces – some of those happy children I played with in the Guatemalan village – June 2018

A little boy fascinated and joyful by my home for the night in his garden in Mexico – August 2018

Rolling through mountains in Colombia – March 2018

Passing the Tropic of Cancer in Mexico – August 2018

A small selection of some of my favourite wild camp spots

Early on in Argentina – November 2017

High up in the mountains of Peru – January 2018

One of those beaches in Costa Rica where time stopped – May 2018

A sweet camping spot by a river in Northern Mexico – August 2018

It's hard to make much out here, but that light in the sky was a near full moon. There was also a big hairy spider out there waiting for me – Arizona, USA, September 2018

An enchanting forest someplace in Washington, USA – October 2018

Welcoming in a new day: A beach I'd slept on the previous night in Mexico – July 2018

A big arms photo in Mexico – July 2018

be protective of the intelligence they have. They would tend towards easy and low-effort successes, with an avoidance of effort and difficulty that may call their intelligence into question. In those people there was often anxiety about performance, and a desire to prove themselves to others. Those with an 'incremental' intelligence perspective, however, would put in concerted effort to improve their intellectual abilities, and would thrive when throwing themselves wholeheartedly into difficult tasks. This belief does not deny there are differences between people in their ability to master certain things, only that with effort we can develop.

This is interesting in itself – suggesting that intelligence operates innately differently across different people. What may be fundamentally true for one person might not be fundamentally true for another. However, what was more astonishing about her research is that when a person was subtly influenced with a story about intelligence being either fixed or malleable, the person began to then think and behave more in line with that theory of intelligence in a subsequent task. For example, those that were influenced to think that intelligence was malleable would take on greater challenges and show more signs of improvement. Those that had been encouraged to believe their intelligence was fixed went on to show less sustained effort when tasks were difficult, and suffered greater setbacks when challenges arose.

And so, as it turns out, there is at least a little truth to both theories of intelligence, and which one dominates within a person depends on that person's beliefs. We behave in line with our personal beliefs about intelligence. However, those beliefs were shaped in the first place by what we happen to see around us, such as how others behave and what we're told. Once our actual intelligence is shaped in line with our belief, what we then see every day tends to reinforce and confirm that belief. We act and behave as if it is true, and it becomes true for us. We become entrenched in our beliefs, and end up seeing and experiencing only what we believe. Evidence to the contrary gets discarded.

Whilst holding a rigid belief might help us feel safe in a world that is complex, it may also act as a block to our own development and that of others. In the case of intelligence, for example, in not believing that intelligence can be developed, we may not only create a block in ourselves for our own development but also be reluctant to help others develop. On the other hand, in not believing that there are innate differences in intelligence, we may hold an unrealistic expectation of ourselves and have disdain for those that cannot develop to the same extent as we have. Either way, there may be less happiness resulting from rigidity in our beliefs.

Back to my favourite happiness topics – personality and money

I've long speculated about how a person's belief about the world might shape their world in relation to other social phenomena. In particular, I've considered this in the two areas I've researched the most in relation to happiness – personality and money.

When I first began work on personality, the consensus academic and public view was that personality didn't change much beyond the age of 30. This conclusion stemmed mainly from ideas of American psychologist William James (1843–1910), and later psychological research carried out in the 1990s.[6] No doubt, given it was a relatively socially stable era, most people's general observations of themselves and others helped cement this belief. Any evidence of personality change was not only said to be small, but was attributed to a natural maturation process across life, rather than the result of anything that happened to a person, or that which they tried to change themselves. As such, why would anyone put effort into trying to change, if they believed change were not possible? However, more recent research (some of which is my own) shows that personality does develop throughout life; changes in personality are linked to sizeable changes in happiness; and personality change takes place in response to things that commonly happen in our lives, such as marriage, unemployment, and traumatic life experiences.[7]

That's not to say aspects of ourselves aren't biologically determined – it's about 50/50, give or take.[8] But it is important to recognise here, by illustrating that personality change *does* take place, it becomes more likely that people will then try to change. With more people trying to develop themselves, more people will actually experience change, and that can open up a potential route to greater happiness. Therefore, changing our beliefs changes how we act. By challenging our beliefs, we may open ourselves up to alternatives that bring us deeper fulfilment; and I know which theory of personality development I would rather believe. Had I thought I couldn't change, would I have still got on my bicycle and journeyed to Bhutan? Probably not.

Let's now look at the money and happiness question in the same way. First, let's suspend all beliefs about whether or not we think money buys happiness. Imagine there is no evidence either way that money buys happiness. Imagine that it is a simple choice as to whether we can believe money is the key to happiness as current mainstream economic theory dictates, or that it is not. If we were to believe money is the key to happiness, then we'd have to act as if it is, aspiring to have ever higher amounts of the stuff if we want to be happier. Our life would need to be constructed around that being true, and we'd pursue money at nearly any cost. However, the logic of that kind of belief is that, if we don't have loads of money (and we probably won't because the world is harshly unequal) then we can't be happy. Note, I'm not talking about people in abject poverty, but rather about having quite a bit, above say US$20,000 for one person each year, and still believing that more will bring them a substantial amount of happiness.[9]

If, however, we believe that things other than money are important for happiness, then our own beliefs won't exclude us from happiness if we don't have loads of money. We'll be able to see with more clarity that there are other ways to meet our core human needs, and that money is one of many strategies to meet those needs. Perhaps we'll spend more time in the present, share more, spend more time in nature, build community, spend time fostering our personal relationships, exercise more, and do the things that we're really passionate about. Maybe one day we'll set out on a bicycle to some faraway place that is unheard of by many people, rather than continue working a job that doesn't fulfil us.

If there were no evidence either way, then I'd prefer to believe the money and happiness story that doesn't put limits on my happiness. I'd prefer to live in a society where the collective beliefs and the stories we tell each other permit more happiness for more people.

However, we do also have evidence. As I've illustrated throughout this book, money does have a role to play in happiness, but above a fairly low level, such that we can meet our basic physiological needs, it is a minor role in comparison to other things.

So, we can make an informed choice about what to believe. Yet, of course, it isn't really about evidence, and it wouldn't be very rational to believe it is.

After a decade of academic research, I came to question the role of evidence in being a catalyst for societal change. It didn't matter how robust my statistics and how convincing my academic arguments were, there was always a reason that someone, usually an economist, could point to something that, in their eyes, would be enough to invalidate what I was saying. It wasn't about listening to evidence, but mostly about those stories that get told and re-told from birth to death. Stories that may have some truth in them, because all stories need at least a little truth in them to go anywhere. But some of those stories aren't doing very much to serve our collective happiness.

This journey, about an unhappy happiness researcher

who cycled to Bhutan, is more about offering a better story, and getting to the core of what we understand ourselves to be, individually and collectively.

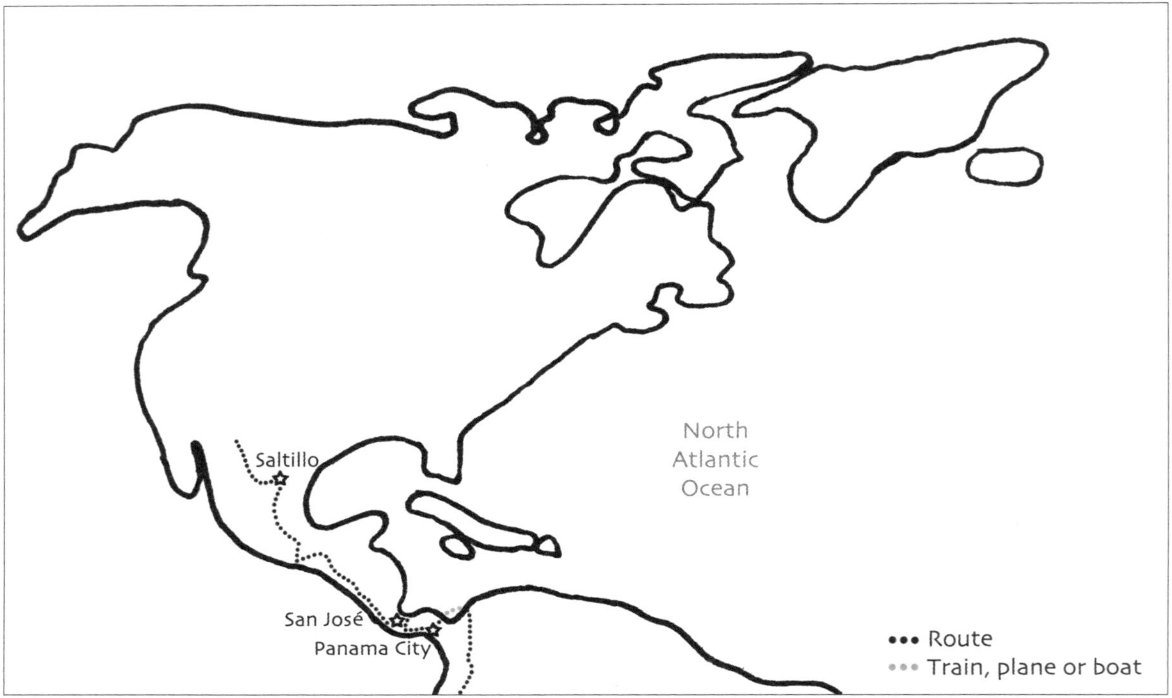

Through Central America and Mexico, and into the USA

CHAPTER 10

Gifts: the worst and the best

"Such a deep rotten fear I have – no faith in the world. And why not? Because of how I grew up and what I observed. In being naïve I could lose everything. (But I missed out on things too)."
Journal entry, 17th November 2017

It was a busy city in Mexico, and they were perfect strangers. They had stopped in their car to ask if I needed help. Sure, I did need help. I hadn't yet found anywhere to stay that night. I wasn't desperate, but I'd begun to appreciate over these last months that when someone asks if I need help, to say "no" would be a lie. There is always something that I could do with a little help with. Not only that, but saying "no" to an offer of help often closes the door to something powerful.

Receiving the gifts

Earlier that day I'd paid a visit to '*los bomberos*' – the firefighters. It's very common for fire stations across most of Latin America to have cyclists that are travelling through stay for a night or two. I'd had a couple of great experiences in fire stations. On this occasion, however, the firefighters were unable to help with a place to stay. Nevertheless, they insisted that I eat before I left. And so, being hungry from my day cycling, I ate with them and we shared a few stories. I wondered what to do next and I looked over a few hotels close by. They were typically uninspiring hotels and though I could have done with a shower, I felt more inspired to journey out of the city into the desert and find a place to put up my tent for the night.

It would probably take a while to find somewhere, because it was a big city I had to leave (Saltillo in the north of Mexico). Nevertheless, I would probably have found a decent spot out in the desert, and be set up in time for a desert sunset. Once set up, I would splash my body with half a litre of water, as had become my customary water washing allowance whenever I camped out if there were no streams nearby, and then I'd cook up some food and write in my journal. At some point in the evening thoughts would begin creeping into my mind as to whether where I was camped was safe. "What if. . .? What if someone comes in the middle of the night? And what was that noise?" Then that same fearful mind would attempt to reassure itself by thinking back to the many other times in which I'd camped out in a random spot just like this. I would remind myself of all the times when I had had similar anxious thoughts, yet nevertheless had woken up the next day safe and very happy. And then I'd give myself a wry smile, as right on cue, I'd hear my mind then consider, "But maybe tonight will be different. Perhaps where I am really is unsafe. Maybe the thoughts I am having tonight are based on something real, and something will happen this time."

So, when these perfect strangers stopped their car on this busy road and asked me if I needed help, I told them that I was looking for a safe spot to put a tent for the night. As luck would have it, they told me, they had a garden where I could do just that, two blocks away. All I needed to do was follow their car and we'd be there in minutes. I smiled deeply at the world.

Yet as I cycled behind their car the thoughts then came: "What if. . .? Who were these people? Could they be trusted? Was this a trap?" Next came that familiar wry smile as I watched how easily my suspicious and distrusting mind got to work on these people: a young Mexican couple with their not yet one-year-old daughter, smiling out of the back of their car. They really couldn't have been sweeter people.

I stayed two nights with them in their home. I camped in their garden, and they gave me a key to their home so I could come and go as I needed in the day. When we went out for dinner together, and I attempted to repay a tiny amount of their generosity and warmth by taking care of the bill, they would have none of it. I was their guest and it had been their pleasure to have me stay with them. Over dinner they suggested a route to my next destination that was much longer and less obvious than I had planned. I listened to that local insight, and there followed one of the happiest weeks of my journey. This was where I started to understand a few things about the power of giving, and more importantly how to accept and receive a gift.

If we want to connect meaningfully with others, then being present in the way I've already described in this book is the first essential step. Then, when we watch and listen with care, we will start to notice that there are people everywhere who would like to help in some small way. Yet, it is rare that we pause long enough to notice or give them the chance to do so.

We all like to help; it's not just in Mexico. Helping others is an innate human need, and when we do give, we often feel good about ourselves – we get that 'warm glow' feeling, as some have called it.[1] Yet fear will often prevent people from offering in the first place. Maybe it will be fear of helping the 'wrong' person – but more often than not, I've concluded, it is a fear that our attempts to help will be turned down, misinterpreted, or rejected. Rejected because that person, who probably does need help, will have their own fears and insecurities about saying yes. Yet, when we begin saying yes, when we begin to lean into others, not out of desperation, yet not fearlessly either, then we see that our receiving is also an act of giving. It's possibly the best gift we can give, for every gift needs someone to unconditionally receive it. And where I come from, we are awash with fear, and there is a dearth of people willing to receive. We are not supposed to look like we need help.

Making space for unpleasant feelings – the fears and insecurities

Sometimes we will feel things that perhaps we'd rather not. Some emotions are unpleasant. This is not a simple case of feeling unhappy rather than happy. The human experience is more fine-grained than that. There are a number of pleasant and unpleasant emotions we can experience in any given moment; from joy, excitement, and enthusiasm to anger, guilt, and irritation. The more we listen, the better we become at naming how we're feeling. Both pleasant and unpleasant emotions, since they refer to how we feel at a given moment, are an aspect of the *hedonic happiness* that I described earlier. Here I am going to focus on the unpleasant emotions – and it would be fair to consider the absence of unpleasant emotions as an aspect of happiness.

Whilst people ordinarily prefer to not experience unpleasant emotions, experiencing them is not necessarily a bad thing; nor does experiencing excessive unpleasant emotions make someone a bad person. The experience of unpleasant emotions is a very normal process and, as I've already described, such emotions naturally go up and down throughout the day. There is nothing wrong with that. In fact, unpleasant emotions can have benefits to our decision making, to our memory, and can make us politer and more considerate toward others. However, the experience of unpleasant emotions does, as may be expected, relate to lower levels of *evaluative happiness,* such as how satisfied we are with life. There is also a strong link between experiencing lots of unpleasant emotions and not many pleasant emotions during particularly difficult periods of our lives. One crucial thing, for the sake of happiness at least, is not to grasp for pleasant emotions, nor try to always avoid the unpleasant ones. Doing so can, in the end, block happiness. Rather, emotions are best seen as *indicators*, and in my experience they are best listened to – a practice which I got much better at after those difficult rides in Panama.[2]

From time to time we experience extended periods of sadness, which again is a normal process. In the moment that we feel unpleasant emotions, it is unlikely that we will simultaneously experience positive emotions. That is, pleasant and unpleasant emotions are inversely linked in the short-term. However, over increasing time periods, this inverse link begins to diminish, and pleasant and unpleasant emotions are generally independent of one another, in terms of how much people feel each of them in their lives.[3]

That being said, overly extended periods of unpleasant emotions are normally an indication of something distressing happening to you, and they are worth seeking support for. Treat them with care – in others and ourselves. Try not to drown them out and ignore them, as many (including me, way back when, as I'll describe later) get into the habit of doing.

One question that researchers use to understand this aspect of happiness is "Overall, how anxious did you feel yesterday?" As with the other questions in this book, to determine someone's overall life satisfaction (Chapter 5) or the happiness they felt yesterday (Chapter 7), people rate how anxious they felt from 0 to 10, where 0 is "Not at all" and 10 is "Completely". (We can also replace 'anxious' with a number of different emotions: pleasant (e.g., joyful, excited, enthusiastic…) and unpleasant ones (e.g., upset, distressed, ashamed…) – and the greater the number of emotions we can trace, the richer our understanding of happiness tends to be).[4]

If we focus on just this question about anxiety, people living in the United Kingdom average about 2.9. Of course, it depends on the day, but as with any question like this, it is asked over a large number of people at different times throughout the year. This tends to account for some people having particularly difficult days and others having good days. On any given day, most people (~40 per cent) score 0 or 1, and somewhere between 35–40 per cent of the population will be having a day that would be considered medium or high in anxiety (a score of 4 or more). Therefore, experiencing at least some daily anxiety is very common.

As with the other questions about happiness in this book, I've considered my own levels of anxiety. Just as with the question on day-to-day happiness, I asked myself the anxiety question every day on my journey, as shown below in Figure 3. Like my happiness, my anxiety was up and down each day, and again I include an average for each week-long period, to show periods when my anxiety was particularly high or low. The dog bite situation was the only time I reached a level 10 of anxiety throughout my journey. Yet, according to the numbers, my most anxious weekly period was early in 2019, just after New Year, as I headed into Laos from Vietnam. My memory doesn't serve me well here as to exactly why. There are just times when I just feel inexplicably anxious, much as can sometimes be the case with happiness.

Nevertheless, looking at the notes in my journal, that anxious week in Laos/Vietnam seems to have come about from a combination of cycling on terrible roads, a couple of punctures, some issues with the brakes on my bicycle, the come-down from New Year celebrations, and a hideous experience with a couple of sneaky leeches who found homes on my feet – all of which took place over just a few days.

Figure 3: How anxious I felt as I cycled to Bhutan

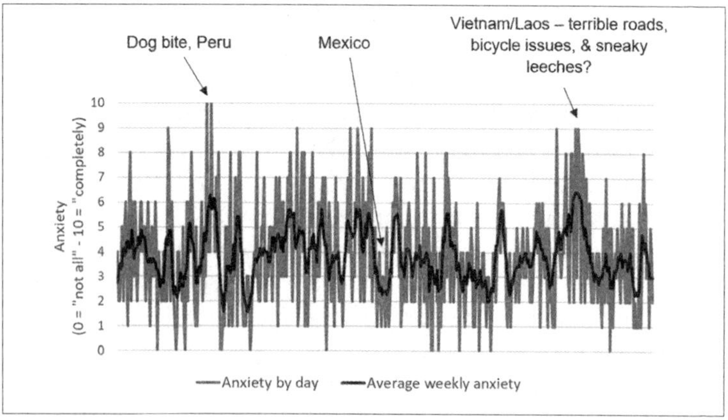

Across my journey, my average daily anxiety level was 3.8. This is much higher than the average of people living in the United Kingdom. On 53 per cent of the days, I scored 4 or more. It was very rare for me to score myself a 0 on anxiety. This might be understandable given what I was doing; plus, there were plenty of days when I recorded both my happiness and anxiety as being very high. Normally, this occurred because of some heart-stopping moment within an otherwise spectacular day. There is certainly truth in Irvin Yalom's words that "anxiety is a part of existence, and no individual who continues to grow and create will ever be free of it".

I have wondered how I'd have felt had I have stayed at home and not gone on this journey. Certainly, my levels of anxiety would have been lower over this period. And yet, I came back less anxious in my life than when I left – in part because I recognised that anxiety, like any emotion, is sometimes just present, and something to be accepted for what it is. It isn't actually a bad thing – it just is – and it is possible, as I'll describe in the next two sections of this chapter, to work with it to understand a bit more about ourselves and the world.

Transmitting fear

I don't doubt that I am pre-disposed towards feeling anxious; however, as with anything, environment and circumstance also play their part. The two interact to shape who we are, and influence how happy we can be. Some of my research on personality has illustrated this. Not only did my research explore how the happiness of people with different personalities responded to things like marriage, unemployment, income changes, and experiencing physical disablement, but also that these experiences can themselves shape and change our personalities.[5]

I remember one day in particular, quite early during my journey, back in the Andes of South America. It was around the time I was letting go of finding happiness based on successfully arriving in Bhutan, but before the dog bite. The day had been much like any other day riding through the mountains, except on this occasion, I felt a high level of anxiety. It was time to find a place to put my tent for the night, but I was reluctant to set up in any of the spots I found. Nowhere seemed quite safe enough to me. There was nothing that stood out to make me think any of those spots were unsafe. Something just didn't feel right. It was inexplicable, and I was thinking, as I often did when anxious to that degree, about heading for a hotel. The prospect felt reassuring, and would probably cost no more than US$5 for a small room in that part of the world.

However, I realised I hadn't felt this way earlier, before lunch. I'd set out for the day with every intention to camp, and I was confident that I would do so. In paying attention to my thoughts across the day, I noticed that the shift in my anxiety had come after a small stop I had made to pick up some bread and fruits for lunch. I thought about the conversation I'd had with a woman in the shop. It had been a pleasant conversation and I had enjoyed speaking to her. In my conscious memory there was no bad feeling emanating from her as a person. Though, just as I was leaving, she looked earnestly into my eyes and said: "*Cuidado, hay mucha gente mala por ahí*", which translates to "Be careful, there are lots of bad people out there." I didn't think much of it at the time.

As I thought back, I had a moment of clarity. I realised that contained within that final statement were that women's fears about the world. In her eyes, she was merely passing on information that she felt useful for a stranger in her lands. Dangers that she thought important for me to know about. Though I wasn't conscious of it in the moment, her fears had stuck with me, and that was a large part of why I was feeling so ill at ease with every camp spot I came across. Her fear had become my fear.

People say such things all the time. I know I used to. On the surface, it looks like someone showing they care. Yet, one has to consider reality. Horrible things can and do happen.

There is always a chance that something will happen, and we must be aware of such risks (with some risks being more real for some than others, because of factors such as their race or gender, or how many questionably necessary expensive gadgets they choose to carry that can create distance between them and local people). Many people's fears come from personal experience of terrible things happening. Perhaps an experience that has not been processed in a way that can be assimilated to the sense of self in the way that, for example, I managed to do with that dog bite. Instead, that experience is shared, recounted, and re-lived – sometimes daily. And when someone tells us something about the dangers of the world, seemingly as they and we think for our own good, it is more a reflection of their own fears about the world. There is, of course, good reason to share our pain with others – but if we are not careful, then we take some of that emotion on, and it becomes our fear too. Fear can be contagious, just as happiness, or any emotion, can be. I ended up camping that night in the Andes, and unsurprisingly woke up safe and happy.

Later on in my journey, I began to understand more about the transmission of fear from others and how to protect myself. On average, my anxiety in Guatemala averaged 5.0. This was one of the highest country averages on my journey. Although I had some wonderful experiences in Guatemala, what dominated my thoughts was that I was about to enter Mexico. And boy, did I hear some stories about Mexico! So many people had something to say about the country. More often than not, stories people had heard – from friends, or friends of friends, or on the news. There were the often-talked-about dangerous drug-running cartels, and so on. The one that people felt compelled to tell me about the most was the story of the two touring cyclists who had been brutally murdered in Chiapas. Chiapas is the first Mexican state after Guatemala, and this murder had happened just two months before I was due to arrive there. Many of the Mexicans I met there were themselves scared of their own lands. *Muy peligroso* – very dangerous, they said.

Overcoming fear (as best I can)

Fortunately, we can do something with our pre-dispositions – we can and do change. Yet, just as with being present, we will be up against it when trying to manage our anxieties in a society where fear is a useful tool to keep us working and buying more than we really need. It is not in the interests of the economy to have people feeling calm and satisfied with their lives. It is better for businesses to tell people what they are missing out on, and what they really shouldn't live without.[6]

It is certainly a great start in the battle against anxiety to come more into the present. It was through watching and observing myself that I had my first inkling as to how fear is passed on to others. From that point, I started watching more carefully in conversations I had with people. I tried not to be judgemental about another's fear, and I would just watch my reaction. After a while, it became easier for me to see when people were expressing their own fears about the world. If I was feeling particularly brave (which wasn't so often), I might carefully ask a person if they have had a personal experience in relation to whatever it was they were telling me to be fearful of – for example, whether they've ever themselves done what I was doing or was about to do. I was surprised at how often there is no personal experience to back up the cautious comment. Often it is what someone has heard through someone else. And with a country the size of Mexico, as well as it being the 'archenemy' of its neighbour to the north, there are countless stories floating about that drive fears about visiting such a place.

Indeed, my time in Mexico turned out to be one of my favourite bits of the entire journey; particularly up in the north, once I'd relaxed more and realised Mexico wasn't anything like people had made it sound. And I suppose that is the other important part of overcoming fear – challenging ourselves through exposure. This is not about pushing down fear and throwing ourselves into things wildly, but about knowing and accepting that fear will often accompany us when we try to do things that have a hope of bringing fulfilment. Through gradually confronting situations that make us feel afraid, we allow ourselves to feel our fear. Eventually that fear becomes less onerous.[7] That doesn't mean the fear disappears, but perhaps we won't feel too overwhelmed to do the things we want to do. When we do something and notice we're afraid, we do just that – we notice it. Then, as I did with those Mexican strangers or those random camp spots, we might give a wry smile and say to ourselves, "Oh, there goes the mind again." Perhaps we'll need to check in with other parts of ourselves, physically and emotionally, as to whether we are in real danger, and then, perhaps, we might just carry on.

In facing the fear comes a real gift

When I arrived in Mexico I was scared. I still intended to cycle through, but I wanted to make for the shortest route and get to the USA as quick as I could. Actually, it is now clear to me that many of my mad heroics on the bicycle, be it the 100-miler in Argentina or the rides of Panama, were in part driven by anxiety – needing to get through a country, my entire journey, to safety on the other side. When I was in Mexico, by virtue of its cultural familiarity, the USA seemed a less scary place to be. However, by the time I'd reached the north of Mexico (with the aid of a couple of bus rides and some hitchhiking), I decided to stay longer in Mexico, heading west rather than north. I ended up joining the USA in New Mexico (the tiny border crossing of Antelope Wells) rather than Texas.

I am happy I stayed longer in Mexico, as I would never have met that young Mexican couple who let me camp in their garden and pointed the way ahead. Like many, they had their hand in shaping this journey for happiness. My travels in Mexico became one family after another helping me. Someone would wave and say hello, and I might stop. With nowhere I needed to be but where I was, we would talk as much as we fancied. The next thing I knew I'd be sitting down to eat tacos or enchiladas with their family. I remained mindful, present, unafraid to say yes, and the world took me everywhere I needed to go. It felt magical, in a very literal sense, and I understood what it meant to be bold and have mighty forces come to my aid. I began having experiences like the one I had in Guatemala all the time. Being alive had never felt so amazing. I was beyond fear.

When people started offering me food, drink, and even money, I was puzzled as to why people gave so freely to me – especially when I didn't seem to desperately need the thing being offered, nor had I asked. I'd worry about what it was that I was bringing to people's lives, and feel guilty because often materially speaking, people didn't have much at all. Yet, they had enough, and they wanted to share what they had. It was important to acknowledge that they wanted to give, and it was for me to simply accept. I gave little back in a concrete sense. Anything I offered was never taken, and would sometimes leave an awkward feeling. It was mostly just me being present with them. That was all people ever seemed to want, and increasingly I allowed myself to go with it.

And what I learnt is that my best gift was just being willing to receive. Humans need to give, and to fulfil that need, some people must be willing to receive. Generosity is an important contributor to happiness, yet to cultivate generosity we need more trust and presence in our societies. Sadly, in too many parts of the world nowadays, these crucial elements of human life have been stifled, eroded. In fact, as I would soon encounter to an inordinate degree, there are some places that can only thrive in an economic sense through distraction, manipulation, and misery. But that's two chapters ahead. First, let's make some space for the wild on this journey for happiness.

CHAPTER 11

A wilder space

"The mountains are calling and I must go."
John Muir

It was a cold, clear day in March, several months before I'd thought of getting on a bicycle for Bhutan. I was sitting in the audience at a conference, listening to someone talk about happiness. It was my turn to get up and speak next.

We'd been sitting in the same room for most of the day. There were a few windows, but they were at the back of the room – a room too big for the number of people in it. I had hoped there would be more. There was the odd glance at one another, and sometimes a small nod of recognition, but eyes were faced forward, flitting between the big screen and the person talking and pointing beside it. Every so often, I swung my head around to look out of one of those windows at the back. I imagined all the things that I could otherwise be doing, rather than sitting where I was. I could see a car park and a few trees out there, and in the distance, bigger patches of green. Perhaps somewhere beyond that green, there was a wilder space for me.

But it was my turn to speak next.

I hadn't even gone outside for lunch. I could have done, but all the food was inside the building, as were all the people. I'd travelled a long way to be here, and I couldn't miss the opportunity to talk to all these notable people mingling together. With hindsight, I would have been happier if I'd gone outside and sat beneath one of those trees, and felt the cool air on my face. I didn't get to talk to many people after all and the food was terrible. As usual at these kind of lunch buffets in windowless rooms, I'd eaten too much, too quickly, and felt bloated. I'd pay for it tomorrow.

But that was tomorrow. It was my turn next.

My palms were damp and my heart was racing. I felt a cold shiver run through me and my hands were shaking. The words I had practised saying earlier in the day were jumbled up in my head now. Yet, this was all par for the course – as always, I'd stumble over a few words, and miss a few lines, but I'd get through it in the end. I just hoped that what I had to say would someday contribute to a happier world. Perhaps that would make the long travel here, during which natural blues and natural greens had passed me by way too quickly, worth it. I took a deep breath and I got up. The air was musty. The fluorescent lights hummed.

All the eyes were on me. It was my turn now.

I gazed out across a room full of people. They were all experts on the subject of happiness – just as I was supposed to be. Some of the people speaking before me and in the audience had been researching happiness for decades, and had produced ground-breaking academic theories on the subject. Before I began to talk and point at the screen as the others had done before me, I smiled. It was a half-hearted smile. I knew that no matter what I did, the faces before me would remain stern.

I also knew that the happiness discovery that I was going to talk about wouldn't come to very much. I had been hawking this one about for a couple of years, and I would go on to publish it in a top academic journal, but I knew it would never be used to make anyone any happier. Nor would travelling a long way to talk about happiness at conferences bring me any personal happiness. This was just over six months before I left for Bhutan, and I knew I couldn't keep on with this kind of work any longer. I grabbed what I could from the moment, and began my talk with a quip about the irony of being an unhappy happiness researcher. Although one person among the crowd laughed, every other face remained dour. I may not have been as alone as I had thought, but it was time to get away from all this concrete and the florescent lighting, and out far beyond those bigger patches of green. I needed to be in a wilder space.

The search for something wilder

It wasn't until my late 20s that I found myself in nature, feeling awestruck. I was doing a personal development course for work up in the Lake District, and before the second day of the course started, I decided to run up a hill close to where I was staying. I'd never in my life done such a thing before. I'd only recently begun running, and I'd also spent much of my life in relatively flat and built-up areas down in the south of England. Mostly in pubs actually, trying to drown out the thoughts of a mind that didn't want to switch off (more on that in the next chapter). Others, who seemed to know what they were doing, had told me they had run up the same hill the day before. And so, I felt inspired to try it myself. I set out on my own very early so that I would make it back for the start of the course. It was still dark when I left, and a nearly full moon was peeking at me through some clouds. Its light glistened on the lake and the silence all around me felt eerie. In this calm quiet, I could hear my pounding chest; my anxiety was strong. This was an unknown world to me – an adventure, the beginnings of a new journey.

It was an easy path – easier than I had wanted to believe it would be – and sometimes, with complete joy, I leapt clear over rocks. The air was fresh, cold too, but that helped keep my body cool. I was so fixated on watching the ground, I hadn't appreciated how high I had run into the sky. Not fully, not until I reached the top. And if the wind hadn't been taken out of me completely as I made my way upwards, it certainly was when I gazed long over the surrounding hills and at the lake down below. The sun was just coming up and everything was clearer. It was like nothing I'd ever seen before (though it did make me think of the train sets I'd peeked at in my Dad's model railway magazines when I was young). To me then, it didn't feel real. Yet, it was real – about as real as it could get, at the top of that hill in that moment, and I took my time being up there. Screw the course, I thought. This was something that mattered, and I needed to make the time for it now and ever onwards.

After that experience I began to find myself up in the hills more and more often. There weren't many big hills near where I lived and worked at the time – Coventry – but I began to venture out of my way to spend time in them. I'd explore them on foot or on my bicycle. I was always humbled in the presence of a big hill, mountains more so, and I began to find more calm inside of me – the anxious thoughts in my mind began getting quieter. When I was on a hill, what did and didn't matter always became clearer and less confusing. I would come back renewed, and with answers to things that had been bothering me for weeks; for a lifetime in fact.

It was never a surprise that the months I would spend cycling in the Andes on my journey to Bhutan would have such a powerful effect on me. As I've described, it was in meandering through those mountains for such a long time that I got my first real glimpse of the happy journey ahead. However, it was the desert-scapes that were the biggest surprise on this journey. I'd never been in the desert before, and I had always understood them to be bleak and uninviting places. Yet, in the weeks that I spent rolling through the deserts of North Mexico and Arizona, ten months into my journey, something within me finally calmed. The dead straight roads in the desert would stretch for miles ahead, the sandy-coloured mountains in the distance changing slightly with every pedal stroke. There was never any boredom, as I was always able to gaze out into yonder and just be with it all. I was merely a guy who happened to be cycling through a desert. Simple – no past, no future; just present. This was a wild space, certainly, and I felt a peace there like never before. Such is the power of nature that even when several masked men brandishing guns showed up outside of my tent – the single scariest moment in my life – I remained surprisingly calm. Yet, since evidence is just as important as a story, before

I describe my encounters with gunmen in the desert (yes, there were two separate incidences of men in the desert with guns), we'll first go through some of the research.

What we know about the far-reaching effects of being in nature

I was certain that nature would be a crucial part of my journey for happiness. It had to be. Not just through personal experience, but also because the importance of nature for overall wellbeing, including happiness, and mental and physical health, has long been known.

Perhaps one of the most famous scientific studies depicting nature as a great healer is the one where patients who had undergone surgery to remove their gall bladder were randomly assigned to rooms with particular views from the windows. About half of the patients' perspective when lying on their bed was an unobstructed view of some trees; the other half looked out onto a brown brick wall. The researchers found that those who had a view of the trees needed to be hospitalised after the procedure for a shorter time, and that whilst hospitalised, they needed lower strength pain medication and tended to be in more positive moods. This research was published in 1984, and since then a large body of research has illustrated that interactions with nature – essentially environments with physical features of a nonhuman origin – ranging from plants to non-built landscapes have clear benefits to our happiness.

Not only are there other examples of speedier patient recovery,[1] but there are also known benefits of wilderness therapy, regularly spending time outdoors, as well as having access to green and blue spaces when living in urban environments. Even viewing photographs or documentaries of nature has been shown to lift a person's mood.[2]

There are several reasons why nature is believed to be beneficial to our happiness. The first is that we have an innate love of nature, that has arisen due to our evolution as a species.

This innate love is called *biophilia*. The basic survival of our distant ancestors would have depended entirely on having a direct connection to nature – for example, how to source food and water from the natural environment, how to navigate and protect themselves from the elements, and so on. Feeling at ease in nature would have been a distinct survival advantage. Urban environments are a relatively new part of the human story and, whilst we might not need a direct connection to nature for our basic survival in a city, we still have that genetic wiring. No matter how we look at it, we are part of nature, and feeling connected to other living things is essential.

A more specific reason is that nature aids stress reduction. When we spend time in nature, there are emotional and physiological responses that promote rapid recovery after a stressful situation. Nature also offers a respite from mental fatigue. Many of our tasks in daily life require prolonged focus and concentration. However, our capacity to direct our attention in such a specific way is limited, and after extended periods we experience declines in performance. Nature offers a break from this focused type of attention. It's possible to experience some of this recovery relaxing in a pleasant room, but in nature there are likely to be other calming factors, such as fresher air and physical movement. We can engage with nature effortlessly, without constantly monitoring a specific behaviour; our time in nature is restorative.[3]

However, despite these known benefits, we don't often spend enough time engaging with nature to receive its full effect. Sometimes this is because of limited access – as it was for me growing up. Nature may be far away, and take time and energy to reach. However, a key reason is that most people underappreciate its benefits. We are known to misjudge the effects of many things on our lives: some things we overestimate in importance; with nature, we are known to systematically underestimate its importance. We therefore engage less than is good for us.

Just as I can relate to the lack of access, I can relate to this general underappreciation of nature too. Most presently, when I've been stuck on aspects of this book and have felt frustrated, only to still be surprised that a 20-minute walk among a few trees can shift my mood completely, and give me inspiration to write again. This same underappreciation was a feature of my experiences growing up. Back then I was unfamiliar with nature, and I could only gauge its importance from the way in which it was talked about by those around me. Nature wasn't regarded as important in my home, and outside of my home, the most prominent messages that I received about what a good life entailed rarely encouraged me to look for my happiness in a natural context. It was only later in life that I had the opportunity to find out its power for myself.

Aside from the direct benefits of spending time in nature, our happiness is reliant on nature's health. We are not separate from nature. From the quarries we mine, to the forests we clear for arable land, we are entirely dependent on nature to sustain us and our chosen way of life. For many people, the way of life they lead is basic, and I encountered many like this on my journey. Sometimes it was a voluntarily simple life, in pursuit of a more convivial existence – people like José Mujica, the Uruguayan president – but most often a modest way of living was largely involuntary. Others, however, have lifestyles that command vast resources from nature. There can sometimes be additional personal happiness proceeding from such heavy use of resources, but it is at best marginal, as we discussed earlier. More crucially, such high levels of consumption cannot be sustained forever, and we have long been pushing the Earth's biophysical boundaries beyond their limit (we'll talk more later in relation to creating an economy centred around wellbeing). Not only is high resource-use a threat to present happiness, via, for example, diminished air and water quality, but such use also jeopardises the happiness of our future selves and subsequent generations.

The sadness from a lost connection to nature

In some ways I consider myself fortunate – I began my life in a built-up urban environment, and then later I was able to explore the importance of nature for my happiness. Although I wasn't as happy growing up as perhaps I might have been, due to the absence of nature, my later experiences have helped me understand myself and the world, and I have become happier as a result. It feels like things have gotten better. I can only imagine how it might feel to go in the opposite direction – to start one's life embedded within nature, connected to it, and to then have that connection violently stripped away.[4] It is impossible to cycle up through the Americas without encountering peoples who have experienced this, or at least have recent ancestors to whom this has happened. It is a very sad thing, but something that is important to look at and acknowledge, if happiness is what we are after.

Shortly before leaving on my journey for happiness to Bhutan, I had been reading a book called *Wild: An Elemental Journey.*[5] The author, Jay Griffiths, is an anthropologist, and she explores the role that nature plays in our lives through the lens of indigenous cultures, and how they find meaning and identity through connection to their ancestral lands. Ancestors walked through these wild places, and the stories they shared with one another were based around the land. Those stories would have helped to remind them not just who they were as a people, but also of their dependency on nature. Griffiths suggests that it is not just indigenous cultures that need at least a little wildness in their lives to remind themselves of who they are. We all do. It is this disconnection with nature, she proposes, that explains much of our modern malaise. I agree.

In his book *Scatterlings,*[6] Martin Shaw, a mythologist, tells us that we are everywhere but nowhere. He suggests that land is not something that we should be laying claim to, but instead we should be surrendering to the vast powers of nature, and allowing the land to claim us. That is a more functional and nourishing relationship, he says. Yet rather than be rooted in the Earth: present, aware, and respectful, of all that we are and where we've come from, we are instead lost in a perpetual search for something. Scattered – yes, I can identify with that.

I have no idea how far I'd need to go back to find personal ancestors that were rooted firmly in the land. I suspect it would be centuries. I cannot be sure whether my ancestors came to live in an urban environment willingly or not. For the purposes of this story, I'd like to believe not, but I honestly don't know. However, what I would suppose is that they probably thought life would be better in such an environment; they came in search of some kind of happiness – perhaps because there was a real opportunity – but I think that's doubtful, as that is not my social lineage. Most likely they were working a piece of land, like countless generations before them, that they did not have any 'legal' claim to. Someone else with more power might have had other plans for that land, such as turning it into more financially lucrative cattle fields. Or perhaps, on top of whatever dues my ancestors had to pay for use of that land to some powerful other, what they produced was not enough to sustain them, and they thought life in the city might hold more promise. Or at least bring a little less unhappiness – a temporary relief from an arduous life.

Perhaps some of my ancestry split off somewhere along the way, and headed out to what was once referred to by Europeans as the New World, the Americas, and made claim on a piece of land there. A piece of land that had never been claimed legally by those for whom it was far from being a New World, but their ancestral home. I'm sure each of my ancestors has their own unique story for migrating, but when they finally arrived wherever it was they got to, most would have felt lost. Disconnected from who they once were; no stories in relation to the land and sky around them; feeling hollow, and having to start all over again. They were to rebuild a sense of themselves in the supposed land of the free – that was the new story.

I thought a lot about these sorts of things as I journeyed through North America. I had an eye-opening encounter with descendants of the prominent Apache leader Geronimo, the last Native American leader to formerly surrender to the US military. He was born in 1829 and surrendered in 1886. His wife and three children were killed by soldiers when he was 28, he broke out of US ordained reservations three times, and his life ended whilst he was a prisoner of war. Geronimo had a reputation for cunning and ruthlessness, and as the Apache in whose company I happened to find myself kept reminding me, would have killed someone like me on sight.

These Apaches had stopped their truck, because they were worried about me being in the middle of the desert on a bicycle on my own. I knew that what I was doing was a bit risky, but by then I felt confident in the desert, and that I had enough water to do what I needed to do. Plus, if the detour away from the main road didn't work out in the way I hoped it would, I'd make my way back to it. I must admit I was a bit worried about being on Apache land without permission, though, they hardly cared about that; they were just kind, as people are, and wanted to help. The only assistance I felt I needed was to know whether the track road we were on would take me where I thought it would. Yet they felt the danger was too great for me, and insisted I ride with them to the next safe spot, which meant going back on themselves. My bicycle and all my gear was piled into the back of the truck, and they made room for me to sit inside. The familiarity of good people going out of their way to help a stranger soothed my soul. They wanted to hear my story – how I came to be where I was. They were fascinated; they shared a little of themselves too.

They weren't sober. It was clear that they had their own struggles. The man on my left kept up his reminders of what Geronimo would have done to a person like me. It was an odd thing to hear, but it wasn't coming from malice. Rather, it seemed to me, from a place of lost pride, and deep sadness about a people that once knew who they were. As a white European man, I felt sadness, and a sense of guilt. People not too dissimilar to me have been, and still are – consciously and unconsciously – complicit in this people's struggle.

On my right was an Apache woman. She had her sadness too. She was dealing with a recent relationship break-up, and the estrangement of her son. Then there was the collective sadness that they all expressed, at the size of a lake we were driving past. Due to water access rights being sold downstream to Arizonian farmers, it had gotten smaller each year. It was not as full as they remembered it to have been in their childhoods. There was loss, and that loss went deep. Nevertheless, they seemed to take a lot from my own story, and got me to that safe spot. We hugged, took some photos, and they went on their way. Although I had met others like them on my journey, this encounter profoundly affected me. I was humbled.

Sometimes it goes beyond wildness

I had two encounters with gun-wielding men on my journey. Both experiences were scarily surreal but also strangely inspiring. The first encounter had been in north Mexico; there were four of them. The night before I had stayed with a local Mexican family. We'd eaten a lot and I hadn't slept well. Where I cycled the next day was so beautiful that I couldn't resist pausing, and putting up a tent to shield me from the midday sun. The plan was to cook up a feast, and then have a nap. It was easy by this point in the journey to just stop and forget about having to be anywhere other than where I was.

It was the middle of the day, and where I stopped was only ten metres from a quiet road; I was visible to anyone that passed by. As I'd unpacked my things a couple of cars passed by, and some of the passengers had gawped. I'd just finished putting up my tent and was standing beside it when a four-door truck suddenly turned off the road and rolled toward me, a little too rapidly for comfort. The windows were tinted and the front grill was enormous. I hadn't expected this, and I looked toward the vehicle quizzically as it got closer. I moved very little. Then, barely a moment after the truck stopped, all four doors flung open, almost in complete synchronisation. Things weren't looking good. My stomach turned. The next moment four masked men holding guns stepped out. They were big men.

First, in such moments, there is disbelief – is this really happening? Yes, all senses checked; this is as real as it gets. My eyes went wide and my legs a bit wobbly. It was so quick and the relief after it went away so strong that I have very few words for it really. For at least a full second there I thought something dreadful was about to happen and I would be the centrepiece of a tragic story that others tell. However, on the whole I remained surprisingly calm, and I imagine it looked that way on the outside too. Part of me thought – if this is my time, then this is my time. There I was, fully in the present, meeting what was before me, and without the sweaty palms that had been so familiar before, whenever I had to get up and give a talk about my research to a sea of forbidding faces. I was out, far beyond those patches of green that I had day-dreamed about in uninspiring rooms. What I did know at that point was that no matter what happened from here on in, it had all been worth it.

As it turned out, they were 'special police' – or at least this was their claim, and they were checking up on me to see if I was okay. Admittedly, it was an odd place to be. I'd never have camped overnight in such a visible place, no matter the country. They asked if I needed any help, and since I didn't, they got in their truck and went on their way. I then cooked my food, laid down, and tried to have my nap. If they were indeed 'special police', why they had to wear masks to check up on me I will never know…

My second encounter with someone brandishing a gun in the middle of the desert was later in Arizona, USA, about three weeks later. It was several days after meeting those Apaches. This time, shots were fired. I had been riding some solid 60 miles a day through Arizona, had passed by the Grand Canyon, and ridden along parts of the iconic Route 66. I was feeling physically strong and confident, but it was time to camp up before entering Nevada the next day. I found a beautiful spot about half a mile from the highway, and there were no buildings in sight. I recorded a small video in which I pronounced myself a happy man.[7]

Sunset was some time off yet, and so I sat, watched the desert meeting the sky in the distance, and let the beauty of the moment envelop me. I started to cook my dinner. Not long after, as the onions sizzled, I heard a car coming up the same track that I had taken. I couldn't see the vehicle, but I was well hidden behind a few cactuses, and I doubted they could see me. I then heard someone get out of the car and close the door. I kept cooking, but remained attentive and curious to the world outside. About five minutes later there was a shot, and then another, and panic kicked in. I was imagining someone squatting down out there, their sights trained on me.

My instinct was to stand up and fully reveal myself. As I did so, I could see a man standing on his own about 100 metres away, holding a small handgun. He appeared to not know I was there. Either I needed to stay hidden, and hope no stray bullets came in my direction, or get his attention to let him know I was there. I listened to my gut and approached, waving my hands and shouting. Even though I was within earshot, he neither seemed to see nor hear me. He fired off another two rounds at what seemed like a random spot on the desert floor. I questioned whether he was sane, wondering if after all I might be better off retreating and staying hidden. I stayed as calm as I could, and kept approaching and waving. I'm glad I did. If I hadn't heard his story, I'd never have slept that night – and maybe never again slept in the desert.

It turns out that in Arizona there is a legal right for citizens to drive out to the desert and, so long as there are no houses close by, pop off a few rounds. The man casually explained this to me as part of our 30-minute conversation, once he'd pulled out his earplugs. He had been just as surprised to see me, camping in the middle of nowhere. Once we'd both got over our mutual shock, he told me about his wife and family, and his very regular life. A pleasant guy. Getting his wild, I suppose.

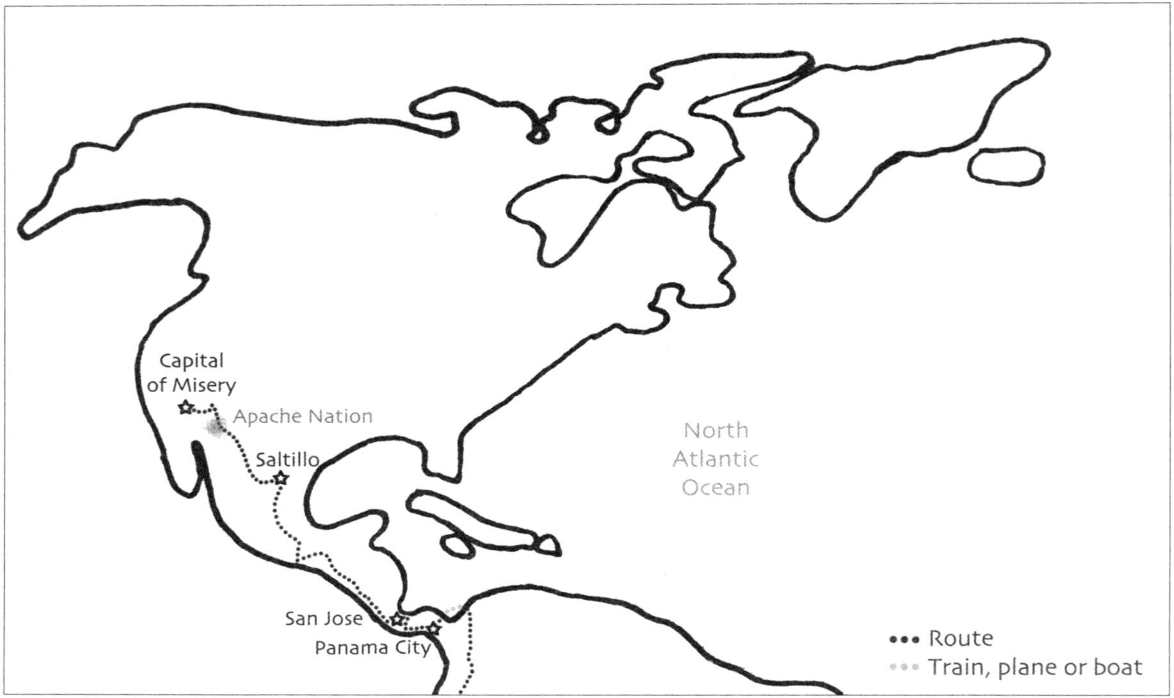

To the Misery Capital of the World

CHAPTER 12

Manufacturing misery

"Sometimes it frightens me just how close I am to being that guy on the streets bumbling about with no shoes and making little sense to those around me."
Journal entry, 7th September 2018

My bicycle was quickly coming apart. And so was I.

It was a terrible arrival into a city where I was going to need all my wits about me if I wanted to survive. Even if I'd been at my best, I might not have coped well. The city I now found myself in was far worse than I imagined.

Throughout my academic career, I'd learnt all about the misjudgements that we humans are prone to make when it comes to making decisions about happiness. Too often we do things that are not in our best interests, and we make the same mistakes in our decisions time and time again. Sometimes these errors in judgment can be downright harmful. I'd also seen with increasing clarity how easily these natural and commonly occurring mistakes can be exploited by others. Perhaps the most painful effect of making these misjudgements again and again is that we'll typically blame ourselves entirely for the unhappy consequences of our errors. And yet, what we might not realise is that it is very likely, somebody will have craftily designed the choice context, so that it is very difficult for us to not to make that misjudgement. That somebody will probably be trying to turn a quick profit. It's just business – their business, not your happiness. Sometimes the two coincide, though often not. The level of manipulation is toxic to happiness in many places. However, I found the level of toxicity in this particular city far too great to bear. My guard was down, and I began to skirt dangerously close to a dark and scary place inside of me. A place that I had not been to for a very long time.

Not a culture that celebrates giving

When I arrived at the hostel where I planned to stay, I was unable to speak more than a few words. I was physically ruined from the day's cycling necessary to get into this giant dustbowl of a settlement (and one that is, unfortunately, no mirage, shimmering up from the inhospitable desert surrounding it). I hadn't felt this terrible in my body since the days of Panama some four months earlier. Once I'd rested, eaten, and recovered a little, I made my way to the nearest bicycle shop to see about getting the parts I needed: a chain/crank-set, a cassette, and a chain – basically, all the essential moving parts that had given up on me on the ride in. I'd known for some time that these parts were long past their best. I may have gotten better at listening to my body, but I'd ignored the warning signs from my bike.

The bicycle shop was small, and it had the smell of fresh rubber and oil that reassures any tired cyclist. I presented Gulliver to the shop assistants, and told them the story of my day. They wanted to hear more, fascinated by the bigger story. It blew their minds that I'd cycled up from Argentina, more than 7,000 miles at that point. They'd never heard of Bhutan. Much of their curiosity revolved around their own fears of carrying out such a journey; they wanted to know whether anything bad had happened, and whether I was ever scared. I told them a couple of stories, and then a little of what I'd learnt about fear from cycling in Mexico, a place they seemed particularly fearful of. I told them too of my experiences of kindness after kindness, and how in the end I'd concluded that sometimes the best gift that can be given is to allow others to give. This idea of giving and receiving gifts didn't land well with them. Whilst one of them looked at me dumbfounded, the other gave a laugh from deep within his belly. I felt self-conscious and awkward.

When we got down to why I was in their shop, they didn't have the parts I needed. I asked if I could use a chain-removing tool to replace the ancient chain on my bicycle with a slightly less-old old chain that I changed maybe 4,000 miles ago and still carried with me in case of emergency. I thought it might make my bicycle rideable for a bit longer – at least so I could look for another bicycle shop.

It's a two-second job to use a tool to remove a chain and changing the chain was worth a shot. The guy did it himself without a moment's hesitation, nor any prior consultation with me whether that was okay. Politely I asked how much that would be. At the back of my mind I was thinking about all the times I had been in far less shiny-looking bicycle shops further south, in Latin America, when I would have said, at the end of sometimes relatively big jobs that had got me out of quite a jam: "*Cuanto cuesta, amigo?*" And nearly every time there would be a shake of the head – "*De nada, un regalo, amigo*" – and they smiled, and I smiled. The opportunity to help a stranger in need was enough payment, and it was beautiful.

For splitting my chain, he wanted $5. I paid it, of course; it's not much. But then, neither was the job he did. Though, "Wake up Christopher," I said to myself, "this is Las Vegas, not Latin America."

In Las Vegas, the idea that the best gift you can give is to allow others to give was always going to be bizarre and laughable. There is no giving in Las Vegas; not unless it aids the taking, of course. In Las Vegas, you are either inside, under the air conditioning, having money cajoled out of you – or you are outside, frying on the streets, the sun sucking out any sense you thought you had. If you're not too dazzled by the glim and the glamour, you'll see that Las Vegas is a deeply miserable place. And if you are taken in, overwhelmed by the show, then plenty of deceptive tricks will be in play to extract all the loose (and not so loose) change from your pockets. Sure, it might be your own hand reaching in there, but that hand is being pulled by invisible strings. Sometimes, you won't be able to stop when you want to, and wish you hadn't started in the first place. There is a total loss of control – even as you know it'll have to be paid for later. And later, it'll be said that it was your choice all along, and you only have yourself to blame. Do you?

Las Vegas epitomises what a society based around happiness would *not* look like. If Bhutan is the happiness capital of the world, then Las Vegas must be its misery capital.

Vegas wouldn't work without the promise of happiness. But it's only the moment-to-moment, *hedonic* happiness we talked about earlier, all smiles and laughter, that is on offer. And obtaining that kind of happiness is made to seem far more likely and longer-lasting than it ever turns out to be. It's not the sort of happiness that will have a person feeling particularly satisfied, let alone deeply fulfilled (more on this kind of happiness is to come).

Any happiness that does come is more likely a temporary relief from anxious tension than anything else – an anxious tension that the casino is carefully designed to bring out in us. I mean, Las Vegas, is hardly a relaxing space where a person can sit calmly. Everything flashes and throbs, demanding attention.

It doesn't normally take long for that momentary relief from tension to fade and become imperceptible. For some people, raising the stakes may get them going again. And they'll be encouraged to 'get going' again and again, until there is very little, or nothing left. For others, they might take refuge in one of the many garish hotels to rest and regather themselves, until something lures them out into the chaos – be it the promise of fun, or fulfilling a basic need like food. Then the heat might start having a go at our bodies, and in the need to avoid that heat the next thing you know you find yourself stuck in a place that you may come to regret ever setting foot in. That is Las Vegas.

Yet, it is not just Vegas where people can't help but act in ways that don't make happiness-sense. The promise of happiness, and carefully crafted environments to elicit certain actions and behaviours are what underpin much of modern life. It is next to impossible to escape. And until my bicycle was repaired, I was stuck in the worst place on earth for such business.

Leaving people alone to make their own 'rational' choices

We humans are prone to making errors of judgement. What we think is in our best interest sometimes turns out not to be. And rather than making that error in judgement just once, and learning to do something different next time, we can go on making that error of judgement, again and again, maybe throughout our entire lives. There are hundreds of known ways in which we are prone to systematically misjudge what is before us.[1] For example, as we can't predict what will happen in the future, we prefer a short-term payoff to one that comes later; we are sensitive to what others think about us, and we have many false beliefs about the world. This goes for most of us, simply because it's the way humans are biologically wired.

In each moment there are decisions to be made. These range from the seemingly trivial to seriously life-threatening. Whilst we might be able to deliberate for a while over some of them, other decisions will have to be made immediately. Some choices, since we've faced similar ones day-in day-out for most of our lives, might be largely automatic. This is how it has always been for us humans, and it is being able to make both quick decisions and careful decisions that has ensured the survival of our species. Often, we'd like a lot more time to make choices in life, but our circumstances won't allow for it. We just do our best, given the little we have and know.

Fortunately, humans have an uncanny ability to make quick and reliable decisions about very complex problems. Rather than our decision process being one whereby we have the opportunity to collect all relevant information, carefully weigh up each option, accurately factor in risk and uncertainty, and so forth, we take mental short-cuts. Often the decisions that arise from these short-cuts turn out to be quite similar to ones we have taken a lot more time over. That is, they enable us to make choices that look *as if* we had carefully deliberated over them, when in fact we did absolutely nothing of the sort. The problem is that there are glitches in these mental short-cuts and sometimes we can get it completely wrong. The outcome might turn out to be far from what we had intended, and very far from being in the best interests of our happiness. It is through this naturally quick decision-making that the errors of judgement we humans systematically make arise.

These errors of judgement are innately human and, though there is nothing wrong with them per se, they can be used by others to encourage us to do things we otherwise wouldn't. Sometimes others deliberately use these innate errors to encourage us to behave in ways that seem well-intentioned – but in all likelihood, the intention behind exploiting natural human errors will not be in line with our interests. When profit takes precedence over anything else, these natural errors of judgement get exploited for monetary gain. Often we're not aware of it happening – especially when it is part and parcel of our culture and has been happening for our entire lives.

Back when I was a student of Economics, there was no mention of these errors of judgement in our textbooks. All the models of economic behaviour that were presented to me had the same underlying assumption: humans are entirely rational in their decision making. According to those economic models, people never made errors that made them less happy overall. Rather, people made choices based on their unique set of preferences that would perfectly optimise the amount of happiness they experienced over their lifetime.[2] We were told that humans had perfect foresight, are equipped with all necessary information, and plenty of time to make their decisions (alongside always wanting more in preference to less). Any outcomes that resulted, it was perversely advocated, were merely a reflection of that person and their desires.

One classic proposition made by economists is that people

get addicted because it is their optimal choice to do so, and that they desire addiction.[3] Based on this simplistic view of decision making (shockingly, still the cornerstone of modern Economics teaching), many economists believe there is no need to actually measure people's happiness, because observing people's choices alone is enough to tell us what brings them happiness. Whatever a person's outcome in life, our impressionable young minds were told, must be what they desired. It was quite some story.

Rationality, as conceived of in Economics, certainly has its appeal. It offers a neat and tidy explanation to human behaviour and as a young student, I lapped it up. No alternatives were presented, and in any case, many of the models I learnt about seemed to accurately predict some of the things that were happening in the world. That helped make a complex world seem altogether quite bearable, and gave some reassurance to my younger anxiety-prone self. After constant exposure to this way of thinking, I came to believe – since we were told it would make us all financially better off and therefore unquestionably happier – in the inherent 'rightness' of behaving rationally, in the way that economic models suggested. I tried to be more rational myself, as I was convinced that the Economic notion of rationality was the surest route to greater happiness. It wasn't long until I began harshly judging anyone – including myself, and especially those close to me – when they did not appear to behave rationally in the way that the models said we were supposed to.

The nudge to rational behaviour

Ground-breaking academic research was carried out in the 70s and 80s, demonstrating that humans are not rational in the way economists believed. It wasn't just a few people, like members of my family, for instance, deciding how to eat and spend, making occasional errors of judgment – but all of us, and with regularity. We are after all humans, not robots. This body of research began to unpick what was actually taking place inside of us when we have to make complex decisions. Though we sometimes behave *as if* we are rational, and quite possibly might believe ourselves to be fully rational, the process that underlies our behaviour is often not. Sadly, research that questioned economic rationality was largely ignored by mainstream Economics when I was a student. There was no psychological realism in our textbooks, and there were no specialist courses to learn about any of this either.

Things are a little different now. What is now referred to as Behavioural Economics has a firm foothold in economic thought. In 2008, after the body of psychologically-informed research had steadily gained impact over decades, an influential book called *Nudge* was published.[4] The main thrust of that book was that whilst people weren't always economically rational, they could be encouraged to be so through influencing the psychological processes behind our decision making. The focus was on promoting policy that would encourage people to act more rationally, in the way economists said we ought to be acting.

One classic example of a 'nudge', that has resulted in a major shift in policy over recent years, and of which many of you will be aware is pension enrolment. From an economic rationality perspective, we have not been saving enough money for our futures. It is said that if we want to have enough money for our retirement to live in the way we've become accustomed to, then we need to individually enrol in a pension scheme. The behavioural explanation as to why we under-save is that people prefer immediate pleasures to delayed ones. When the default option is not enrolling into a pension fund, we collectively save too little for our retirement (this is considered irrational economic behaviour). People don't *opt in* as much as they rationally should. However, if the default option is instead switched – so that a person is automatically enrolled into a pension fund, although opting out is still possible – then people tend *not* to opt out, and savings for retirement end up being much higher, using this very simple default switch (rational economic behaviour).

The key to this approach is not to infringe on a person's

ability to make a different choice if they so wish. Therefore, rather than tell people what they can and can't do, people are instead given a nudge in the direction of behaviour that is desirable from a rational perspective, by subtly influencing the environment in which the decision is being made. In the case of pensions, many might prefer a pension system supported by general taxation. However, others argue, often those with more money who don't want to pay more tax, that such a system infringes too much on people's freedom to choose for themselves. By defaulting someone into a private pension, a person still has the choice to opt out. This approach to policy is known as liberal paternalism. It is paternalistic – as in somewhat authoritarian – but still allows freedom to choose. And framed this way, the mainstream economists could accept the findings of the behavioural economists. It didn't threaten the centrality of rationality in economics, but rather, maintained economic rationality as the ideal behaviour for any self-respecting human. (And those that weren't rational, in the way they should be, could be coerced into behaving better.)

Economists, psychologists, and philosophers have debated the ethics of nudging people. Do governments have the right to coerce people into making decisions that make them better off? Who gets to decide what behaviour would make someone better off? And indeed, better off for whom? There is well-intentioned care in this nudge approach, but it misses a far bigger issue. How ethical is it to permit the widespread nudging to which we have all been constantly exposed throughout our lives? Much of what the behavioural economists have tried to bring to Economics and government policy has long been familiar to businesses and marketers. The errors of judgement brought to light by early behavioural economists have since been intentionally used to convince people to behave badly – to do things that are very far from being in the interests of their own happiness. We will all be familiar, for example, with the subtle default switch that goes on when paying for goods online –at the checkout, we're defaulted into certain options, such as faster delivery, that are of course, more expensive and more profitable for the business we're buying from. Up-next videos default to play automatically when we finish watching something, because this keeps us seated in front of a screen (and therefore, in front of yet more adverts), rather than attending to an important but nourishing task that we've been putting off all evening. Las Vegas is an extreme, but this sort of manipulation for profitable gain will always be prevalent if the focus of society is to grow the economy, rather than the people's wellbeing.

Because it is private organisations using these psychological tricks, rather than the government, we somehow deem this approach to be ethically acceptable. There is always a choice, we are told – yet why do the choices that better serve our happiness always seem to be so psychologically difficult to make, and often very well hidden? And wouldn't it be fair to say that one reason we save so little for the future is because so much energy is put into encouraging us, often deceptively and imperceptibly, to take immediate short-term pleasures rather than delay.

Keeping something dark hidden

It surprised everyone, none more so than myself, how easily I consistently obtained the highest grades in our Economics exams, despite being without doubt the meanest drinker on my university campus. On the final day of our first-year exams, in which I achieved the best marks in the entire year group, my behaviour whilst drinking got me kicked out of every bar in town. That was just the afternoon warm up. Later that night I was kicked out of the student's union and that resulted in a banning from that establishment for the second time that year, only a few weeks after being allowed back in. My behaviour would turn out to be so atrocious that night that the police were called, and not for the first time in my life, I would find myself waking up in a cell with a pounding headache and a whole host of emotions I couldn't pin down. Though I was first rate at making sense of rational economic models, I could make very little sense of myself.

Things are very different now. As I write, I've just cleared 16 years without alcohol passing my lips. I have had plenty of time to find compassion for a younger self who was doing the best he could with what he knew. And, like anything, most of what I knew came from the people around me. I had no reason to not trust the messages I came across each day about how to live a happy life. And so I reached for the 'nectar of the Gods', as my Dad would often call it. Drinking, among other things, was just what you did in my world. It held a magical appeal to my young self, because it completely changed people. It made them smile and laugh when ordinarily they didn't. Plus, once I got a taste for it, alcohol did offer me some kind of happiness – the kind that is nothing more than a temporary fix.

In the end, despite the early promise, alcohol brought me far more misery than happiness. And when I woke up in those cells, or in one of the many and often frightening predicaments I found myself in over the years, I knew for certain that I was miserable with how things were turning out with my life. Yet that didn't stop me from reaching for another drink again and again, or any number of other quick fixes, for that matter.

It will be clear from this book that I am prone to anxiety, and it was a crushing anxiety that I was trying to escape when I drank. I wasn't aware of why I was doing it at the time; all I knew was a feeling of anguish and hopelessness. I had scary thoughts about the world around me, and worries would reverberate around my head all day long. Drink made all of that go away, at least for a little while. I was inhibited and self-conscious around other people. The more I drank, the less I thought, and so an inhibited, awkward self transformed into a confident and fun self; one that some people seemed to rather like. The anxieties disappeared, and so long as I took a beer or two to help me get out of the house in the first place, I wasn't destined to sit nervously in some corner of the room for the rest of my life after all.

However, I didn't have enough faith that I could be the person I needed to be without that nectar flowing through my body. Plus, the quantities I seemed to need got vaster and vaster. As my drinking worsened, so did my feelings about myself. The anxiety pounded at me when I woke up from whatever state I'd gotten into the night before, and along with the anxiety came a powerful rage. Other drugs came swashing into the mix, and things began to get very messy – a relationship collapsed, there were grave financial troubles, low physical energy, a lack of interest in life, and shame – oh gosh, so much shame. All were a cause and a consequence of my attempts to self-medicate for something happening that I didn't understand. I was trying to do my best – but this didn't feel like my best.

I kept my internal struggles to myself. No-one around me spoke about their own battles, although I would often wonder whether others were, like me, concealing difficulties. Or perhaps at root – which I resigned myself to be the truth of it at the time – there was simply something innately wrong with me; a thought that had long tormented me. And the belief that there was something wrong with me only compounded my anguish.

A toxic environment and the dark nudge

The truth is that there was nothing fundamentally wrong with me. At age 24, after repeated attempts, I finally had my last drink. It was difficult in the beginning, but once I remained sober for long enough, I began to understand why I had come to depend on drink in the first place.

Anxious thoughts, as I highlighted two chapters back, are common; chronic low mood also. For example, in any given week, one in six people are experiencing a common mental health problem such as anxiety and depression. Each year, one in four people in the UK will experience some kind of mental health challenge. In 2018, there were 6,154 suicides (16 per day) in the UK, and it is estimated that 10–25 times that number attempted suicide.[5] Mental health is certainly talked about more openly these days. In fact, it's a growing public concern, and it is becoming evident how much it blocks a person's capacity to find happiness.[6] Unfortunately, however, mental distress, much as is the way with unhappiness, is primarily discussed as if it is an individual's fault, rather than a societal issue. Rather than have compassion, we are quick to point the finger at the individual and blame them, and them alone, for their misery. Blame never helps. What we see in others often lingers deep within all of us, and what I've come to understand is that when we point the finger at others, we escape having to looking at ourselves and the society we are part of.

Individual choices are, of course, an important aspect of our struggles. Yet, if some choices that would better serve us are kept well-hidden, whilst other choices that are not beneficial are misleadingly visible, then we have to question why the environment in which we make those choices is as it is. It is not for the sake of our happiness and mental health. It is designed for the sake of profit. A few prosper financially (though are not necessarily themselves happier) from this set up. Most of us might keep bouncing along, no sadder and no happier, and still longing for that deeper fulfilment. Yet, it is those that are the most vulnerable that often end up suffering much more.

The rule I had to give myself in the end was simple. No alcohol. Ever. I had to eliminate alcohol from my choices completely. There was a part of me – let's call it, though I don't think it true – the rational side of me, that would like to have had only a few drinks when I went out. Yet, it never turned out that way. I'd always be tempted into drinking much more than I initially intended. Alcohol was too readily available in my environment. It was also too sweet and fun-looking, and waking up with a lack of memory for several hours from a night out was too socially acceptable. After a time, I came to accept that moderation was not one of the choices on offer to me. It was either stop altogether or spiral deeper into my misery.

Once I stopped drinking, there was a huge void in my life. I hadn't begun researching happiness at that point, nor had I been taught anything of our irrational economic nature, much less considered how it applied to the world around me. Yet somehow

I found a way through. I could just about recollect the hopes and dreams for happiness that my five-year-old self had once held on that orange-swirl of a carpet. I felt a tremendous grief for that part of myself. I knew that I deserved better. First, there had to be compassion – yet once I'd nursed my wounds a tiny bit, I began to get a better glimpse of what this five-year-old boy had been up against all his life: having to deal with an environment in which it was in someone else's interest to convince me to feel and think things that would encourage me to act in ways unlikely to bring me much in the way of long-term happiness.

Whilst in the last few decades, behavioural economists have academically demonstrated hundreds of ways in which we are prone to decision-making errors, these same errors have been used to influence people to behave against their best interests for far longer than a mere thirty or forty years. Most of the time we are quite unaware of the psychological tricks being used to coerce us into wanting, desiring, and craving things.[7] And in our desire to survive financially – because we never do feel like we have enough – we'll both exploit and be exploited. We can call this the *dark nudge*.[8] It's everyday business. In my view – and it is not a popular view among behavioural economists, since it might jeopardise their now firm footing in Economics and limit their influence in policy – a dark nudge can do far more damage to societal happiness than a few behaviourally-informed policy interventions could ever hope to rectify.

Struggling in Las Vegas

There is perhaps no better place to witness the *dark nudge* than in Las Vegas. I went there on my bicycle, with my eyes wide open to witness it. Given all I'd learnt up to this point, I thought I would be able to spend time in Vegas – on the streets, in shows, in casinos – and be able to watch what was before me with a calm curiosity; just as I had done when viewing many of the infamous films depicting the city. However, it wasn't that simple, and I found myself feeling rather mentally ill. It was a far cry from pedalling through the mountains of Colombia, camping on beaches in Costa Rica, or hanging out with Mexicans in a street plaza. By the time I arrived in Vegas, I had been journeying for 11 months, and had learnt to be more present with what was before me than ever before in my adult life. I was much happier for it too. However, I wasn't quite ready to be so exposed and vulnerable to an environment that operates by promising a cure to the tension that at one point I believed was an innate part of me.

Las Vegas reflects an extreme of what many of us contend with every day, and to which we sometimes succumb. There is the promise of a quick fix wherever we look. Whether it is a getting-rich-quick scheme in our email junk box, the bombardment of advertisements for more possessions, more alcohol, checking our phone just one more time, more this, more that... Our innately human errors of judgement are preyed upon – whether it be our inability to predict the future, our tendency to take immediate pleasures over delayed ones, our sensitivities to what others think about us, or our fears about safety, among many others. There is perhaps no starker example than the built-in addictiveness of social media apps. In fact, designers of those apps have borrowed tricks directly from the slot machines of Vegas, such as bright colours, refreshing mechanisms, sporadic rewards, all of which keep us using for much longer than we know is ideal. This prolonged use keeps us in contact with more adverts – and that's good for business.[9]

Yet, this hard-to-avoid profit-driven environment rarely delivers the kind of happiness we are led to believe it will. We are left wanting. Abandoned to our usual struggles, perhaps with a new and devastating addiction on top of them. And then comes another suggestion that something else, in a conveniently placed position just as we're about to check out, will this time *really* do it for us, now and forever. We might not be sadder, because this kind of thing is the stuff we've faced all our lives, but we are no happier either. We get through it, in the hope that maybe next year will be better. Hope gets us through, hope keeps us playing.

On some instinctive level, I have always known that *dark nudges* were present in my life. With sobriety, my awareness sharpened, and I began to see with increasing clarity how much the societal structures I thought were supposed to support happiness did not. In fact, anxious-prone though I may have been, living in a society where heightening anxiety makes solid business sense, alcohol was a way of numbing myself to thoughts and messages that were not my own.

Some years after I stopped drinking, once I had done a lot of deeper personal work and was clearer-headed, I came to the conclusion that it was down to me to safeguard myself against making the systematic mistakes that others were banking on. Essentially, though I didn't know it at the time, I began *nudging myself* – appreciating my own potentialities for decision-making errors, and using those potential errors to bring about decisions that were good for my happiness, rather than someone else's bank account.

Some things, like alcohol, I began to ban myself from ever doing. Beyond the short term, some things are just too destructive. Other things I began to refuse to own or buy myself, but might contemplate consuming if offered as a gift, such as playing a computer game or eating a sugary good. My favourite thing – that I still do – when I see something I want to buy, is to walk out of the shop and touch a tree before I go back and buy it. It allows me time to think about why I want something, and whether I really need it, rather than get lost in a commercial world that promises instant happiness. If it is online, the same applies. When I get anxious, I remind myself that it is okay to feel that way, and sit with what is coming up inside me. I have no television. I avoid things in shiny wrappers.[10] There are a whole host of other things that I do to support myself. I still get it wrong and do things that don't serve me – I am human; and I am continuously working on being a happy one.

However, given the pervasiveness of the *dark nudge*, becoming a happy human is no easy thing for anyone, economic-psychology-happiness expert or not. I'd prefer it if I didn't need to be so vigilant and guarded – it takes energy I don't always have. I want to feel relaxed out in the world. But, at root, these protections are all an effort to bring greater happiness to my life in a society where happiness is not the priority. Once I'd quit my job and began rolling around on a bicycle, it became easier to make decisions that were bringing greater happiness. I was away from it all. Dropped expectations, being present, telling a different story, confronting anxieties, dealing with challenges, receiving gifts – I no longer had to constantly side-step the temptation to fall for someone else's version of the good life. I was relaxing into a new sense of self, and I suppose I didn't realise how much I was doing that until I'd reached Las Vegas. When I arrived there my guard was down, and I quickly felt just as anxious as I had been when I was younger. It was horrible.

Once I escaped Vegas and made it to the Californian coastline (with the help of one of my favourite hitched rides), there was a lot of learning to be done through reflection. I became thankful for the experience – but whilst I was there, I didn't find many safe spaces, spaces where I felt I could breathe, and where it was enough to just be me. In Vegas I was back to being constantly on my guard; merely surviving. I want to be in spaces that have health and happiness at their centre. Fortunately, as I'll describe in the next chapter, I came across quite a few on my way to Bhutan: places that give me genuine hope.

CHAPTER 13

Happiness havens

"I feel like I'm in heaven – such an amazing day on the bike and so happy and grateful to have a camping spot where I feel safe."

A journal entry, up in the mountains of Peru: 9th January 2018

On my journey for happiness there were some places I stayed for a fair while. They were real gems – sanctuaries. They not only allowed a little mental and physical recuperation, they were places I could have stayed much longer and been lastingly happy. They were personal happiness havens, in that they nourished me whilst I was there, and just knowing they exist reassures me and gives me hope that there is another way.

It wasn't so much the places themselves – it was more about the people that had created these havens, and importantly, whether I was moving with just enough lightness to be able to share in what was being offered by them. In another time, with a different version of me, things would have been different. I'd have found other places. I have faith that there are plenty of havens out there.

These are not 'this season's must-see' kinds of places. If we can remain in touch with what our fundamental needs are, and be willing to stay a while and be present with people, then we'll find havens all over the world. Maybe they're not even that far away from where we sit now. Perhaps, if we're lucky, we have one right where we are. If not, then perhaps we can step towards co-creating them...

#1 Cusco, surrounded by mountains and relishing presence – day 60 to 73

The first part of my journey was dominated by thoughts of arriving in Cusco. As I've described in earlier chapters, it wasn't easy to shake the 'needing to be *there* by *then*' mentality that would drive me on each day, and sometimes into struggle. I wanted to be in Cusco for Christmas and New Year's, and spend it with a friend who was living there. It was two months into my journey, and it was joyful to hang out with someone familiar for a while, deepen in my relationship with them, and reflect upon those early days of my journey. However, it wasn't only my friend being there that makes Cusco such a special place.

Cusco is an old Incan city set high up in the Andes. It is big and busy, and usually I struggle to find happiness in such places. Many people find it difficult to be happy in big cities, with the reported levels of happiness being typically lower than rural environments. Despite being surrounded by people, there can often be more loneliness. Nature is lacking, and people are time-pressured.

Cusco, however, felt different to other cities I've spent time in. With large mountains surrounding it, nature feels ever present – I only needed to look out of my friend's apartment window to find the calm that such majestic sierran beasts provide me. A short walk would take us out of the city and into those mountains.

One thing I noticed throughout both Peru and Bolivia, more than in other places on my journey, was people's capacity to just sit with themselves and be with the world around them. Not everyone was like this, but more than enough to notice differences across cultures. People would just sit – practically no distractions, certainly no phones to touch and scroll through – just them, just there! It was uncanny to watch, and also inspiring, because they seemed to know what was going on around them. Someone always seemed aware of the stranger, which was ordinarily me, coming onto the scene, and they'd be ready to greet me – just a wave or a nod, some small recognition of my presence in life's dance.

Cusco attracts a lot of tourists, and it is still a big city, so this presence in people was less than compared to other, smaller places I passed through. However, it was still enough to calm the tendency to rush about, and it felt easier and more natural to talk to local people than in other places I've been. Tourists were also a bit more open and friendly than in many other places too.

When I came to leave, I felt sad. I could have stayed longer, maybe a lifetime, yet when it came to it, I was certain there would be a whole lot of happiness to uncover ahead of me.

#2 Costa Rica, tropical farm work – day 199 to 209

I was hopeful I'd find a happiness haven in Costa Rica, and as I described earlier, I slowed down whilst there. After the heat exhaustion and near-collapse on too many occasions in Panama, the few restrictions I imposed on myself enhanced my happiness. I sat on more beaches drinking coconuts and talking to more people. I also spent an extended amount of time volunteering on a small tropical farm, several hundred metres up in altitude, overlooking a distant volcano.

Each morning on that farm I worked for several hours, and then I would spend much of the rest of the day talking to the other workers. Or I would just sit on a hammock, reading, writing, and every so often looking up at the volcano in the distance. I didn't have any specialist farming skills, but that didn't matter.[1]

It was run by a friendly Costa Rican couple who showed me all I needed to know to work with the land. I learnt a lot, and what I was doing was useful to the farm. I also had a chance to confront some of that vulnerability I have around being in groups, by putting on a communication skills workshop.

Over the years I have developed skills that foster deeper communication between individuals and between groups.[2] For the first time in my life, I decided to share some of these skills. There was enough support and encouragement for me to do this, and it helped my confidence so much that I ended up developing this workshop to share with others I later met on my journey. Again, it was sad to leave. I thought about staying longer, and never ever returning home.

#3 Coahuila, a state in Mexico where I made peace with the desert, and felt the love of its people – day 279 to 286

Mexico was one of the highlights of my trip. I was amazed by the curiosity and kindness of the people. Whenever I stopped – which after Costa Rica was a lot more – people would come and talk to me to find out who I was and discover what I was doing. They asked if I needed any help; I was invited into people's homes to eat, to sleep sometimes, and I even camped in a few people's gardens.

One time I found myself as the reluctant focus of everyone's attention at a *fiesta*. I'd heard music from the side of the road and stopped to watch for a bit, then was invited to join in. Admittedly, my Spanish skills – vastly improved after spending ten months on my bicycle in Latin America – made me an attractive guest to many I met there. But what was crucial here was how open I now was to people, and to the gifts they offered.

Coahuila, however, has a particularly special place in my heart. Not only did I find myself at peace in the high desert – it was beautiful to cycle, and cool enough at night in my tent to sleep well – but I met some wonderful souls there. There was one place, an enchanting village called Viesca, where I stayed with a family that deeply nurtured me. They showed me around their village, made me feel at home, and treated me as if I was family. I sometimes wished I was.

I only stayed a few nights with them, and it was beautiful. Part of me wonders what could have happened had I stayed longer. What if I'd have tied up my steed and hung up my boots?

What if? I'd have been happy; I am certain of it.

After I reluctantly left Viesca, I ran into some television journalists. They'd seen me cycling along and were curious about my story. I spent about an hour or so with them; my Spanish was just about good enough by then for both a live interview and to record some footage for a news item they would later air on Mexican television.[3] I love watching and re-watching the short piece they did about me. It was a superb reflection of the love I felt, and still feel, from the people in that part of the world. I still get regular messages from some of the people I met there, and sometimes those who just saw me on television.

On my last day in Mexico there was one family that drove past me on the road, and stopped just ahead to speak with me as I passed. They'd seen me on television, and they offered me a ride to somewhere close to the US border. I was happy enough cycling, but why turn down the gift and a chance for connection?

#4 Oregon, USA, intentional togetherness – day 353 to 361

An intentional community is one in which a group of people have chosen to live together, and it typically has a high level of social organisation. Often there is a shared purpose or vision – such as environmental sustainability, spirituality, or social and political reasons – and this helps to unify people.

My experiences in such communities have so inspired me that one day I would like to commit to being part of an intentional community myself. What appeals to me the most is the sense of togetherness in such communities, and that is important for happiness. I think intentional communities are particularly important in individualistically-orientated cultures, where familial bonds are less strong.

I've seen a lot of different types of intentional communities over the years. On this journey I had already spent time with some communities in both Peru and Nicaragua. All these communities are unique, because there is no set way of doing things. Much of a community's success depends on the people present, the strength of their shared vision, and their willingness to work towards that vision.

There is no perfect community, and often they don't last very long. Yet, the one I was fortunate to spend a week at volunteering in Oregon was, for me, pretty close to being perfect, and had lasted a long time. In exchange for working in their abundant garden, I was fed delicious food and had a place to sleep. The people I met there enriched my own life, and I felt inspired by the life they had created for themselves, and were sharing with me whilst I was there.

They started their community some 40 years ago, and though there had been a little bit of coming and going over the years, they were a very stable group. What I was moved by the most – and that I've not seen in many intentional communities – is that the shared vision was not about a political ideology, but simply about being committed to one another. Just that; and they worked unswervingly through whatever arose for them – which included a healthy bit of deeper challenge.

If I don't one day return to try and stay at this community forever, it'll be because I've developed something very similar in my own part of the world. I'm hoping the latter is the most likely, and I'm certain that the time I have spent with this particular community will help me in that process.

#5 Island of Sumba, Indonesia – sometimes there is nothing like real family – day 471 to 478

I had never intended for my journey to take me to Indonesia. However, when I was journeying somewhere in Colombia, my brother successfully applied for a job there.

My brother has expertise in permaculture – which is a type of sustainable agriculture system and has an overarching philosophy associated with it that venerates land, people, and fairness – and he primarily works in tropical and sub-tropical parts of the world designing and cultivating permaculture farms. It is often difficult for him to find paid work doing his specialism – in this job he would be working at a hospitality school on the remote Indonesian island of Sumba. He would be teaching permaculture to 60 or so young students, mostly in their late teens, and running a small farm.

When he got the job, I began to consider, since I would be closer to that part of the world at a later point on my journey, whether I should visit him. And then, since the people of Indonesia report having more positive experiences throughout their days than any other non-Latin-American country (they rank 6th, with the other nine top ten being Latin America countries, see Table 1), it seemed like a doubly worthwhile place to visit on my journey.

I'd call it more of a holiday because, after I'd managed to reach Bangkok with Gulliver, I left my bicycle at a hostel and flew to Sumba. This time was mostly about being with my brother. We have always had a strong bond – those very early years sharing that swirly-orange carpeted room had a lot to do with it. Wherever my brother is, I could stay for a lifetime.

Whilst there, I met all his students, and I gave them a few classes on happiness. That said, I don't think they needed much teaching, as they were the happiest bunch of students I've ever encountered! When I asked them to rate their own levels of satisfaction in life on a scale from 0 to 10, they averaged 8.7 – a high level of evaluative happiness by any standard. The average across Indonesia is 5.2; the average in Finland is 7.7. And as well as reporting high evaluative happiness, they were always smiling and laughing.

I presented them with a few theories about happiness. A simple model for happiness based around fulfilling needs is Maslow's *Hierarchy of Needs*.

Maslow's model suggests that there are a set of universal human needs that must be fulfilled for happiness. These needs include, physiological (e.g., breathing, food, water, sex, sleep), safety (e.g., security of body, employment, resources, health, property), love and belonging (e.g., friendship, family, sexual intimacy), esteem (e.g., confidence, achievement, respect of others, respect for others), and self-actualisation (e.g., morality, creativity, spontaneity, problem solving, lack of prejudice, acceptance of facts). Though it is not true that these needs must be fulfilled sequentially, as Maslow's model suggests, the model does serve to highlight an important point – that happiness comes through *fulfilling needs* rather than *acquiring stuff*.[4]

Often we confuse needs with strategies to meet those needs. Something is only important to the extent it meets the need. If we think in terms of needs, we realise that there are multiple ways to fulfil those needs, and this enables greater flexibility in how we do so.

This relates to the example I gave about money and happiness in Chapter 9, and in believing we need tonnes of money.

People say they *need* money. In an economy where nearly everything has a price-tag, this is understandable – however, it is easy to forget that money is not a universal human need in itself, but a strategy which may help us to meet those needs. However, beyond meeting basic needs such as physiological and safety-related necessities, money is a less effective strategy than, for example, building a strong community.

This is why, once a certain income level is reached – as I've been highlighting throughout this journey – ever higher amounts of money often do not correspond to very high levels of happiness. Money is mostly used inefficiently, and often to the detriment of others, to meet needs for esteem and status. We can also meet such needs through doing good things for others in the local, national, and international community.

This residential school on the island of Sumba was one of a kind. What was abundantly clear to me was that the reason these students were so happy was that they were meeting all of their needs, including the self-actualisation one. This school was a happiness haven for those students, and it was an important part of my journey to be a part of it for a week.

#6 Being with self and others – surprising learnings from my happiness scores

My final happiness haven is unlike any of the previous ones I've described in this chapter. It is no fixed place. I did not realise at the time, nor foresee how big a happiness haven I was carting around the world. I didn't get round to looking carefully at my daily scores for happiness and anxiety until I returned – and when I did so, the scores indicated that, for the sake of happiness, I should have been out in my tent much more than I was.

As I journeyed, I would either find a free-camping spot and sleep in my tent under the stars, stay with people I had just met or already knew, or stay at a hotel or hostel I had paid for. Of the three, I was least happy when I stayed in a hotel or hostel. This comes as no surprise intuitively.

However, what did surprise me is *just how* much happier I was.

Figure 4: Daily happiness and anxiety by type of lodging

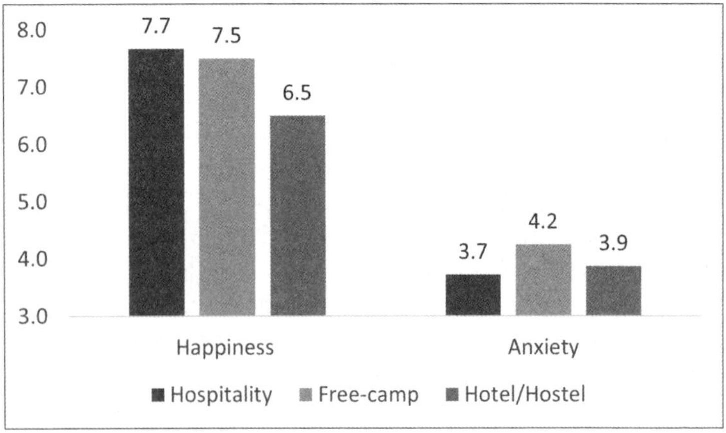

As Figure 4 shows, my daily happiness was as much as a whole point lower when I stayed in a hotel or hostel (although 6 also illustrates that anxiety was much lower too, explaining why I checked into hotels and hostels more than I perhaps should have for my happiness).

And looking at these scores, I wish I'd done it more. What is better than gazing at a desert, mountains, or a tropical beach, as local market-bought food slowly sizzles to feed a well-worked body and a happy head and heart?

Figure 4 shows that the same could be said for my experiences in receiving hospitality. At the beginning of my journey, I didn't know how to be receptive to help from others. I was either too focused on reaching some destination by the end of the day, or anxious about having general conversations with people that may have led to help. If I had known these differences would be so large, perhaps I would have put a lot more effort into camping and/or connecting with others; and the costs of the journey would have been lower, too.

Of course, another way of explaining these scores is that I just stayed in hotels when I had a difficult day. This is certainly true to some extent. Sometimes the day had been so terrible, I just wanted to be on my own and to feel safe. However, there were plenty of days that weren't so challenging, and I felt so anxious about camping that I opted for a hotel.

I spent the night relaxed, but was it fulfilling?

Did I connect with others, myself, or nature?

Was it a happiness haven?

No, not even close.

Who can say whether I was right to listen to the anxiety on those nights I chose a hotel?

I do know that there were times when I felt dreadfully anxious about camping or speaking to a stranger beforehand, but I did it anyway, and had the most beautiful experiences – waking up happy, safe, and free.

What can we learn from such happiness havens? Can we build an entire society that has the wellbeing of people at its centre? I think we can – and, as I was also busy exploring on this journey, there are plenty of promising things afoot at national and international levels that could make a big difference. Some of them are already having an impact.

CHAPTER 14

Towards a wellbeing economy

"I like that there are service station attendants here. It would be easy to see it as an unnecessary job, but it creates connection and gives everyday meaning to people's lives. In the UK it is about cutting costs and making money, and so these sort of jobs go. We need to bring them back."
Journal entry, 19th December 2017

I am not sure exactly when the Wellbeing Economy Alliance (WE-ALL) began, because I was too immersed to pay much attention to anything beyond my journey. However, I first heard about this intriguing organisation when I met with Costa Rican government officials, about six months into the journey.

The meeting in Costa Rica had been set up through an academic contact. I didn't make much of a secret of the cycling journey I was on, and I was anxious about how I might be perceived by these officials. Yet, my openness about the journey proved to have been wise, because I had little choice but to attend the meeting wearing shorts, flip-flops, and the one freshly ironed, though slightly faded shirt I had carried with me around the world for such occasions. As I'd hoped, the Costa Rican officials were curious about my undertaking, and my nervousness remained unnoticed.

My intentions for the meeting were as loose as my attire. I wanted to share ideas, build connections, and see what might develop from there. With the Costa Rican president having just come into office, winning an election in which LGBT+ rights had become a central campaign issue, there was a great deal of excitement in the air about how Costa Rica would further evolve as a nation. This was not only through recognition of the progress that Costa Rica had made towards the United Nations Sustainable Development Goals (SDGs) in recent years, but also the pride with which Costa Rica had obtained levels of happiness and health comparable to countries with much larger economies (e.g., the USA, the UK, Spain, France, and so on). As I've described previously, Costa Rica has implemented some very progressive policies over the years.

When talk in the meeting turned to WE-ALL, and the hopes that the Costa Rican government would become directly involved, I tried to not make it too obvious that I didn't yet know anything about it. As I now know – and as I suspected at the time, given its descriptive name and curious abbreviation – WE-ALL is a 'collaboration of organisations, alliances, movements and individuals, working together to transform the economic system into one that delivers human and ecological wellbeing'.[1] I was embarrassed about my lack of awareness during the meeting, given that all my work had revolved around wellbeing, and it was the subject I was there to discuss.

It is important to say here that wellbeing is a word that often gets used in place of happiness. There are three main kinds of personal happiness – the moment-to-moment hedonic kind I described in Chapters 7 and 10 (pleasant and unpleasant emotions), the evaluative kind from Chapter 5 (an evaluation of life overall), and what we call a *flourishing* kind of happiness, that I'll come to in more detail later, concerned with purpose and meaning. However, the trouble with happiness from a political and policy perspective is that, when talking about happiness, people tend to think mostly of the moment-to-moment happiness, and less so of the other kinds. Wellbeing covers all three kinds of happiness and more. As well as including personal happiness, wellbeing also incorporates a wider sense of what is required to enable people to find that personal happiness. For example, it additionally concerns the infrastructure to meet basic needs, as well as the societal and ecological context within which we make our choices. Wellbeing sounds much less exciting than happiness, yet it is the favoured word used when discussing policy. It focuses debate, rather than distracting people into thinking 'happiness policy' is just about encouraging people to laugh and smile all the time.

Though I did not know anything about the WE-ALL when it came up in conversation during the meeting in Costa Rica, I did know some of the people who had been involved in establishing the organisation. I had long been aligned with the idea that the purpose of an economy should be to deliver sustainable wellbeing, and my academic research had highlighted the inadequacy of our present economic system to do so. Therefore, over the years I did what I could to build links with people involved in policy. So, initial embarrassment aside at my ignorance of the organisation, talking about WE-ALL's aims was natural and easy for me. How do we get beyond a world that has mostly been framed into a highly competitive 'us versus them', into a world that is about all of us together? A WE-ALL world? Indeed, I felt a tiny bit of tension in me finally relax, knowing such an organisation existed. At last, I thought: an influential organisation telling a different economic story.

Getting beyond growth – re-purposing our economies

There has long been talk about the purpose of economic growth. For decades – despite dire warnings from as far back as the 70s that there would be environmental consequences to economic growth without limits – it has been advocated as an unquestionably good thing; a panacea to cure all ills. It was also advocated that the best way to achieve economic growth was through an unrestrained free market, and that governments, since they impeded private organisations seeking out the biggest financial returns, needed to minimise their involvement in the economy. So we were told, and so we believed. Yet another story.[2]

We shrank our governments and cut our taxes. Despite most of the direct benefits of economic growth being accrued by those that were already very rich and very powerful, those riches, we were again told, would one day trickle down to those with less wealth, and make all of our lives better. It sounds very simple. It hasn't worked out like that; not even close.[3] It was another believable story, yet with scarcely any truth in it. These ideas were based on the economic models I talked about in Chapter 12, where all the complexity and realism of life had been stripped out. Not only were there crude assumptions about human behaviour (more is always better, perfect foresight etc.) but also no consideration was given to our place in the wider ecosystem, and how much our survival depends on nature's health. Nevertheless, the conclusions that arose from these economic models did align with the interests of those that were rich and powerful, and so these ideas were cherished and propagated, until most of us believed them and our lives were organised accordingly.

As Robert Kennedy once put it, Gross Domestic Product (GDP), the total sum of all the goods and services that are produced and consumed within a country:

> does not allow for the health of our children, the quality of their education or the joy of their play. It does not include the beauty of our poetry or the strength of our marriages, the intelligence of our public debate or the integrity of our public officials. It measures neither our wit nor our courage, neither our wisdom nor our learning, neither our compassion nor our devotion to our country, it measures everything in short, except that which makes life worthwhile.

He said this back in 1968, just a few years before the King of Bhutan informed the world about the Bhutanese concept of Gross National Happiness.

In essence, if we are trying to track whether life is improving for most people, knowing how big an economy is doesn't tell us very much. It gives us some idea as to the picture of human life, because undoubtedly economic growth can and has brought real and lasting benefits to people's lives. However, there are also costs that are rarely accounted for (environmental and social), and these costs are not borne equally. Hence, the picture painted by economic output is a very incomplete one. It is one single number – and all that is worthwhile in life cannot be boiled down to one single number. Life is much richer than that. And yet – what we measure matters, and if economic growth is all that is measured with any rigour, and if our political debate is dominated by the question of whether the economy is increasing in size or shrinking, then our lives begin to revolve around little else. *We must grow economically – or else*, apparently!

One of the more prominent international attempts to critique the use of GDP to measure societal progress came in a 2009 report commissioned by then French president Nicolas Sarkozy. The report was overseen by esteemed economists Joseph Stiglitz, Amartya Sen, and Jean-Paul Fitoussi; two of whom have won Nobel prizes in the subject. It was some 300 pages long, a fairly tedious read – but in essence, the report addressed a broad range of inadequacies of equating economic output with wellbeing. This included what they called classical issues, such as accounting for changes in quality and the use of market prices to reflect value, as well as grave concerns that no account was made for either inequality or sustainability. Sure, the numbers are going up but why, who for, and will this jeopardise our future? The report made a number of recommendations, and the debate about going beyond GDP as an indicator of progress (which had begun on the political fringes long before) began to gather momentum.

A few years later, the Organisation for Economic Co-operation and Development (OECD), created their *Better Life Index*. This was a real break-away from the past for this organisation, because the OECD is an international institution that had done much to champion economic growth above anything else over recent decades. The Better Life Index sets out a framework by which countries can consider progress beyond just economic growth. Income and wealth are, of course, part of that framework, yet so are ten other areas of our lives, including housing, health, education, work–life balance, jobs and earnings, civic engagement and governance, social connections, environmental quality, personal security, and people's own reports of their happiness and wellbeing. The research is clear that an increase in income and wealth does not go hand in hand with improvements to any of these areas of life. Therefore, if people – or only some people – experience increased income and wealth, yet their own or other people's health, work-life balance, social connections, and safety worsen, then can we really call this progress or development?

None of this is to say that there has been a huge uptake in the use of the OECD's Better Life Index to guide policy throughout the world. We are collectively fixated on growth, and we fear not growing. Our economic and political system is predicated on constant economic growth. The story is that we simply must grow. And sadly, many can't yet picture a world in which we aren't growing our economies.

Progress in Canada

There is no doubt that Bhutan is exceptional. It has fascinated and inspired many to consider a different approach to progress, and has fed into the conversation about repurposing our economies. However, as I would discover when my bicycle and I arrived in Bhutan, the country is very far removed from the societies of most people. This makes it easy to disregard what the Bhutanese have been doing all these years, and call it unrealistic or unworkable. Yet, as I was exploring on my journey, in Costa Rica and elsewhere, it is not only here where bold attempts have been made to redefine the purpose of our societies.

Some countries, such as Canada – where I would arrive

after a year on the bicycle – had begun developing their own alternative indicators of progress long before the OECD got serious about doing so. In Canada, what has come to be known as the *Canadian Index of Wellbeing* began its development in 1999, when experts got together to ask "What would it take to create a tool to measure the wellbeing of Canadians?" Ideas from that were taken forward to begin an extensive process that, as well as harnessing expert advice and research, included public consultation to discern what Canadians themselves thought constituted a good life. The Canadian Index of Wellbeing, rather than being a political project, evolved into a citizen-driven initiative that is guided by Canadian core values. Unsurprisingly, it wasn't just the economy that people cared about. Crucially, the Index has clear and direct links to policy, which helps those wanting to know how to make choices that improve wellbeing locally, regionally, and nationally.

The Canadian Index of Wellbeing is an exemplar for national wellbeing indexes, and when I reached Canada I was hoping to learn more. On my journey I managed to set up a meeting with the director of the Canadian Index of Wellbeing, Bryan Smale. Whilst it was too cold for shorts and flip flops for that meeting, I'm confident that if I had been wearing them, they'd have been fine, because I'd met Bryan before. Back in 2015, I'd invited him to give a talk about the Canadian Index of Wellbeing at a conference I organised in the Scottish Parliament. I thought there was a lot Scotland could learn from Bryan.

We spent several hours talking – about the challenges and successes over the years, what the future held for the pioneering wellbeing index, and what other countries could learn. We also talked about my journey, which he had been following as I'd progressed up the Americas. Like me, and countless people I had met, he couldn't quite believe I'd cycled up from Argentina: a little each day directed toward something that felt purposeful had gotten me a long way. Much as it has been with the evolution of the Canadian Index of Wellbeing.

Bryan and his team have been chipping away at this Index

for years, and they are in constant demand to help implement it at local and regional levels. There has been some real change as a result. What is quite clear from the Index is that, whilst the economy has grown over the years, other aspects of life in Canada, such as health, democracy, time use, leisure and culture, and the environment, have largely stagnated or actually worsened. Could that be classed as progress? Despite the Index's impact on Canadian society over the years, perhaps more through shifts in the conversation and policy at the local and regional level, the Index is yet to supplant the national policy obsession with economic growth and become a key part of discussion. More radical change is still needed.

Countries repurposing their economies

In 2018, a handful of countries declared themselves to be Wellbeing Economy Governments (WE-Go). WE-Go is an initiative instigated by WE-ALL, and includes governments that have a shared ambition of building *wellbeing economies*. What this means is ensuring that an economy works in a way that serves the wellbeing of the people within that economy, rather than just growing every year, irrespective of whether people's lives are improving – essentially building societies in which profit is not prioritised before people, or the planet we all have to live upon.

Founding members of WE-Go include New Zealand, Iceland, and Scotland, and more recently Wales and Finland have joined this small collective. Those I met in Costa Rica were hopeful of being part of this set of countries when it launched. I thought they would have been from what we spoke about in our meeting, yet no doubt there were unforeseen political barriers. However, in the next few years this set of countries will grow in number, and it may just be the catalyst for change that we need. The wellbeing economy presents us with a different story about what's important – an economy centred around people, not profit.

Current WE-Go members have made some bold steps in

recent years that others are slowly replicating. New Zealand, for example, are in the process of establishing what are known as *wellbeing budgets*. Ordinarily governments make spending decisions based strictly on financial costs and benefits. This is a particular problem when some costs or benefits can't be equated in monetary terms, because that cost or benefit would be left out of the calculation. A *wellbeing budget*, on the other hand, encourages decisions to be made based on whether a policy delivers overall improvements to people's lives. Although there are lots of logistical issues to work through, this is the closest an economically rich country has come to looking a bit like Bhutan.

Iceland, as well as being the country that has been the most successful in calling international financial institutions to account following the financial crisis in 2007/8, now have a set of indicators to track national wellbeing linked with the SDGs. SDGs are a collection of global goals outlined in 2015 by the United Nations to offer a 'blueprint to achieve a better and more sustainable future for all'. They are part of the conversation about redefining progress.

I know Scotland well. I set off from here on my journey, and spent years living and working here, contributing to the country. Like Canada, the Scottish government began to develop a wellbeing framework before the OECD's Better Life Index. In 2015, this wellbeing framework was enshrined into our Constitution via the Community Empowerment Act. Successive Scottish governments are constitutionally obliged to report on and review this framework; in the latest review, the Scottish framework was concretely aligned with the SDGs. The Scottish Government still needs to have a public conversation, and state its wellbeing intentions more overtly than it has been doing, but that is another step for the future.[4]

Wales, the latest WE-Go country, has my favourite piece of wellbeing legislation, and one that I hope will become widespread throughout the world one day – a *Future Generations Act*. If the idea doesn't become widespread, then future generations are in big trouble, because this Act essentially brings the concerns of future generations explicitly into the policy discussion. Some cultures have long understood that some provision needs to be made in our decisions for those that are unable to come to the table, most notably the voice of yet-to-be-born generations. The sullied Apaches I met in present day Arizona certainly knew this. And when I reached Canada, I would encounter the concept of '*putl'lt*', which comes from the Nuxalk people. The Nuxalks were one of the many tribes in North America largely eradicated by a dominant culture of endless acquisition that saw itself superior in all ways. Yet, within that dominant culture there has never been much time for *putl'lt*, which translates in English to mean 'everything belongs to those not yet born'.

The legislation enacted in Wales encourages reflection on how decisions we make now will have consequences for those in the future. There is currently talk of enacting this across the entire UK. A major problem we have to contend with is ensuring any happiness and wellbeing we have now is sustainable – not just for future others, but more and more pressingly, for ourselves into the future too.

Without busting the planet

Whilst mainstream economists have kept with tradition in believing that all economic growth is good – because it allows people greater choice, more freedom, increased consumption possibilities, and therefore greater happiness – other economists have posed strong challenges to the growth imperative and underlined the importance of organising our economies to meet other goals.

Kate Raworth, an economist at Oxford University, suggests that a model for a healthy economy ought to look more like a doughnut than one that grows infinitely bigger every year. In her 2017 book, *Doughnut Economics: Seven Ways to Think Like a 21st-Century Economist*, she highlights some key ways in which current mainstream economic thought has got it disastrously wrong. It is a fairly accessible book as Economics books go, and well worth a read. The key thrust is that the goal of our economic system should not be to grow forever; instead, we need a system that not only enables people to obtain life's essentials, but to do so in a way that doesn't threaten the Earth's life-supporting systems. Those life essentials are not too different from the areas of life specified in the OECD's Better Life Index, Bhutan's Gross National Happiness Index, the Canadian Index of Wellbeing, or any number of country-specific wellbeing indices. Earth's life-supporting systems include, for example, having a stable climate, fertile soils, and a protective ozone layer, with these limits being evidence based.[5]

According to this model of sustainable development, we are all developing countries, because no country is close to meeting the needs of its people within the means of the planet. For example, a country like Germany, although largely meeting its population's needs (11 of 12), overshoots on most of Earth's biophysical boundaries (5 of 9). Germany does better on the doughnut model than most countries that – using outdated economic definitions – would be considered to be 'developed'. The United Kingdom, whilst similar to Germany with respect to overshooting the Earth's biophysical boundaries (5 of 9), struggles to meet population needs (8 of 12). The United States, though meeting slightly more population needs (9 of 12), transgresses more biophysical boundaries than any other country in the dataset (7 of 9). This is unsustainable.

Countries that are typically classed as 'developing countries' such as Indonesia or India, for example, fail to meet population needs, but do not transgress most of the biophysical boundaries of the planet. Then there are the countries that are typically classified as 'emerging economies', including China, Russia, and Mexico – who are neither meeting population needs nor staying within planetary boundaries. The doughnut model suggests that all countries need to aim for the sweet spot of the doughnut, whereby population needs are met without putting undue pressure on the planet.

Whatever we are achieving with our lives, it must remain sustainable within our own lives and those of future generations. No country is yet at that point. The country that is perhaps the closest is Vietnam: there, they meet 6 of the 12 population needs, but they overstep only one of Earth's biophysical boundaries. When I came to pass through Vietnam on my bicycle later in this journey, I thought about this a lot. I didn't manage to meet anyone involved in policy, but my sense, from what I saw and what I have read, was that their 'success' was more by chance than clear intention.

However, this way of assessing sustainability is a little crude, because the transgression of a biophysical boundary is treated the same across countries, irrespective of how much that boundary has been transgressed. For example, Costa Rica marginally transgresses most of the biophysical boundaries, whereas the United States overshoots them by a long way. A better way of catching the same idea as to the sustainability and efficiency of an economy in a nuanced way is via the *Sustainable Development Index*.[6] According to this Index, in which development is balanced with sustainability, it is Cuba (0.86 out of 1) that tops the list, followed by Costa Rica (0.83), and then Sri Lanka (0.83). Of these three, it is only Sri Lanka where both CO_2 emissions and material footprint could be considered sustainable; Cuba and Costa Rica are close, but fall just outside.[7]

United States places 160 out of 164 (0.18) on the Sustainable Development Index, ahead of Australia (0.15), United Arab Emirates (0.11), Kuwait (0.10), and Singapore (0.08). All have unsustainably high levels of CO_2 emissions and material footprint, and – excepting Australia – don't have outstanding levels of happiness by any of the measures I've described in this book. Although citizens of both Cuba and Costa Rica have a higher life expectancy than those living in the USA, per-person CO_2 use and material footprint are at least four times smaller in both countries. We have also already seen that citizens of Costa Rica are happier on average than in the USA (there is no comparable data for Cuba), illustrating the extent to which a large economy need not be essential for a better life. The United Kingdom is 132nd (0.40), marginally behind Germany (131st, 0.40) and New Zealand (128th, 0.44). Bhutan, still a subsistence economy and not always meeting population needs – as I'll describe more once we arrive there on a bicycle – is 69th (0.64), on account of low life expectancy, low income, and minimal years of formal schooling. In Vietnam it is similarly so (43rd, 0.71). With the exception of Uruguay, South American countries do very well, all having high levels (>0.7).[8]

Making people happier

Many countries now have national programmes to measure the happiness of their citizens. The Office for National Statistics in the United Kingdom began asking questions about happiness in 2011. They ask four questions:

- How satisfied are you with your life nowadays?
- How happy did you feel yesterday?
- How anxious did you feel yesterday?
- To what extent do you feel the things you do in your life are worthwhile?

These are the exact same questions that I've outlined in this book, and asked myself throughout my journey. Over the last decade, according to these metrics, people in the United Kingdom have generally been getting happier.[9]

That these questions are asked in a national survey is an important step forward. In so doing, they have helped spark debate as to what is the goal of our lives. And yet, that doesn't mean change has come at a policy level. Relevant as these national happiness indices are, they don't offer any insights as to what can be done to influence them. Like the happiness league tables that are released each year, they are interesting, but what can we actually do with them? There are no links to concrete policy actions, and these types of measures do not account for whether the happiness at a given point in time is sustainable. In addition, there will be natural ups and downs, sometimes in opposing directions for different types of happiness, that are not easy to know how to respond to. And, of course, you can't force people to be happy.

Rather, it is better to create the conditions that we *know* foster greater happiness. That is: that people have access to life's essentials, such that they can seek happiness for themselves with the right mix of the different kinds of happiness – the moment-to-moment kind, the evaluative kind, and the meaningful flourishing kind that I'll uncover in two chapters' time. And then embody those conditions that we know foster greater happiness within national wellbeing frameworks. Not only are there natural links to policy in these frameworks, but they have come about through extensive public consultation, and are backed up by research that I and others have carried out over decades. These frameworks enable different choices, and they are helping to shape global and national stories of what it means to be human – conditional, related, and interdependent.

CHAPTER 15

Alone and broken

"No-one has acknowledged my presence today – not a hello, or even a nod. What does that mean? I'm OK alone. I am. I've gotten good at it."
Journal entry, date unknown

Sometimes when I was a child, my Dad and I wouldn't speak for days on end. And when we finally did resume speaking, there was never any attempt at reconciling what had happened in the previous days. No-one sought to understand why there had been so much upset in the first place, the tears were ignored and quickly forgotten, and the harshness of the punishment never questioned.

That was just how it was, and I went along with it. What choice was there? I was only small, and I had to survive. I adapted to what was around me. I didn't have any better ideas at the time. Neither did Dad. Like anyone, he's had his own struggles, and blaming him – or anyone else for that matter – has never gotten me very far.

That doesn't make what happened right, but if we humans want better relationships, with ourselves and with one another, then we are going to have to get beyond ideas of right and wrong. We've got to be prepared to get really deep into it.

And whilst my Dad didn't physically accompany me to Bhutan, he nevertheless came along. He came along in a way that completely surprised me, given the state of our relationship before I left; and as the journey progressed and unfolded, we got right into the heart and soul of things together. What happened between my Dad and me as a result of this journey is unparalleled.

Colder, wetter, windier... and lonely, again

I remember the day well. There was a line of trees along each side of the road, and with them came the ever-divine smell of pine. The clouds hung low in the sky, and there was a light mist. It wasn't hot as it had been further south, barely even warm, in fact. I was reminded of the lands that I had long ago left and sorely missed. I stopped by the roadside to gaze over the mouth of the river I'd just crossed. Some birds flew overhead, and they squawked at something. At me perhaps? I found a little joy in the thought that they might have squawked at me, but that brief pleasure wasn't going to be enough to get me through yet another difficult day on the road. I felt supremely glum. Tears were close.

I'd been battling strong northerly winds and heavy rains for nearly a week. It wasn't so rough today, but it looked gloomy around me, and that seemed a perfect mirror for what was happening inside this sore body of mine. It was one year to the day that I'd set out on this fateful journey, and I had been hoping that the anniversary would give me some cause for celebration; that my mood from recent days would lift a little. Yet it had the opposite effect, and things felt heavier than ever. There was no point in moving these legs any longer; there was something going on inside, and I needed to look at it. I knew it was going to be big.

I had by now been cycling north up the west coast of the United States since Malibu, California. Canada was not far away, and neither was winter. Further north it was only going to get colder, wetter, and windier. The roads were always busy, and often hazardous. Cars would come close – perhaps deliberately, I don't know – but the spray of water and noise would sometimes really get to me. Conversations had become rarer. Long gone were the days where I'd feel like a minor celebrity, journeying through remote villages in Argentina or Mexico, when I'd have plenty of people welcoming me into their lives. Here, I was alone and lonely. And this was all too familiar.

When cycling about in all sorts of places and often camping where it is quite desolate, time alone is inevitable. Yet, no matter how good we think we are on our own, and how much we might say we prefer it, aloneness has its limits. After a year on a bicycle, I was well past that limit, and I suspect, given the rates of people reporting loneliness in modern society, many of us have long past the point where the going-it-alone mentality is serving our individual or collective happiness.[1] I found an unremarkable spot by the side of the road and set up my tent, behind a few trees and out of sight of cars. I wanted shelter and a little warmth for what I was about to delve into. And once my tent was set up, I got into my sleeping bag and zipped away the world outside. The tears began flowing.

Longing for love

It was the contrast that did it, again – a contrast that helped me see something that I otherwise could not have properly seen. Something painful from my past was revealing itself in the present. This has always been the greatest block to my happiness, and when it happens, I've learnt to stop and look carefully into it. Painful though it can be to do this, it helps me understand how I came to be who I am, and removes something of the block, so that it is not so difficult next time. The last time it happened so intensely on this journey was Las Vegas – there, I'd found myself immersed in that manifestly manipulative environment, and my mental health struggles of the past had come blazing to the fore. Rather than drown those anxieties out as I would have done before, I gazed as best I could at my struggle, and understood something I had long needed to. This time, though, the struggle was arising from being truly and deeply loved.

Like many people, I've struggled in my relationships with others. Through others I have experienced many of my greatest joys in life. Yet, alongside those great joys, deep anguish has not been far behind. Rather than work at finding a way, it has often seemed easier to step away, live alone, stay single, not commit, and separate. Who doesn't find it difficult to not place blame on others when things go horribly wrong? Or to not react with anger and frustration when we hear someone else place all the blame for what happened on us? By going it alone, there is the hope of greater happiness or, perhaps more accurately, less misery – at least in the short-term, because one day comes loneliness, that has fast become a scourge of our time; a profound barrier to a happy society.

I want to be loved. I don't mean worshipped for something that most of the time I am not and cannot be, despite my strivings – but being accepted for who I am from this moment to the next; held and supported. I want to feel that whatever difficulty I am facing, that I am enough simply as I am. I am sure that all of us have this desire, deep down.

I've had difficulty in receiving this kind of love from others, and offering such love to others is just as difficult. And, perhaps more importantly still, offering it when there doesn't seem like much of the same being reciprocated. Therein lies my deepest struggle. I hear Jesus excelled at offering love unconditionally. From what I understand, Buddha did a fine job of being able to accept and love what is, too, as have many enlightened beings that have beautified this planet.

It had been five days since I'd left that community in Oregon, described a couple of chapters back, where there was an unerring commitment between the people. This community had an exquisite sense of togetherness that I had never seen before. At least not beyond the small room with the swirly–orange carpet I inhabited with my brother when I was a young boy. I'd certainly dreamt about such togetherness ever since, and given what I'd already experienced on other parts of my journey up until now, I hadn't completely lost hope of experiencing it again.

Actually, I'd say that, given all I had gone through up until that point, I was just about ready to witness it in full. After everything I'd learnt, I was aware and open enough to appreciate it when it finally appeared. The really amazing thing was just how easily I found it to be wholeheartedly part of that togetherness during my short time in the community: a testament to them, and a testament to how far I'd come in remembering who I was and what I needed. It is in my nature to care and be cared for, and those beings in the Oregon community only ever asked me to be me. I was enough, much as I've always been enough. I know this deep down, just as you will know it, deep in there; and although I'd done my best over the years to cultivate that on my own, it really helps when those in my life are strong enough in their own love to remind me that I am indeed enough, too.

Being enough

A crucial ingredient of knowing one is enough is to receive that message from others. If others imply that we can only receive their love if we fulfil certain criteria, be it behaving or looking a certain way, obtaining some grade, or having a certain type of job, then fulfilling that criteria is often what we will attempt to do. Sometimes, depending upon what we do, we may be labelled 'bad', another time 'good'. This is what the humanist psychologist Carl Rogers called 'conditions of worth'.[2] The idea is that if we don't meet these conditions, we won't receive the love we need, from the people from whom we need it most – our parents, for example. When we are children, our physical survival depends upon doing what we can to feel accepted. Outside of the immediate family we receive other messages, possibly very similar ones, that remind us how we ought to be, and what it will take for us to feel accepted and loved by others.

One day these conditions might come to be part of our identity. As well as these conditions being essential to receive love from others, they also become essential for us to be able to love ourselves. We internalise them – "I am only a good person if and when I have/do/look like this or that..." – and we find ourselves expecting these things of others too. If we manage to meet those conditions, then perhaps life can be more or less okay for us. However, we may end up having to spend much of our life anxiously trying to maintain these conditions to receive the love we need. Perhaps what we would rather be doing, because it brings more joy to the world, is throwing a ball about with our little boy.

In any case, the conditions imposed upon us are often about doing better than other people, or how we did last year in some area of life, such as school, work, sport – and such a game of performance never ceases.[3] Plus, someone else's gain becomes our loss. And vice versa. So we keep striving, despite having little hope of ever meeting those conditions, and may find ourselves just getting through all or part of our life feeling largely unloved. That can be painful; even depressing.

Carl Rogers suggested that our psychological difficulties are largely borne out of trying to fulfil the *conditions of worth* that have been placed upon us by others – including our friends, our family, our communities, and our societies. We indicate to each other, in both subtle and not-so-subtle ways, that we are not enough as we are. That we must do and be certain things; things that are often not in keeping with what we want ourselves to do and be, deep down. This conditioning process from others links with why we often experience much less happiness than we expect when we strive to achieve certain goals – as I described earlier, when a few months into the journey high up in the Andes I let go of finding happiness through achieving my goal of arriving in Bhutan on my bicycle.

This is not about blame and judgement, because normally others aren't intentionally trying to make us feel miserable for not fulfilling the conditions they expect of us. Rather, they may think it is in our best interests that we try to fulfil them, since that is the life they and those around them have come to believe will bring the most happiness. (That is, if they ever achieve these things themselves, which they possibly won't.) But not achieving goals yourself doesn't stop you believing that those goals are the recipe for happiness. These conditions have been fully internalised by those around us and they may believe they are helping us. We may believe they are helping too, if we've fully internalised the conditions of worth. Yet, rather than resort to blame, because that just plays an unloving game, our aim is to understand the process as to how and why we got to where we are.

Loving: from theory to practice

This conditioning process is certainly not all one way either – from them to me, from them to us. Most people, including me and probably you, are complicit in it too. I know that I've internalised an idea of how people should be, for example, making rational choices or being grateful, and doing so has often prevented me from finding fulfilment in my relationships. Some, however, do know how to love in an unconditional way, and they have been working at it consciously most of their lives. It's a practice – the art of looking at something or someone and not judging. Just seeing a person as they are. That doesn't bar having emotions come up in response to what's happening before us. It's simply not judging, not labelling; it just is. A little bit like being mindful and in the present with what is.

Though it is difficult to be unconditionally accepting, it is something that we can move toward being. Being more mindful is a good start. Carl Rogers believed that for us to be able to introspect, break down our conditions of worth, and experience personal growth and happiness, it helps to be in the presence of someone who unconditionally accepts us. They send a message with their being that we are enough as we are, and they enable us to see ourselves more clearly. We can, of course, focus on finding acceptance within, if we know what we're looking for – or indeed not looking for. Some say that within is where love and acceptance has to ultimately come from anyway... Yes, ultimately, of course. However, it is a hell of a lot easier if others can furnish us with unconditional love and acceptance at the same time. We don't seem to be making it very easy for one another at this point in human history.

I first came across the theory behind unconditional acceptance many years ago when I moved from Economics to

Psychology. I'd not encountered anything like it before, yet it was another psychological theory that made a lot of sense. At least it made a lot of sense in theory. It would take many years for me to begin getting anywhere close to putting the theory into practice in my own life. It is not easy to switch off and reverse a conditioning process that has been going on our entire lives, and go out into a world where we are confronted with messages that we are not enough. That said, it is not completely impossible either, and being a little more unconditionally accepting has certainly brought more happiness to my life.

At first, it was a case of acknowledging that many of the things that I had chosen to do with my life were not really my choices. I had simply gone along with expectations of what a little boy was supposed to become. Not to cry, to do as he was told, do well at school, to be lively and sociable, and to work hard. I'd done unbelievably well in that conditional sense, and whilst I changed a few things here and there to bring more happiness, I mostly kept on playing that conditional game. Yet, after a while, I began to look deeper – and with time, what I realised I most craved in life was to be able to look at my Dad with total and complete love. The way I used to, as a small boy, before I began seeing him as an ogre. He is no ogre, just a man who has his fair share of struggle and needs love like the rest of us; it took this journey for me to fully appreciate that.

Sobriety was a definite leap in the right direction for me. I started to really make progress with unconditional acceptance when I began to practice mindfulness to get in the here and now. I noticed a little shift within me – I was able to watch more and react less to others. Over the years, a few people came into my life who were able to see me more clearly than I was able to see myself. That helped me appreciate aspects of myself that I had not liked very much. There was also a little therapy and some communication courses along the way. I learnt to see my emotions and not be frightened by them, in the way I had learnt to be in the past. I found a way of expressing my emotions without laying blame and guilt on other people. I took ownership for what I was feeling and why, and communicated it without judgement. Others' emotions became less scary too, and I learnt to listen to people without taking it personally or making what they were saying about me. I took little steps; just changing a small thing here and there. There were times when I really messed up. Or at least that was my assessment of what I had done. However, some people were more forgiving than I was to myself, and that helped.

The appeal of going it alone

These days, if we don't want to work on our relationships then we don't have to. We can walk away. And we often do walk away, because we believe that somewhere else, and maybe with someone else, we will find more happiness. Perhaps we really will this time… yet in all likelihood, the same inability to perfectly love an imperfect other will rear up. There is nothing wrong with always walking away, but as a path to greater happiness it can have its limits.

Material wealth is in abundance in many parts of the world. If we want to move to a new city, start a new relationship, or live alone in an apartment, then it is not as difficult to do as it once was. It is expected even. There is a greater freedom of movement than ever before. This is fantastic, where it has allowed people to get away from abusive families and relationships, as well as enabling greater expression as to who we are as individuals, i.e. breaking out of oppressive conditioning. However, has that freedom also reduced the threshold by which people are prepared to face difference? Has it blocked our ability to find compassion and understanding? Has it driven us to isolation?

I can't answer these questions with any authority; I'm no sociologist. Just a guy alone in a tent with his tears. However, I can and did once look at lots of data to see what brings people the greatest happiness, and I have introspected pretty deeply as to why I've neglected what is most important in my life. When it comes to the data, our relationships with others are quite simply the single most important contributing factor to happiness in our lives. As I highlighted near the beginning of the book, being married, for example, has an associated happiness-effect equivalent to US$100,000 each and every year. It is not about being married per se, but whether a person has supportive relationships in their life. If our relationships are unsupportive then we are likely to be less happy. If our relationships are supportive then there is a good chance that we'll be happy. The importance of relationships in our lives is consistent across different cultures, and all the kinds of happiness I've outlined in this book.

Yet, despite the importance of our relationships for happiness, we may not prioritise them. We may not have the time, and often, if we do have the time, we do not have the skills that would enable us to develop them so that they are mutually supportive. No-one has taught us. Role models of co-supportive relationships are few and far between. Well, actually that's not true, there are plenty, it is just they are not made visible in a society predicated on the exchange of things, rather than our relationships with one another.

Dearest Dad

As I lay huddled alone and cold in my tent with my tears, I kept thinking about my father. I was reminded of the times that I had hidden myself as a small boy in a cold cupboard, wanting nothing more than to be loved by him for what I was – tears and all. After that week of profound togetherness at the Oregon community, I had thrust myself back into an individualistic culture that was not too dissimilar to my own. It was a shocking contrast to what I had experienced in the previous week, and that contrast made it all the more visible, and painful. I felt sick and tired of this kind of aloneness in my life. In that Oregon community I had seen something beautiful. Something of how it could be. It was the practice of the theory that had inspired me all those years ago, and by being held securely in that love for a very brief time I felt something re-birth within me. What

I realised in that moment was that what I wanted the most was to be at home with my father. To go back to the source of my biggest struggle. To keep offering my love when there didn't seem like much of the same being reciprocated. And after all these years, I saw that I was at last ready and able to do that.

I'm not saying my Dad didn't love me. Far from it. It was just very difficult to see sometimes. Deep down I knew he did; he must have. Yet, I suspect he needed my love more than I needed his. And it has long been that way – he's a man with a large number of conditions – internal and external. There is no right or wrong of it, at least not as far as I am concerned anymore. Back then I just didn't understand what his struggle was. Yet, it was the same struggle that I would go on to have, that many of us have: how to make our way through a life that sometimes makes no sense at all. If there is no sense to life – and I don't fundamentally believe that is the case (see the next chapter) – it is always easier when we have others by our side in support.

This realisation about my father didn't come out of the blue, because more than anyone, my father had really gotten behind my journey. What I was doing on a bicycle was far more relatable to him than my academic career, and my journey allowed something to shift between us. Our relationship strengthened as I journeyed. Before I left, we'd struggle to spend more than ten minutes on the phone together once or twice a year – yet as I journeyed, we'd find ourselves talking for more than an hour, and regularly. We opened up to one another, we listened more. In fact, I spoke to him more than anyone else back home throughout my journey, and when I wrote a blog post he'd often be the first to comment on what I'd written.

I'm still touched to this day when I read his response to a blog post I wrote around this time about how sad I had been feeling: "Oh Christopher, this makes me so sad to read..." Now there is a human, I thought, and I could see him as clear as day. What shifted between my Dad and me over the journey is without a doubt the best thing to have come from it, and has been a big source of a deep, enduring joy ever since.

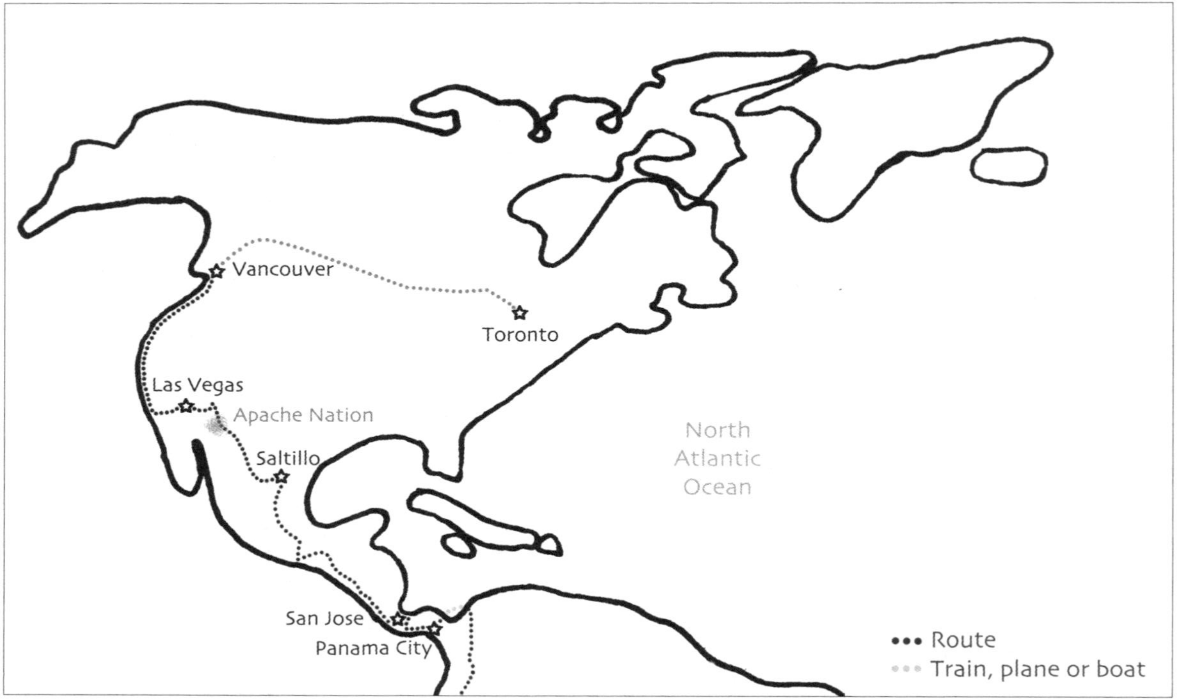

To Toronto and a personal journey for happiness ends

CHAPTER 16

A life on purpose

"Do not strain yourself trying to improve this world. First completely know your Self. Then your actions spring from this spontaneity, from this depth, from this understanding, from the Real. And they will shower blessings upon this world. Be the One who is eternally free, happy, whole."

Mooji[1]

If this journey were just about more pleasure and less pain, then I would have given up long ago. If it were only about achieving a goal, then I would be foolish to continue in the belief that some satisfaction would come when it is achieved. No, this journey had to be about something much bigger than me. And when there is something beyond the self in what one chooses to do, therein lies a happiness that can and will endure.

I wanted to come back from this journey feeling complete. I didn't know exactly what being complete would feel and look like, nor when that would be. I just knew that at some point, I would know that I didn't any longer need to haul myself and a few things on a bicycle across unfamiliar lands. That I no longer needed to wander the earth, getting into adventures. A point would come when I would know that I had all I needed to return home, to create a life that had happiness at its root and centre – irrespective of the distractions that could and sometimes would disrupt that ultimate aim.

Since I'd long ago let go of expectations of happiness upon arrival in Bhutan, and that I had also become more attuned to myself, I was prepared to feel complete when the time came. I was open to it being long before I reached Bhutan. And so it was, as I rode up the west coast of the Americas into the wind and rain, a year into my journey, and with my Dad in my thoughts, that this cycle journey felt complete. I didn't need to do this anymore. Certainly, not for my own sake.

I remember getting my first inkling that completion might be on the horizon way back in Guatemala, eight months into the journey. Learning how to be present – in the way that I described earlier in this book – was key to feeling like I could return home complete. There had been sizeable shifts within me that made seemingly magical experiences possible and likely, just like the one in the Guatemalan village. The journey unravelled further in Mexico, when I became attuned to other peoples' gifts. I hadn't thought that I would need to continue for much longer after Mexico; and once I'd left the community in Oregon, basking in the immensity of the togetherness there, I knew there was little more that I could personally get from this journey. It was home time – deep breaths, and back to Dad and all those I'd left behind. Back to that less-than-ideal culture that obsesses about the economy. Back to all of the challenge that inevitably arises – and I was ready to stand firm in what was important, for a life centred around happiness and wellbeing.

A journey naturally unfolding

As I've already described, at the beginning of this journey I found it difficult to share much about what I was experiencing. I had written a few articles about my intentions, and shared them on my personal blog about happiness, but there had been no bigger announcement beyond my circles. Not only was there little time, but I was overwhelmed with the anxiety around what lay ahead and what others might think and say about what I had chosen to do. At the time of departure, I thought there was some chance I'd be back after a few weeks, realising I'd made a big mistake, or that it wasn't as achievable as I had thought. That would have made me feel more embarrassed than embarking in the first place. Back then, it was about getting out the front door – trying my best at something that was important for me to attempt to do, and to trust that everything would work itself out, as and when it needed to. Trusting that in my boldness to act, those mighty forces would come to my aid. This was my journey, and if there were to be any happiness lessons, then I wanted them to unfold in their own time and manner. There is little point in forcing anything. In my experience, forcing things rarely seems to have the desired effect.

As the journey evolved, I wrote and shared more. I'd only ever written as an academic before this journey began, and the academic style of writing is dull. Not many people read academic articles, except other academics. There was a lot to learn about writing in a way that people can relate to, and that meant opening up to the personal. That meant being vulnerable, and though that vulnerability invites people in, the thought that someone might judge and jeer can also invite anxiety.

With time, however, my confidence in what I was doing increased, and I began to share more as the journey progressed. When I bought my first smart phone in Costa Rica (to replace that old one my brother had given me that just about took photos, and sometimes struggled to turn on), I began to share my journey more widely on social media, and people were curious. About then, I also made some stickers with links to my blog, that I sometimes gave to people I met who wanted to know a little more about what I was doing. People didn't think the journey was at all ridiculous, and I began to believe maybe I really could reach Bhutan one day after all.

I soon began to display the hashtag for my journey, #AdventuresInHappiness[2] on the back of my bicycle every day. I'd get a few new followers to my personal blog here and there, and once in a while someone I didn't know wrote a touching email about how I was inspiring them in some small way, through some words I had written about my journey. I loved it whenever anyone connected to my journey. It encouraged me to open up a little more each time, and with my anxieties around unknowns and what others might think diminishing, I began to feel safer about doing so.

In Mexico things really came alive, inside and out, when a group of journalists I came across in Coahuila – one of my happiness havens – saw me riding by. There I was on Mexican TV! It wasn't planned, it just happened. It was surreal and, if it had happened earlier in my journey, I'm not sure I would have been ready to have done it in the way I did. This was the natural unfolding in motion.

I'd been writing one particular article about my journey for months. The plan was to share it more widely than through my personal blog. As an academic, I'd written about happiness for *The Conversation* a few times before.[3] This article I was writing about my journey, though, was far more personal than the ones I'd previously shared. It was a long piece, and described why I had quit my job as a happiness researcher, and ended up attempting to reach Bhutan on a bicycle. It depicted my personal dance with the happiness research that I'd come to know so well, yet had struggled to live by. It took several months to write it, and I finally felt happy enough with the article to have it published on the site, just at the point when I had that feeling of completion and that it was time to come home. It felt weird to write about this attempt to cycle to Bhutan knowing I'd probably be coming home soon and never arrive there. I confessed this to the person who was editing the piece. They said it didn't matter that much. What I was writing about was still relevant to their readers, and we would just change the ending to account for the 'uncertainties' of the journey ahead.[4]

However, at the time of that confession, I was very certain I would be going home; and by the time article was published, I'd arrived in Vancouver and already booked a five-day train ride over to Toronto. From Toronto I intended to cycle to Montreal, where I would take a direct flight home. I got on that train and switched off – my personal journey really was complete. It was a sublime train journey – through snow-covered Rockies, across the

Prairies, and past the Great Lakes. To cover such a great distance without any pedal strokes felt odd, but I took the time to pause and take stock of my journey. I was heading in the direction of home, and that brought a smile to my face. There was a little sadness that I'd never get to see the mountains of Bhutan rise up before me, as I approached them slowly on my bicycle. Yet, I was certain heading home was the right thing for me to be doing in that moment, and I knew that seeing those mountains appear would never be quite as joyful as I imagined it would be.

By the time I arrived in Toronto, the article I'd written had picked up some attention (some 20,000 views in its first week). Alongside it, there was an article in *The Times*, with a picture of me on my bicycle taken by Carlos, the Uruguayan road worker who gave me some of his cool orange fizzy drink over a year ago. A radio station in the UK wanted me to do a live interview for their listeners. It was the conversation I had with the radio presenter that finally swung it for me. It seemed there was something fascinating to people about this journey I was on, and by one day reaching Bhutan my journey would be infinitely more interesting to people than were I never to do so. And through reaching Bhutan – whether I found happiness or not when I arrived – I would have a good chance of sharing some ideas about happiness. Perhaps in doing so, I might fulfil my forever-held deeper life purpose of making the world a slightly happier place. In its own natural way, the journey was continuing to unfold. I couldn't have planned it to be this way. Those mighty forces were at work.

A purposeful kind of happiness

Aristotle, the ancient Greek philosopher, who said that happiness was the "whole aim and end of human existence", spoke of two kinds of happiness. There was the *hedonic happiness* – the pleasure and pain we feel moment-to-moment. Hedonic happiness is a useful happiness to pay attention to, but it is elusive. Such happiness will come and go. And we can often find ourselves in misery if we only try to grasp for pleasure and avoid pain all the time.

The other kind of happiness that Aristotle spoke of was what he referred to as *eudaimonic happiness*: the result of people following their best inner nature. Aristotle conceived this kind of happiness, all those 2,500 years ago, to mean following cultural ideals of excellence of his time, such as being wise, brave, and temperate.

In the world of happiness research, we still talk about *eudaimonic happiness*, although these days it is more commonly referred to as *human flourishing* – somewhat easier to say, and perhaps more relatable. The *flourishing* kind of happiness is different to both of the other main kinds of happiness we've talked about already.[5]

Human flourishing refers to whether a person leads a purposeful life, has supportive relationships, has high self-esteem, and is optimistic about the future. The idea is that these are universal human needs, and if these are not fulfilled, then it makes it difficult for a person to feel good about their life for very long. That is, we may well achieve the goals we thought were important, and feel satisfied about doing so (i.e., we think we're happy when we reflect on our lives overall – *evaluative happiness*) and experience pleasure (i.e., we feel happy in the moment – *hedonic happiness*), yet once these experiences dwindle into the past, we can be left still wanting.

This human flourishing kind of happiness is more prescriptive than the other two. It states the areas of life that are important to flourish – namely having meaning and purpose, relationships, self-esteem, and optimism – rather than letting us decide for ourselves. However, a lot of research has gone into establishing that these elements are at the core of what people really care about. In addition, as with the other kinds of happiness, whether a person is flourishing in this more prescriptive way is still based on their own perceptions of those areas of life. This kind of happiness expresses deep fulfilment.

Plus, it was this kind of happiness, and not the hedonic happiness, that Aristotle was referring to when he spoke of the "whole aim and end of human existence". It was this kind of happiness that I had been yearning for, ever since I lost it as a young boy. And it was the kind of happiness that, as I sat on that train from Vancouver to Toronto, smiling contentedly, I now had. My life was full of meaning and purpose, my relationships had gone deeper, my self-esteem was high, and I felt optimistic about the future. This was what I had set out on this journey to find, and I had found it.

One very simple question researchers use to understand this kind of happiness is "Overall, to what extent do you feel the things you do in your life are worthwhile?" It is similar in structure to the other three happiness-related questions I've talked about in this book: overall life satisfaction, and happiness / anxiety experienced throughout the day. Again, people are asked to respond to this question on a scale from 0 to 10, where 0 is "Not at all" and 10 is "Completely".

Several months before I set off for Bhutan, I would have given myself a 5 for this question. I couldn't see the point in many of my day-to-day activities. Nowadays, I would struggle to give myself less than a 10. Life feels worthwhile – unerringly so. It is worthwhile, but not because I made it to Bhutan with my bicycle in the end. My life was always worthwhile – I just didn't do many things that made it feel that way much of the time. Not only was I disconnected from my wider purpose in life, but – before I left on my journey – most of the things I was doing did not feed into the limited sense of purpose that I had. My wider purpose in life became starkly clear to me in Toronto, and when that happened, there was little choice but to continue on toward Bhutan – just as there had been little choice in setting out on this absurd escapade in the first place. I was complete in a personal happiness sense, but through continuing the journey, I recognised I had some chance of contributing to something bigger than that.

The happiness of others

The title of one of my earliest pieces of research was "Do people become healthier after being promoted?". An important question, no doubt. Many will face the prospect of a promotion in their lives, and they'll often take it, perhaps unhesitatingly. However, to the surprise of both me and my PhD supervisor at the time, what our research showed was that, though promotion had no effect on physical health, there tended to be a deterioration in a person's mental health. Upon publication of these results, and whilst I was still only a student, I found myself thrust into the media spotlight to talk about what we'd discovered. My PhD supervisor, whose research has never been far from the news, stepped aside and encouraged me. It was a scary and overwhelming experience, yet I didn't resist, because I thought that sharing what we had discovered was worth overcoming any unpleasant feelings of my own. I thought that I might have contributed to someone making a life decision that would bring them more happiness; and enabling someone else to find a little more happiness seemed like a meaningful and purposeful thing to be doing with my time. When I did that piece of media, I was opting for wider purpose rather than personal pleasure. (Although, once it was all done and the anxiety had passed, I admit I ended up getting a very pleasurable buzz from seeing my name in the newspapers, alongside a quote I'd given about my research.)[6]

Over the years, talking to the media went on to become a familiar part of my research career.[7] It was always accompanied by anxiety, but overall, I enjoyed doing it. It was also one of the things I felt compelled to do. Not for academic reasons – as it takes time and there is no academic incentive to do it – but so that it would make all those days spent alone in front of a computer, or overcoming countless publisher rejections worth it. Deep down, I hoped that my research would be of some small use to someone, somewhere, at some point in time. That was mostly blind faith. However, publicly sharing my research was the second most effective way I thought I could bring more happiness to the world, and so I kept publishing articles and talking to the media about my research, whenever the opportunity arose.

In the meantime, I focused on what was *the* most effective way of increasing world happiness: changing things about my own life.

With time, I began to question whether my research would be of any use to anyone – yet, whether it was or not, it was reassuring to know that I could at least make use of what I was researching, and increase world happiness that way. Bringing more happiness to the world via changes to my own life became a concrete personal purpose. I got happier and happier, until the day I saw that my ability to obtain greater personal happiness in my own situation had reached its limits. With a wavering personal purpose, the blind faith that my research might help others find happiness just wasn't enough on its own. In fact, I was fairly convinced that my academic articles and any of the related media coverage were doing nothing to change a society fixated on the economy, rather than happiness and wellbeing.

An important reason I was unhappy back then was that my work had lost meaning. If I wanted to further embrace the research I knew so well, and make better choices for myself, I had to quit my job, in order to do something else that felt more purposeful to me. That I was able to do so – i.e. I had enough financial resources stashed away, sufficient physical capacity and confidence, support from friends and family, and an open and diligent disposition – gives me reason to feel fortunate.

And so, I'd gotten out of what I was in, and had begun cycling – and here I was in Canada, with close to 10,000 miles of cycling in my legs, wondering whether there might be a chance to bring the world a little more happiness if I continued.

The importance of uncovering purpose and meaning

What is purposeful and meaningful for one person doesn't need to be purposeful and meaningful for another. Purpose and meaning are not objective; they are very personal. We may look to established belief systems for our purpose and meaning, and the purpose and meaning people find in those belief systems explains why those with religious or spiritual beliefs tend to experience more moment-to-moment happiness, and have higher life satisfaction levels than those who do not hold such beliefs. Believing that we might be floating around in an existential void can be a scary prospect, and most of us wouldn't like to embrace it for too long.

Filling our lives with purpose and meaning is undeniably important. For example, the presence of meaning has been shown to account for over 30 per cent of a person's life satisfaction (*evaluative happiness*) and nearly 25 per cent of their moment-to-moment positive emotions (*hedonic happiness – positive*).[8] Purpose and meaning are what keep us persevering when we are struggling. As Viktor Frankl, a survivor of the holocaust and psychotherapist, put it, 'If we can find some meaning to put at the centre of our lives – even the worst kind of suffering becomes bearable.'

How do we discern what is purposeful and meaningful to us? Perhaps it is easier just to accept someone else's explanation as to why we are here. Maybe we prefer to distract ourselves from considering our purpose by continuously seeking pleasure, or through unending busyness. That's not to say these things can't be purposeful in themselves. Yet, like most people, I've had my share of experiences trying to deal with my existential woes in these ways over the years – and they've always resulted in greater torment eventually.

Purpose and meaning have always mattered to me. In trying to make sense of my existence, I have sometimes found myself doing some things that made more sense to me and brought more sustained happiness than when I did other things. I didn't know it at the time, but the things that made the most sense were often directly related to what I've now come to understand to be personally purposeful and meaningful. As the years and the pedal strokes went by, and as I became less afraid of what I might find, I challenged myself to look beyond the apparent reasons I did certain things. It is invaluable to take the time to question what is really important to us. When we know what it is that's important, then we can align ourselves to that more fully. And we'll be undoubtedly happier for it in the long run.

A question along the lines of "Overall, to what extent do

you feel the things you do in your life are worthwhile?" has been used in various studies to better understand happiness. The extent to which something feels worthwhile helps explain why we do things that don't seem to make us happier, in either an evaluative or hedonic sense (i.e., increase our life satisfaction or moment-to-moment happiness).[9] For example, much to some people's surprise, having children doesn't, on average, increase people's evaluative or hedonic happiness. Often people feel worse in these respects. Less satisfaction, less pleasure, and more anxiety. In some ways, it is a mystery why we still have children! However, doing things for our children often evokes a sense of meaning and purpose in our lives. Similarly, we may find a job to be inherently senseless, bringing us no joy in itself, yet it enables us to provide for those we love, and it is in the providing for others that we find our meaning. Or, children aside, maybe the job itself is not particularly pleasant day-to-day, yet it feels inherently purposeful.

None of this means we don't do things we find both unpleasant and meaningless. Sometimes we make mistakes, and get trapped by a system that is not designed to bring much pleasure nor purpose. Yet, there is always a reason why we do things, and if we get to the root of why that is, then we may discover different opportunities to meet the deeper need for purpose and meaning in our lives.

Purpose whilst cycling to Bhutan

I've found that by asking whether I feel my life is worthwhile has helped me unpick what is important for me. On my journey to Bhutan, I took this further, by asking – alongside how happy and anxious I felt each day – how worthwhile I felt the day had been, on a 0–10 scale. This is an adapted version of the earlier question about how worthwhile we feel our life is overall. Similar questions have been used in the context of whether the things we do in our daily lives feel meaningful, purposeful, or worthwhile. Asking myself this question each day drew my attention to what I found purposeful in life, and encouraged me to align my journey with that wider purpose. My daily scores and a seven-day moving average can be seen in Figure 5.

Figure 5: The worthwhileness of each day as I cycled to Bhutan

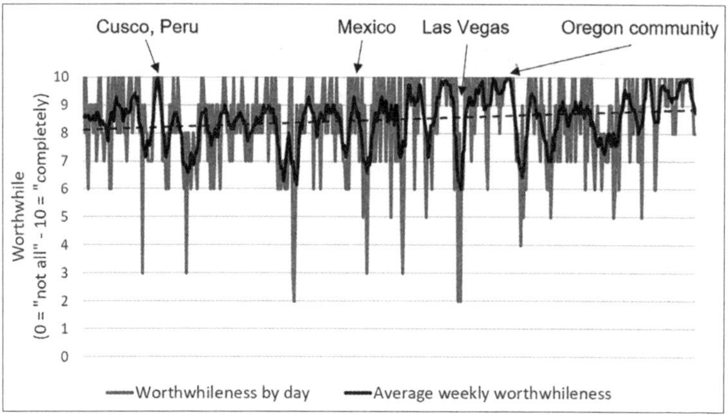

As should be clear from this illustration, I scored a lot of 10s on this question. My average across the journey was 8.5, and on 77 per cent of my days, I rated the worthwhileness of my day 8 or higher. On only 4 per cent of my days did I rate this question 5 or lower. This is compared to *daily happiness feelings* (as in Chapter 8) with only 44 per cent of a score of 8 or higher, and 18 per cent of 5 or lower. What this means is, that whilst I wasn't always experiencing a lot of pleasure on my journey, what I was doing day-to-day felt meaningful and purposeful. What you'll notice is that, even when there was pronounced difficulty, the worthwhileness of my day diminished below a score of 3 only a few times. I could nearly always find something about my day that would make it feel purposeful. It was finding something purposeful and meaningful in the dog bite that helped get me though my struggle there. And, when I look back now, that dog bite experience abounds with purpose – in the end it became a crucial part of my journey. Without it, maybe I'd never have made it to Canada. Finding purpose is such a crucial component of resilience when dealing with a crisis – purpose keeps us going, purpose gives us grit.

In scoring this question each day, I began to understand what was really important in my life. This shifted my attention to doing each day the things that would tap into that wider purpose, and as the journey unfolded, my days gradually began to feel more worthwhile – that's illustrated with the upward-trending dashed line in the Figure. The days that brought me the most purpose were those when I took care of myself, and I shared with others. For example, camping in nature after a hard, but not too hard, day cycling. Or the days when I'd taken the time to stop and talk to people along the way, who had beckoned me into their lives for a short while. Or when I slowed down, and stayed somewhere for an extra day or two, because someone asked me to.

These activities naturally gave me a lot of pleasure too, even though sometimes, when I camped out in the wild or put myself into social situations, they were also accompanied by greater anxiety.[10] There were also days that, whilst not being necessarily pleasant, still felt purposeful. For example, it wasn't fun to spend most of a day in front of my laptop writing a blog post about the journey – yet doing that felt like an important part of my journey, and I'm glad I did it. Nor was it fun when I directly confronted some past or present difficulty I was having, such as what happened in Las Vegas. Yet, with these small everyday actions, I felt like I was contributing more happiness to the world – and that made me feel like my days, my life, were worthwhile.

Not self-sacrificing

Before this journey began, I hadn't realised the depth to which the happiness of others was such an integral part of finding purpose and meaning in what I did with my life. I see now that the happiness of others lay beneath the drive to keep writing and publishing about happiness as an academic. Yet back then, the core purpose of sharing happiness through academic writing was so mixed up with other things – how much I published, whether I published in the best journals, administrative responsibilities, how much I was paid compared with others, whether to take a promotion or not, and so forth – that I doubt I was fulfilling that purpose very effectively.

In addition, it is questionable how much happiness can be shared with others if we aren't first happy ourselves. If that is the case, I've asked myself often, what is there to really share with others? I've often wondered whether the reason happiness research doesn't seem to be taken too seriously is because so many of those that conduct the research aren't exactly poster-children for their own conclusions. It seemed to me that to be a successful happiness academic you are required to do certain things (work very long hours, outperform others, deal with bureaucracy and academic politics) that don't bring much in the way of personal happiness. I often think about all those stern faces to whom I have presented my research over the years in rooms with little natural light and terrible food. It never did add up.

The bottom line is that happiness cannot be an entirely selfish, hedonistic pursuit, nor should it be one in which we sacrifice our own happiness to make others happier. Both can be harmful. Our own pursuit of happiness can limit others' capacity to be happy; not only those that we care about the most, but also our own selves in the future. Such a pursuit can leave us feeling empty inside. Happiness – the enduring kind – comes about when we are so deeply aligned with ourselves that our actions bring forth happiness for others, as well as ourselves.

Cracking on with it

After hanging around for a few days in Toronto – which included taking a very worthwhile trip to the University of Waterloo to meet the director of the Canadian Index of Wellbeing, discussed in Chapter 14 – I wrote on my personal blog: "We need to create societies where we can all live better, happier, and healthier lives, and if my journey to Bhutan can help spread a message around that need, then perhaps I should keep pedalling on."

What I saw in myself in Toronto was a being full to the brim with happiness, in a way I had not experienced since I was a five-year-old sitting on his swirly-orange carpet. Sure, I missed all the people back home, and I was desperate to have those long lingering hugs, often only experienced with those one knows deeply. However, I knew that after 12 months on a bicycle exploring happiness, I now had the skills to be happy almost anywhere. I was enough. I was fully aligned with what was important to me, and I knew exactly what I needed to do to have the best chance of bringing more happiness to the world.

From Toronto, I flew direct to Hong Kong. The story of an unhappy happiness researcher cycling to the happiness capital of the world was back on. I really was going to make it there after all. Well, at least to the border...

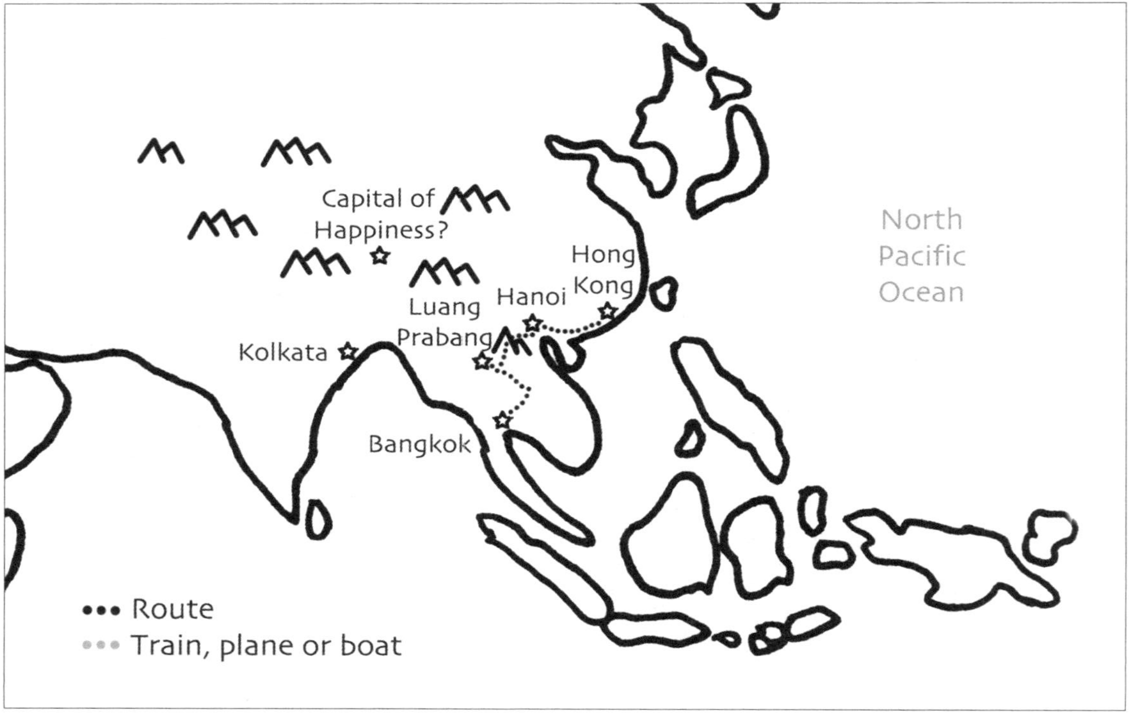

From Hong Kong to Bangkok

CHAPTER 17

The end in sight

"Women with their top hats and beautiful coloured scarves. Dogs trying to fuck one another; white people trying not to notice other white people; ice cream man wearing his uniform and passing his time contentedly in the sun. There is a lot of watching and waiting in Bolivia. No one seems in a hurry, or trying to make a fast buck. All the businesses the same – just waiting and accepting what comes."

Journal entry, somewhere back in Bolivia, date unknown

The best way I can describe the moment was like suddenly waking up from a dream. The Laotian mountains I was riding felt eerily familiar. Not quite as big as the ones I had been riding through exactly one year ago in the Andes, but big enough. What exactly had happened in the past year? Who and what was I now? From what you've read up to here, it may sound like I knew what was happening inside of me, and on some level I did – but back then I could hardly put words around much of what I was experiencing. It didn't always make complete sense at the time. I was immersed in this journey.

The pattern for me was that I would begin to understand one thing that had happened, only to have something else happening right before my eyes that demanded my full attention. Throughout my journey, I had often been in what psychologists call *flow* – a state of being where we are fully engaged in a challenging activity, such that we temporarily suspend our sense of self and of time. As I rode up and down this range of mountains, I wondered whether this past year had really happened. Was I still in the Andes next to that illustrious Huachuma? Was it I who had experienced these things, and not somebody else I was reading about, or had been watching? It didn't seem real. No, I had to be dreaming.

I pinched myself, and it hurt! This couldn't be a dream. I'd been pinching myself throughout the journey – and the world had pinched me back a fair few times too. It had taken a bite out of me too, I still remembered. I had certainly been awake – more awake than ever – and time and space had ceased to matter, in the same way they had done before I'd left.

What these mid-sized Laotian mountains did, just as much as make me think about an earlier part of the journey, was remind me that I needed, one day, to get back to the mountains I'd fallen in love with in Scotland.

It was becoming warm enough to make a journey up into the Himalayas possible, and by my calculations, I had a good chance of being in Bhutan for that year's International Day of Happiness – 20th March. Then I could declare my journey officially over and go home. And that, more than anything, would be a relief. All this movement, enriching though it can be with conscious intention, gets to be exhausting. Eventually, the deeper learning stops, the insights do not come, and continuing ever-onwards seems to be driven by something resembling addiction, rather than meeting an innate human need. It then becomes much more important to allow ourselves some time to stop, to breathe, and fully integrate all that we've now become.[1]

Beyond Hong Kong

When I set out on this journey, I had no idea what my route would be in Asia. I first had to get there – which, until I finally decided to book that flight to Hong Kong from Canada, just two days before arrival, had been uncertain. I'd long let go of making rigid plans, as that's not how the best moments of a journey tend to happen.

When my bicycle and I landed in Hong Kong, those Laotian mountains weren't even on my radar. I was certain I'd figure it out as I went. Despite having cycled up from Argentina to Canada, I was nervous, particularly because I was about to encounter a whole different culture, with no language skills for this part of the world. However, I'd learnt by now that for me, being worried was par for the course. Even when I take others' warnings with a pinch of salt, there was still going to be a residual bit of uncertainty that will draw some concern. That's only natural; I had no expectation it would go away – my duty was just not to get too lost in my mind's endless play, and stay present enough to hear whether any of my other senses were telling me I needed to worry.

There was one major practical consideration for the next months – to stay far enough south to keep warm. It was now December 2018 – 13 months since I'd begun – and at such a time of year back home, I wouldn't have been cycling much, let alone camping. I knew that so long as I stayed in southern China and Southeast Asia, and didn't venture too high into mountains, I would be warm enough. Once things warmed up, I could work my way northward until I somehow got to India, and then one day I would at last get to see the mountains of Bhutan rise up before me, and the end would be in sight. I had plenty of time for this final part of the journey. All I needed to do was stay fully aligned with my now firmly established purpose – completing the journey for the sake of sharing a curious story about happiness. I would know how to act and when.

To some extent, this part of the journey was an integration. All the major lessons about happiness had been lived and learnt – now was simply the time to put those lessons into practice. To fully embed being non-expectant, present, able to give and receive with abundance. To know that personal and situational challenge would come, and I would be able to meet it. To deepen my unconditional acceptance of whatever and whomever was in front of me. To live life *on purpose*. And the more I could practice what I'd learnt the better, because soon I would have to return to a culture in which I had never been encouraged to practice these things in the first place.

That said, there were also a few new things to explore about happiness in this part of the world – the Buddhist culture, for one. Many of us will be familiar with the Dalai Lama, who, despite being exiled from his Tibetan lands, has made countless pronouncements on happiness, and has inspired many throughout the world to consider seeking happiness through compassion. We may also have come across Thich Nhat Hanh, who has established monasteries outside of Southeast Asia, and encouraged mindfulness and peace in his teachings.[2] Or perhaps we may have read Alan Watt's classic, *The Way of Zen*, and been able to appreciate Buddhism through a western lens.[3] I was also curious about Vietnam, in particular. This country, as described earlier, comes closest to meeting population needs without overstretching our planet's environmental boundaries. I wanted to know what this meant for people's happiness.

Did it result in higher numbers on happiness questions?

And if not, then why not?

I also wanted to see how I felt in a culture so different to my own.

Would what I'd learnt in an earlier part of my journey be easier to apply here, or more difficult?

There are also many beautiful things in this part of the world; things we will be told we ought to see while we are in that place. But after a while on a bicycle, I came to see beauty everywhere and, as it turned out, the most beautiful things I saw were the things that others weren't looking at.

Our travel habits have a cost

As I mentioned at the beginning of this book, it costs US$250 a day to visit Bhutan (unless the visitor is Indian, Bangladeshi, or Maldivian). This makes Bhutan a very exclusive travel destination; only those that can afford it will be admitted. In a vastly unequal world, this doesn't seem very fair, and many people will feel aggrieved by it. Ironically, it is often those who ordinarily can travel when, where, and how, they want that seem to be especially aggrieved. And if it were any other way, I don't think Bhutan would have been named in 2020 by *Lonely Planet* to be the best country to visit. The reason the Bhutanese have restricted travel access to their country is because it helps in preserving its unique Himalayan Buddhist culture. If access weren't restricted, things would naturally change, and most likely it wouldn't be such a coveted tourist destination.

Tourism brings expectations as to how things should and could be – what's for dinner and where to sleep – that are not always in keeping with how permanent residents would like it to be; and also, not in keeping with the culture those very tourists have come to see and experience.

At its worst, tourism can mean big hotels with modern conveniences, and commercial chains we know too well, selling foods familiar to international travellers. Those things can quickly come to dominate – and whilst we might be satisfied, we may also start to wonder why we came.

However, the tourism effect can also be subtler, as local restaurants sell food that appeals more to visitors, centrally located housing is converted into holiday homes, western throne-like toilets replace the more physiologically aligned squat style toilet, and a few more stalls spring up, selling mementos that people feel pressed to buy. Sure, it seems to bring resources to local people, and we might wonder how these communities would survive without tourism. Yet, of course, there wasn't always mass tourism, and the locals were surviving fairly well before. In fact, they were immersed within the culture we might just about still be able to discern.

What was once sacred has become, out of economic pressure, an often contrived commodity. And, whilst we'd like to believe we are bringing benefits to the local community, it is often the case that much of the economic benefit will go to external investors, or just into paying inflated rents, higher than they otherwise would have been, were there no pressure to convert space into accommodation for tourists. It is hardly fair. Nor is it likely to bring much in the way of sustained happiness.

The US$250-a-day visa for Bhutan is a product of its happiness policy. The idea is to create a high-end sustainable model for tourism. It preserves a culture that has long existed, which is deemed an important pillar of Bhutanese happiness. Those that do come must pay – a lot. They also receive a lot, because the US$250 a day is inclusive (full catering, a car and driver, plus a personal guide), and all tourist sites are unblemished and even sometimes deserted. It's unfair. It's exclusive. Yet, for what the Bhutanese are trying to achieve, it seems necessary to them, and I respect that. But it had meant that I had been wondering to myself what I was going to do personally, about cycling into Bhutan.

As I travelled through the Americas, I had written many letters to various people in Bhutan, explaining to them about my journey. I thought my journey would interest the Bhutanese: I thought I was doing a lot to bring healthy attention to the country that I hoped they'd find valuable. I wanted my visit to Bhutan to be in a professional capacity, rather than as a tourist, and that was my proposition in my letters – I wanted to give in a way that was not financial. Yet, all my letters fell flat, and were often ignored. This indifference was an important factor in my earlier considerations about going home from Canada. The Bhutanese weren't interested in my journey.

When I arrived in Hong Kong, I still had no idea what would happen when I reached Bhutan. If I wanted to enter the country, I would need to be prepared to pay the going rate. Yet, as a happiness researcher who'd carved a career for themselves by showing that the link between money and happiness is very small, as well as having undertaken this humble journey to explore this point, I questioned not only the worth of paying so much but also my authenticity in doing so. I thought it unlikely spending time in Bhutan would bring me much happiness, or at least not much more than elsewhere. The price of one day in Bhutan would be sufficient for multiple weeks of cycling in any other country on my travels, and probably bring a lot more happiness.

One idea I was therefore considering, as I cycled around China and Southeast Asia, was to simply cycle to the border and there to declare my journey over. After all the journey was to 'cycle *to* Bhutan', and that was enough for me to go home and share the story about doing so. To cycle all that way – what would turn out to be over 12,000 miles (nearly 20,000km) – and not go into the place I had based this entire journey around would have taken some courage. But if there were no other options that aligned with what was important to me, I was preparing myself to do it.

Being happy on route to Bangkok

Although I pondered now and then about getting into Bhutan, I was mostly focused on being happy once I'd left Hong Kong. I stayed with a British ex-pat whilst I recovered from my jet lag, and sorted out a visa for China. I intended to cycle through southern China, sticking more or less to the coast, crossing into Vietnam, and then to Laos. From there, maybe I'd head to Thailand, and then up through Myanmar. However, I was thinking it more likely I'd head further south to Cambodia, and eventually over to Bangkok. I was thinking about skipping Myanmar altogether, on account of visa border restrictions and recent genocide,[4] instead flying to Kolkata in India from Bangkok.

Most of my experiences in Southeast Asia were a mixture of things that had become familiar throughout my trip – the generosity of strangers, having to pacify my anxieties, the odd insight about happiness related to where I was, and the occasional challenge here and there. And so in reciting this part of the journey, I'll be brief, highlighting only a few key things about happiness – including the long overdue and uncomfortable acceptance that touring around the world on a bicycle is far easier if you're a white man than if you're not.

The curious case of China

I was anxious on my first day of cycling in China. I left the city Zuhai, which rolled into another city and more urban areas. The roads were busy, the surroundings heavily built up. Lots of the high-rise buildings I passed were fewer than ten years old; I imagined what it would have looked like 20 years before. China has seen phenomenal economic growth over the past few decades, and many of the places I cycled through would then have been simple paddy fields. When it comes to the economy and happiness, China is a curious, yet telling, case. Despite the rapid rise in material living standards, that has lifted millions out of poverty, happiness in China has declined. This includes how people on average answer a life satisfaction question, as well as increases in suicides and incidence of mental illness.[5] This is worrying.

Some conclude that there are several important reasons for happiness declines in China. The first is owing to rising inequality, and the widening gap between the haves and the have nots. Second is the reduction in social support, as traditional structures have been quickly dismantled to make way for free-market economic reforms; the third is limited political freedom. Some feel that that the pace of change in China has been too quick for people to adjust to; though there is conjecture that people in China will catch up psychologically with these social changes sooner or later, and in the long-run, people's lives will improve. In part, China seems to represent an extreme example of what happens when there is a blind focus on economic progress – people might suffer, at least in the medium term. Time will tell what will happen beyond that.

However, societal struggle rarely seems to inhibit that unerring human desire for giving. After I'd ridden a nervy 20 miles on that first day, I met a Chinese man on a bicycle. We shared no common language, but that didn't prevent us from figuring out on a map that we were going in a similar direction. We cycled together for about 30 miles, and he showed me the best route to my destination. Along the way we stopped, and he insisted on buying me lunch (using universal sign language to communicate – the gesture of spooning/chop-sticking food to the mouth, followed later by a disdainful look as I reached for my wallet at the end of the meal). After lunch, he wanted to ride my bicycle for a little bit. I guessed it was so he could get a feel for what it was like to ride with the weight I had. We switched bikes for about ten miles, and I was glad to not have to carry my usual burden of gear for that time. It was a funny and touching experience, and deeply reassuring to the nerves with which I had begun the day.

People in China were friendly. Plenty of people stopped me and insisted on buying me a meal. Sometimes those that bought me food didn't want to eat themselves. They were content enough to watch while I ate, and we delighted one another with our attempts to communicate using hand gestures. Smiles and laughter are powerful tools.

It was also in China that I came across a striking pink baseball cap abandoned by the side of the road. It was a cheap hat, yet I love pink and the one I had on was frayed beyond belief. That pink hat became mine. (The pink sky on the front cover illustration was inspired by that hat!)

One of my biggest fears throughout my journey was having a major bicycle malfunction in the middle of nowhere. I was particularly worried that it would happen in a land where I couldn't speak the language. I can think of nowhere better for that fear to have been realised than in China.

I had become fed up with the bigger roads, and I headed out to the countryside. In a couple of villages I rode through, there was clear struggle – impoverished and worn-out looking people – but mostly I just saw people living their lives as best they could, and sometimes showing joy in seeing someone like me pass by on a bicycle. The roads were sometimes terrible, and somewhere along the way, I lost two spokes from my rear wheel. I had spare spokes but not the tools to remove the rear cassette (the cogs on the back wheel). The bike was rideable, but not for very long on those bumpy roads, with all the weight I carried on the rear of my bike. I tried to get local help, but in that part of the world, a bike mechanic is someone at the side of the road with a wooden box of fairly knackered-looking tools. Certainly not the specialist tools I needed to fix my problem. In the end, I managed to hitch a ride with two Chinese men; they went well out of their way to take me some 50 miles to the nearest city, where there'd be a bike shop. I was confused as to what they were doing and, when they went a different way than the map indicated, I must admit I was very worried as to where they were taking me. At one point I thought I might be better off doing a runner from their car with whatever I could carry. They picked up on my agitation, and it all went weird for a bit. When I was finally dropped off, not far from a bicycle shop, I felt ashamed of myself.

Through Vietnam with joy

I entered Vietnam on Christmas Eve 2018. Christmas isn't traditionally celebrated in Vietnam, and I felt sad not to be around people I cared about deeply at this time. I made a perfect plan: I'd get some Vietnamese currency and ride off into the hills, to spend a few days at peace with myself in nature. It didn't work out like that. Some high-level serendipity took over.

There was no money coming out of the bank machine. I tried another, and then another. It was the same story everywhere, and each time my body tensed. I went into the bank, and waited without any clue what I was going to say or do. I tried to communicate the problem, but it was difficult. However, there was one young Vietnamese man working at the bank who spoke excellent English; he went out of his way to help me. He explained that it wasn't a problem with my bank card specifically; it was just a general shortfall of cash in the town, and I'd have to wait until it was replenished. Then, when he came outside and saw my bicycle loaded with all its things, he became really curious – and that's when he went far beyond the role of helpful bank-teller, and deep into being human. He invited me to stay that night with his family.

That night I slept on the floor of his family restaurant. However, that was only much later after he'd taken me to a Christmas-themed corporate event. In his spare time, between working in a bank and running a family restaurant, he taught break dancing, and he, along with some of his students, were the main act for the night. I ate very well at that event too. Sometimes there is nothing we can do but smile at what life has given us – maybe give our body a pinch, enjoy the magic, and just get on with being happy – satisfied, smiling, and with purpose.

The next day (Christmas Day, of minor consequence to the Vietnamese), I sat and ate breakfast with him and his family. His two daughters were about the same age as my sister's then two-year-old and six-year-old daughters. I felt a deep joy being with these Vietnamese girls, having thoughts of my nieces many thousands of miles away, as they enjoyed their Christmas morning in the presence of people that loved them.

I rolled on through to Hanoi. A powerful city – I loved the intricate nature of its older areas, and winding dark alleyways, full of all sorts of peculiar things going on. Strangely, it reminded me of some of the old-growth forests I'd camped in cycling up the west coast of the USA. There was something deep and mysterious about the place. Getting in and out of Hanoi on a bicycle, with all the traffic, mostly motorbikes, was intense. Being present and aware is essential – it was good practice. (Although it was also occasionally terrifying, and I shrieked a few times.)

After New Year in Hanoi, I headed south. I hadn't slept much and felt rundown. I headed to a town called Ninh Binh, where there are lots of temples and some interesting geology. It was nice enough, but I didn't get much connection there. I was just another tourist; I had picked up a cold and felt ill, and I soon wondered what good I was doing for anyone, including myself, in spending too much time there. I ate and looked at stuff. Sick or not, it was time to move onto Laos. At that point, I still thought I might head back into Vietnam further south.

Laos and the re-awakening

Northern Laos is fairly mountainous, and it was there that I began thinking back to where I had been one year previously: the point on my journey when I'd realised that, if this journey were to take its natural course, i.e. reach Bhutan, then I'd still be on a bicycle in a year's time. Well, there I was, one year on. It seemed so long ago – far longer than a year. The self I then was seemed so distant to me. How much longer would it be from here? Certainly I couldn't imagine another year living off a bicycle. Though, if I decided to cycle home, perhaps it might be...

After a few days in the mountains (with a mix of terrible roads, punctures, brake issues and leeches, which combined to produce the most anxious week of my journey, as described in Chapter 10), I headed south to a city called Phonsavan. I'd already been learning a little about the struggles of the Laotian people during the second Indochina war (the Vietnam war). Laos is the most heavily bombed country in the world, and still to this day there is a high density of landmines, which had worried me whenever I was looking for somewhere to put up my tent. Phonsavan is home to a megalithic archaeological landscape, known as the Plain of Jars, dating from the Iron Age (between 500BC and 500AD) – the sort of thing people like to go and look at when in the area. For some inexplicable reason, perhaps relating to the things that had happened the days before, but probably something deeper, I had a horrible panic attack upon arrival to this small city. I got stuck for a few days, unable to leave the hotel, and unable to make a decision about what to do next.

I took a bus to Luang Prabang, a town which is one of those places a person might feel they 'have to go to'. Although, as I figured out upon arrival, it wasn't a place I 'had to go to' at all. Not because it wasn't pretty – it was stunning – but I struggled to see the soul of the place. That's what mass tourism will often do to a place.

There are beautiful people and places everywhere, but when commercial interests dictate how people interact, in some places it can be hard to see the deeper magic. People appear either subservient, or out for the hustle. It was difficult to get the kind of connections that I had become so familiar with throughout my journey; the kind of connections that, over the course of this journey I had come to realise, I feel lost without, no matter where I am.

Racing through Thailand

I took the bus back to Phonsavan and got back on my bicycle. The plan was to head south, and as I rode, I'd decide whether I needed to head all the way down to the Angkor Wat temple complex in Cambodia.

I decided I did not need to do that. No matter how much I thought I might be missing out if I didn't go, deep down I knew it wasn't true. In fact, if we want to look at life in terms of 'missing out', then whatever path we take, we'll miss out on something. In the last 15 months I'd seen what I'd seen, and I'd missed what I'd missed.

And so, it was onto Bangkok in Thailand: flat and hot – and so I raced right on through. Folk were friendly to me as usual. I was invited to camp in a few Buddhist monasteries, and to my eternal joy, I saw some wild elephants along the way. There were no physical challenges to speak of. I was head down and riding free.

However, whilst in Thailand, my journey was challenged. Nattavudh Powdthavee, a famous Thai happiness economist – who had been an avid follower of my progress – asked me on social media: "Do you think that people have been especially nice to you because you are White?" Powdthavee (who has been living and working in the UK for some 30 years, and is both a co-author and a friend[6]), went on to say that he knew "from having friends and families in Thailand, that Asian people tend to 'look up' to Westerners more than they would to others. I just wondered whether I would have had the same treatment if I was the one cycling instead!"

Over the entire 18-months of my journey, I saw no more than ten people on cycle tours who weren't white. That's out of at least a few hundred total touring cyclists with whom I crossed paths, going somewhere or another. Most of the cyclists I saw who weren't white were cycling in or close to their own countries of birth. For example, some Colombians near to Colombia (a country where cycling is popular and there is a diverse ethnicity), one Chinese man cycle-touring in China, and a couple of Thai men touring in neighbouring Laos. I saw a handful of touring cyclists that weren't white on the west coast of the USA, a very busy cycling route. Along there I could easily see 20 or more touring cyclists a day. Most were headed south (and white), and would pass by on the other side of the road from me. We'd wave, sometimes stop to talk. One man who wasn't white, a US citizen of Mexican descent, was partnered with a white women, and they were planning to head all the way to Argentina. Then there was a Korean man cycling around the USA, another Korean man who had joined forces with a Mexican man to head south to Mexico, and a Black man cycling on his own.

It's not as if people of colour are unable to cycle across the world – yet what is clear is that they generally don't. I am certain that if we took some of the crucial moments in my journey, forgetting for a second that I may not have even put myself in the moments in the first place were I not white, the responses I met would have been different. I am certain they would have been less positive.

Would I have camped on a random piece of land without permission in certain countries if I were a different ethnicity (or a different gender)? Probably not.

How would I have been received in some parts of South America? With warmth and with trust? Not according to my Peruvian friend, who looked after me for a couple of days whilst I was in his city.

Being white carries a privilege throughout the world, one that – by virtue of that privilege – I can hardly appreciate. Embarrassing as it is to admit, there is a part of me that denies the reality of that imbalance outright, and would like to think that race does not matter in how I relate to people. Mostly, that's because I don't experience negative racial bias every day, and that's a natural part of having privilege. However, a good part of it is that I sometimes don't listen, and I invalidate other people's lived experiences. For example, a friend might tell me about a micro-aggression they experienced that day, which they believe to be racially motivated, and I find myself inwardly thinking 'surely not?'

And now here we are, in Chapter 17, considering race in a directly meaningful way for the first time. If I weren't white, I wouldn't have been able to wait until Chapter 17 to discuss it. Not being white would have to have been part of this journey from the start.

Imagine if that boy sitting on that orange-swirly carpet were Black. Would he have found his way out of South London and into prestigious universities, to become a world-leading expert on happiness, one day setting off to journey to Bhutan on a bicycle? As it was, being a white person coming from a working-class background, it was already touch and go...

If I were a person of colour, my sense of happiness would have been dictated early on by that identity, and my conforming or not conforming to the social narratives that differ by race and culture. I'm aware that I'm dealing with race late in this book, but the truth of it is that how others perceive someone of my race means I haven't had to face the same challenges in life as others. I have not yet figured out how to write about what I have *not* experienced. Perhaps in the next book, I'll have found a way to bring race in from the start. And so here I am, primarily highlighting the absence of considering race throughout this book. There are countless books out there that tackle uncomfortable truths about race, and I highly recommend them.[7]

Nevertheless, I am certain that the key challenges of happiness are the same for each and every one of us. Some who are of certain races will have greater challenges interacting with their own and others' cultures, and other issues of intersectionality – systemic biases that may keep them trapped in struggles that others may never experience. One thing I hope to have conveyed in this book is that there is plenty to learn about happiness from the many non-white cultures I journeyed through on a bicycle. I have done my best to erase ethnocentrism in the perspective on happiness I present in this book. There are core underlying human needs, and some cultures are, at present, doing a better job of meeting them than others. There is much to learn from every one of us.

My Thai economist friend and I ended up having an important discussion on race. Personally, I found it illuminating, and I'm glad he asked me the question. It also gave me a concrete inroad into highlighting an issue I could have all too easily left out completely.

We didn't solve any issues on race in our discussion, yet in true academic style, we both agreed we'd need an RCT[8] to test some of the hypotheses on race that our conversation had thrown up. I interpreted that to mean that soon my friend would himself be cycling to Bhutan in the near future. He has not yet saddled up. I don't blame him.

As I arrived in Bangkok, the subject of race was still heavy in my thoughts, but I was looking to the future and making concrete plans for the journey ahead.

The plan was to take a quick break from the bicycle to spend time with my brother in Indonesia, in one of the happiness havens I described in Chapter 13, then take a flight to Kolkata and spend a month cycling in India, until I reached Bhutan, just in time for International Day of Happiness on the 20th March. And then I would head home.

At that point, the path ahead seemed easy.

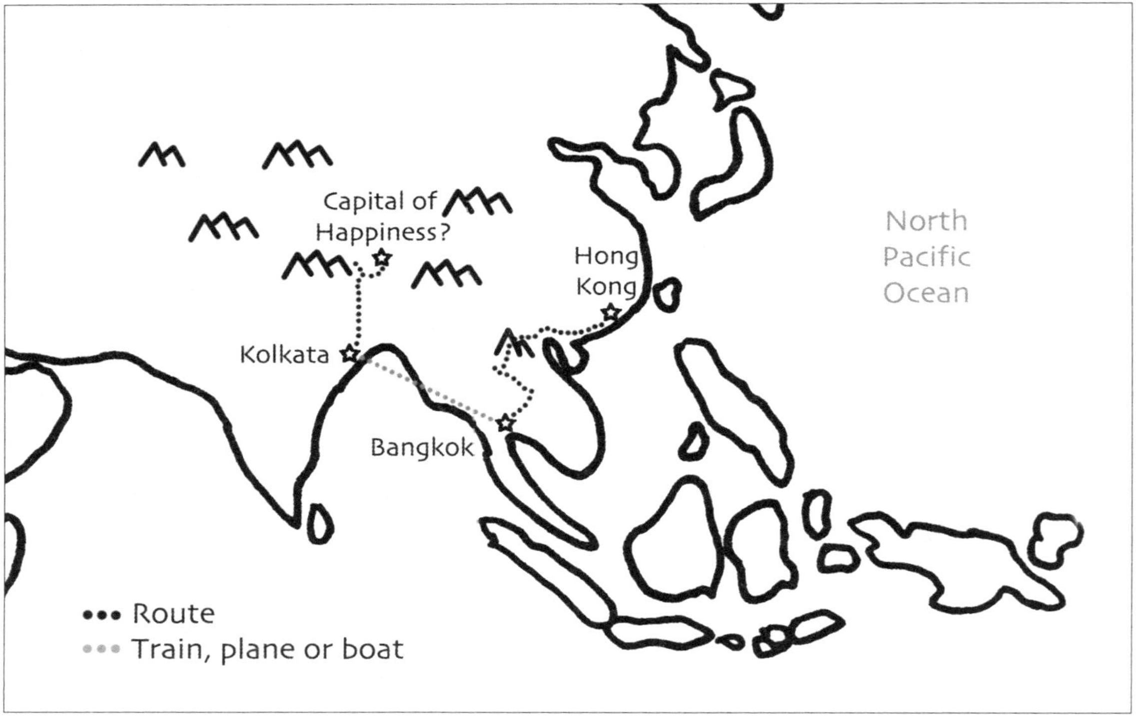

The final push onward to the capital of happiness

CHAPTER 18

One final challenge

"There is one within me who is more myself than my self."
Saint Augustine of Hippo

It is about now that we arrive at the blissful moment I described in the prologue. However, you'll now have a much better sense of the many layers beneath the experience I described. Sometimes I imagine that I wrote this book in that exact moment, and that I'm still there even now. In some ways, of course, I am still there. Other times I've wondered whether the real purpose of this book is to do some justice to a moment that goes beyond words.

What had unexpectedly triggered my moment of bliss was that I had begun playing some music through my phone. There were a few songs that always touched me whenever I played them as I journeyed – they'd remind me of times gone by, and of who I was. Yet, overlaid on top of the time and the person that once was, when the song was first heard, there is the recognition of a self that is now somehow different, that has changed and grown. What was most extraordinary, in that moment looking across those mountains, was that at my core I saw that nothing had ever really changed. Only that in that moment I connected with the timeless wonder of the small five-year-old boy who lives inside of me. A wonder that has always been there, and that has kept me going through the darkest of times.

It was also a moment for others too. Yes, there were the smiles of all those I'd encountered and the help I'd received, but more than anything, those delicate tears were for my Dad.

A father with whom I'd done battle for most of my life. We'd never taken the time to wonder at the world together, until I began this journey. In that moment I could see the five-year-old that he once was too, with his hopes and dreams, sitting on some carpet in some place and time, and his eternal wonder. And I could see with pristine clarity that at his core, he wasn't any different to me. There I was, with a wide-open heart full of compassion and joy – for myself, for my father, and everything beyond. What I was experiencing then was a happiness that went beyond numbers, as all true happiness surely must. Like all *truly* happy moments, it wasn't willed for, it just arose. It arose when I was ready for it. And, with all that I had confronted about myself and the world, I really was ready for it.

At this point, however, I was not quite in Bhutan; although after an epic 18-month journey, I was very close. As I sat there, I thought about how easily things can go awry – a chance encounter sends a journey in a whole different direction. Something slightly different changes everything – be it a different choice, a change in circumstance, or a chance encounter. I wondered about how my journey would have been if I'd not brought that extra pair of underwear that I hadn't really needed after all. Would I have gone slightly quicker at points and had different experiences?

Maybe I would never have met Juan, an intriguing local soul I'd met in a juice bar in Peru, who shared his insights on life during our short encounter. Or Judd in Arizona, who after more than five decades, finally had an opportunity to pass on to me some of the hospitality he'd himself received, when he rode his motorbike from Europe to India back in 1958. Or Lisa; or Bholu; or Yana; or any number of souls I encountered in the briefest of moments. Souls who, upon connection, gave my journey a whole different script. Who else might have come my way instead? Now that I was where I was, I wondered whether being bitten by that stray dog needed to happen, perhaps preventing something far worse further along the road. How different would my journey have been, had the specific challenges I encountered not occurred?

As an academic, I'm not supposed to go for such things, but in that moment my journey felt fated, wholly predetermined. It was as if something inexplicable had been holding me in its loving and tender arms all along, and had finally delivered me to exactly where I needed to be. In my boldness to act in a way that I was compelled to, those mighty forces had come to my aid, just as Goethe, the long-dead German polymath, had told me they would. It could have been another way. Yet it wasn't. It was *this* way.

It was an exquisite moment, and I slept peacefully under the stars that night. The next day, as the mountains greeted my waking yawn, I thought things would just get better and better over the next days as I made my final approach to Bhutan. Of course, it didn't happen that way. That's not how these kinds of stories go. There would have to be one final challenge. A challenge in which all the happiness learnings I'd discovered up to then would be tested, before I could make my full entry into the Kingdom of Happiness. And when this final challenge happened, I was distraught – mostly because I only had myself to blame for it. This was no chance occurrence. However, it had its funny side, so I made sure I laughed about it too. I then presented a deep, resounding smile to the universe, found a love for myself and my bicycle that I never knew I had, and let go one last time of ever arriving to Bhutan on a bicycle. And it was about then that an Indian fellow with a blow-torch showed up!

Mad, old, charming India

There is no question – India brought forth more happiness in me than any other part of the journey. My self-rated daily happiness (8.0 out of 10) and worthwhileness (9.6 out of 10) scores confirm it.

Perhaps it was because India's streets are full of bicycles, and that offered me some reassurance as I rolled on through yet another unfamiliar land. However, it could have been because in India the food is largely vegetarian and, as that is my dietary preference, I feasted there in a way I hadn't in any other part of the world. There were rich aromas and enchanting colours, greeting me around every corner. Or maybe it was the ease with which I seemed to tap into the spiritual and cultural depth of the place – whether it was crossing the path of a holy person or a holy cow, or crossing a holy river, and into a holy city. I was mesmerised.

But most importantly for happiness, as it always turns out to be, there are India's people. Never before have I encountered such a depth of curiosity, nor such an incredibly humbling welcome. Barely a day went by where I didn't get an invite for a chai tea by the side of the road – only five rupees a shot, which equates to about ten cents, or five pence in British money, but a generous gift from a local person. It was my pleasure; and it was their pleasure. Even when there was no shared language (which was often the case in the remote places I travelled through), the desire for human connection was evident, and people did not shy away. Through the intense gazing of eyes, a small smile, or a little wobble of the head. People saw me. And I looked back with curiosity and kindness in return. I really saw them too.

None of this is to say that India could be considered a happy place on the whole. Being able to roll through on a bicycle is far removed from everyday life for most people. When I was interacting with people, there were smiles and laughter, which is what will most likely be offered to a traveller passing through in many parts of world. However, there is much that the foreigner on a bicycle will not see. If we are to consider some of the happiness metrics covered in this book, then India does not do well at all. With respect to evaluative happiness, Indians rate their lives on average 4.0 out of 10, placing them 140th in the world out of 156 countries. Though 69 per cent of Indians say they laughed and smiled a lot during the day, only 59 per cent said they enjoyed themselves. On the positive experiences index, hedonic happiness, therefore, they rank 94th out of 143 countries.

I was not too far removed to have a sense of why. The streets may be full of bicycles, but the roads are manic and harrowing. As electrifying and delightful as the aromas and colours can sometimes be, there are also smells and sights that evoke feelings of disgust and anger. There is spiritual and cultural depth, yet there is also visible poverty and struggle. It ached my heart to witness it. There is great disparity, and one can only imagine what happens to people's frustration and anger behind closed doors. The inequality between genders is undeniable.

You might well ask, therefore, how could I have found personal happiness there? The struggle in peoples' lives that I did and didn't see aside, India is not an easy country to cycle in. India was the most challenging country of the entire journey – demanding everything of me. India asked me to be fully present and aware on her harrowing roads. India asked me to come and dine on her side streets, reminding me to not forget that one hand was to be designated clean for eating, and the other dirty for cleaning my backside. India asked me to lean into her people's well-meaning but intense curiosity, when a moment's pause on the bike would have me surrounded; and a dozen or more eyes would watch my every move – no words sometimes, just stares. I am certain I could not have begun my journey there. I arrived in India on day 483 of my journey on a bicycle, and I was able to meet India exactly as she was. My time there was electrifying; although let's not discount the truth that my high happiness scores were also, in part, because I was in the final throes of a journey for happiness.

A daily cycling life in West Bengal – Kolkata to Siliguri

India is a big place, and I could only take in a fraction of her beauty one moment at a time. Kolkata is in West Bengal, and I didn't need to go out of that state to finally reach the border with Bhutan; however, when I landed in Kolkata, there was still a month until the International Day of Happiness. There was plenty of time. I still didn't know at that point whether I was going to obtain a visa to enter Bhutan. Although I had hopes of going in, I was still preparing myself to get to the border and call the journey complete.

I'd head north – not too fast, but not too leisurely either, until I reached Siliguri, the closest Indian city to the border of Bhutan, just 100 miles by road. If I made it there with enough time, I thought, perhaps I could make a small trip to the Indian state of Sikkim. Sikkim is up in the Himalayas, and neighbours Bhutan, sharing a similar Himalayan Buddhist culture. Like Bhutan, Sikkim was once a kingdom, but became part of India in 1975 and the monarchy was abolished. Some consider it an annexation – an unwelcome occupation by India. Darjeeling, world famous for its tea, is also up in the Himalayas, and before the British came along, was part of Sikkim too. The British involvement was certainly an annexation.

As I rode up through West Bengal, I met some fine people and ate some fine food. Each day I'd start my ride with no real hurry – packing up my tent, checking out of a simple hotel, or a occasionally leaving the home of a stranger that had become a dear friend. The first stop of the day would either be a chai (Indian style tea) with a few sweet biscuits or poori (a deep-fried bread accompanied with some sort of curry). I always went to the busy places, where food turnover is fast and numbers indicate some sort of quality – I ate plenty of street food and was not sick once. Eyes would stare – heads would wobble in a quintessentially Indian way, and smiles would follow. Occasionally someone with just enough English would show up, and we'd talk; others would listen to my unfamiliar words, have their questions given to me in English, and my answers translated back into Hindi or Bengali. Someone might ask for a selfie – a word that transcended the language barrier – and I always obliged. When I felt like my work there was done, I rode on. Lunch was always a thali (a plate of rice with dahl, a few vegetable curries, maybe a chapatti or several), as much as I could eat – continuous refills at no extra cost as is typical in local places. Then I'd find a place in the shade and lie down, with my belly as full as a belly can be. Maybe I'd ride on, maybe not. That would depend on whom I met next.

There was not much to attract mass tourism in the kinds of places I cycled through. That's no bad thing – but in some sense it's a shame, as there is so much to sit watching, and ponder. The practice of being present feels easier in some places, observing the hustle and bustle of daily life, emotions rising and falling. I would sit for hours just supping on a tea, or wandering about the streets, flowing with whatever was before me. No matter where I am in the world, I will never tire of seeing a local market. That's the first place I go to connect to the soul of a place. Life emanates from there – the business of exchange between *people*, rather than the business of profit (often at the expense of people we will never see).

On to that blissful moment

I reached Siliguri with plenty of time to spare. I had two weeks to cover just 100 miles. Siliguri is like many Indian cities – completely chaotic and exceedingly delightful – but a few days were enough. I would have time for a slight detour, to make it to Darjeeling, and then into Sikkim, before sweeping back toward Siliguri and finally onto Bhutan. I expected it to be something like a celebratory victory lap.[1] I expected it to be plain sailing. I smile now for my thoughts then.

It was on my way to Darjeeling from Siliguri that I camped up and had that moment of pure, unadulterated bliss. There were several immediate things that had set up that exact moment in all its perfection. The hard slog of going endlessly upwards into the mountains was part of it. I had extra buoyancy on account of what had happened that morning: for one, I found out that my visa for Bhutan had been approved. Due to my journey and the media I had up to that point attracted, I had made the case for a special visa. It was a long process, that had begun back in December 2018, when I received one of those random emails I sometimes got from someone inspired by my journey. His name was Sangay, and he was from Bhutan. He asked if he could help in any way, and so began a conversation. Sangay was the founder of a tour agency (Nobventure), and he told me about a special media visa I might be eligible for on account of news attention I could bring to the country, and that he wanted to help me to obtain it. We wrote letters, filled in forms, and fine-tuned a travel itinerary to align with the request for this special visa. It took some time, and the process was uncertain – but we were successful, and that was the day I found out.

Also that morning, I'd had a radio interview with Paul Ross (then at UK's talkRADIO) about my journey. It was the second interview I'd recorded with him, and Paul indicated that he wanted to talk to me a third time, on the International Day of Happiness in two weeks' time, when I arrived in Bhutan. Then, before heading into the mountains and up towards Darjeeling, I'd had my head freshly shaved with a razor and my beard neatly trimmed. I wanted to look smart for the victory lap.

That wonderful moment up in the mountains was also preceded by a conversation with four curious local teenagers. They spoke English well, and just before the sunset we took some photos of one another. That perfect beautiful moment was backed up by a day full of happiness – present-focused, and aligned with my journey purpose, connected with others near and far, basking in nature. It was an ideal set-up for the tears that were to come, once I pressed play on the music I had on my phone.

Then came that final challenge

A few days before Siliguri I'd had some problems with my pedal. There was an annoying clicking noise, and looking down, I could see the pedals looked knackered. I'd re-fitted new and good quality ones back in California, and I thought they would last a bit longer than they did. I bought some new ones in Siliguri. These pedals were inexpensive and low quality – though I can't blame that for what would happen. I fitted them myself, but I'd assumed when I bought them (without checking) that I could fit

I was just rolling through and got an invite to this local fiesta in Mexico – August 2018

Help your soul, free your mind

It was hard to believe that I'd reached the Golden Gate bridge all the way up from Argentina – September 2018

The story of how I became a happiness cowboy

On Mexican TV: '*Sólo quiere ser feliz*' – 'He only wants to be happy'. Check out the news broadcast (https://youtu.be/ie1YZW-44FQ), which captures me looking generally tatty, cycling in flipflops (non-matching ones because I used to find odd ones as I journeyed), having enough Spanish to give the interview, and a clear love for tortillas.... this is probably the coolest I'll ever be.

Above: In Mexico and close to the US border – August 2018

Left: High in the mountains of Laos and deciding to get the journey done – January 2019

A Christmas morning with my bank-telling, break-dancing host and his daughters – Vietnam, 25th December 2018

Shortly before a moment of bliss on the way up to Darjeeling – March 2019

Teaching happiness to Indonesian students – February 2019

Behind a photo at the Gross National Happiness Centre in Bhutan. I might be smiling but secretly I'm wishing I didn't get up that day – March 2019

My second day in Bhutan and the most spectacular day I have ever experienced on a bicycle

My Bhutanese guides, Sangay and Kunzang, and I stopping for a picnic on our way up to the Tiger's Nest Monastery

Talking with Bhutanese media about why I journeyed to their country on a bicycle

The journey to Bhutan on a bicycle finally complete but the journey for happiness ongoing

Important men to whom I gave the Bhutanese Khadars I was bestowed with upon arrival

The man who planted the seed for the journey, Matthew Hopwood – April 2019

And a dear father who planted the seed for life – May 2019

Back in Scotland beside one of my favourite lochs, nothing more needed – July 2019

them with a standard Allen key tool; without the correct tool, I could only get the pedals screwed on finger-tight. It wouldn't matter, I thought, because pedals are reversed-threaded; they'd tighten as I rode. I read something online about this to reassure me... I also read another article warning of the danger that insufficiently tightened pedals can strip the screw-thread. I'd just stop at the first mechanic I saw and get them tightened.

I rode up to Darjeeling (at least 2,000 metres of climbing), and then over to Gangtok, the capital of Sikkim, another 2,000 metres of intense climbing. I still hadn't bothered to get those pedals tightened. Other things on my mind, like being fully in that bliss perhaps... Once I came down from Gangtok and was out of Sikkim, I would have only 100 miles before Bhutan, and four days to do it, before my visa began. I'd get to the border and rest up for a day, before cycling into Bhutan and up into more mountains. This was going to be easy.

It was about then that my pedal started feeling strange. I thought I'd better get it tightened immediately, which I did. But it was much too late, and the pedal soon fell off. The screw-thread had been stripped. However, it wasn't the screw-thread of the pedal itself that was stripped, but the crank arm (which the pedal screws into). Now I couldn't just buy a new replacement pedal, and sufficiently tighten it this time. No, I would need to get a whole new crank arm – and I was certain I wouldn't be able to get what I needed locally, or even regionally. The cycling part of this journey looked like it was over. *So near.*

This was gutting. Although I'd not cycled every inch of the way – sometimes taking buses, hitching rides on trucks, taking boats, and of course flying over oceans – it was torment to think that I wouldn't be able to cycle the last 100 miles. It was also comical. I spent a little while, anxious and self-loathing, trying to think of a solution. One of those options included ditching Gulliver back in Siliguri and renting or buying a new bicycle to finish the journey on. Yet what a harsh betrayal! I soon got back into the present, gave a great smile to the universe, and surrendered to whatever awaited me. I'd get to Bhutan alright, and I was resolute that I'd get there with Gulliver. If we had to jump on another bus, like we'd done before in times of difficulty, then that was what we'd do – together. I hadn't fully appreciated the beautifully crafted piece of steel that I sat upon every day until that moment. It was a blessing that it happened, just so that I could feel that level of gratitude.

When I think back to this situation, I find myself thinking once again about fate. I wonder what would have happened if I hadn't surrendered and let go one more time. How would things have otherwise transpired? Would I have managed to locate a man with a blowtorch, confident he could weld my pedal back onto my bicycle? Maybe, maybe not – choice, circumstance, and chance. Whatever the outcome, I would have been okay. It was, after all, never really about cycling to Bhutan. And this felt like a weird final test, to see whether I truly believed that. I sincerely did, which is why I think it worked out in the end.

By the time I found my Indian welder, and he'd got the job done, I had a few hours of light and a full day to make 100 miles. The last few days had been hectic, and I'd not slept that much, but I was reasonably well rested, and I knew that as long as the pedal held up, I could do that kind of distance without too much difficulty. I rode a little into the night on that first day, which was quite scary on Indian roads, but I managed to get a third of the way to Bhutan.

The next morning as I set off, with hot sun to my side, a man named Mukesh pedalled up alongside me. He asked me where I was going. I offered him the biggest grin I've ever given another human being. He had just asked me a question I'd been asked countless times by curious folk on my journey. I'd answer it in one of two ways – with where I was trying to get to ultimately, or with where I was trying to get to that day. I was always torn as to how to answer because I could never be sure which answer would match what the person was after – there had been plenty of places on this journey where people hadn't heard of the tiny Land of the Thunder Dragon. They'd only look at me puzzled, rather than curious. However, on that day, the answer was the same thing regardless. And it was the last time I would be able to say to someone that I was "cycling to Bhutan". It was exactly 507 days since I'd left Edinburgh. As I began cycling those last 70 miles, I wondered at what point I would see the mountains of Bhutan rise up before me. For a long time now, I had been imagining such a moment...

CHAPTER 19

A happy human? On a happy day? In a happy place?

"There is often much more than we can ever know going on beneath the surface of another's triumph. If we are not aware of that possibility, then we might easily become distracted from our own process – to doubt whether how we are feeling is how we should be feeling."
Blog post, 24th March 2019

I had been looking out for mountains in the distance all day long. Those mountains were to signify that Bhutan would at long last be in eyeshot, and I had played and replayed seeing them in my mind many times throughout this journey. I would imagine how I would feel when I finally saw them, with the possibility of the moment becoming more and more real as the months went on. On that final day, I couldn't get the idea of those mountains out of my head – I thought I'd see snow-topped peaks from miles out and they'd get clearer and bigger as I got nearer, and that I'd grow increasingly jubilant.

There were some beautiful moments throughout that final day – there had been meeting Mukesh in the morning, a long lunch stop that left my belly fattened-full with dahl and rice, and plenty of chai tea with curious locals – but every time, once the moment had passed, I'd come back to thinking about those mountains. I squinted into the distance, and wondered when they would finally make their appearance. Surely it had to be soon, I thought. And each time, as I imagined the moment of catching sight of those mountains, I would feel excited.

It wasn't until I reached the outskirts of the Indian-Bhutanese border town of Jaigon that I could trace a very faint outline of something that looked like mountains in the distance. The heat was thick, and visibility wasn't very good. At first, I questioned whether it might just be the shading of clouds. By this point I was tired – not so much from the day's cycling, but from the mental gymnastics I'd been doing trying to stay present. I'd tried my best to curtail my anticipation about what would lie ahead in those mountains, knowing that if I didn't, I had a good chance of tainting the moment when it finally arrived. And so, when I finally accepted that what I could see must be nothing less than Bhutanese mountains, the little elation I felt was loaded with guilt due to what I'd done to myself all day.

Yet, it does get better! Despite not being as thrilled as I had hoped, I then spent the next hour trying to capture a photo of my bike and me, looking ecstatic – as I was supposed to be – in front of those just-about-visible mountains. Whilst I tried to get that perfect picture, I flipped erratically from joy and disbelief at finally being where I was, to frustration and impatience, as each photo didn't quite convey the joy and elation that I thought it should. Deeper down, however, as another part of me watched this dance play out, I was smiling, just as I am now in recollection. Perhaps it needed to be this way. Not so much for the personal relief that this journey was more than a destination, but to remind myself that no matter the depths I go inside, and what I learn from the world, I am simply human – my emotions will flow; I will sometimes grasp and avoid; and I will want things to be different from how they are.

Once I realised I'd taken more than enough photos, recognising later that all of them were perfect in their own way, I found myself a hotel so that I could settle in for the night. It was hard to sleep, and I began to wonder whether, in three days' time – on the International Day of Happiness, when I would declare my journey officially complete – I would be a happy human, on a happy day, in a happy place? One of those was certainly true, but about the other two, I remain dubious.

Was I a happy human in Bhutan?

On the first day in Bhutan, after I'd met my guide outside the hotel in Jaigon and cleared the border, it was midday and already hot. It was then a relentless 2,000+ metre climb on the bicycle, up to a small town called Gedu. I cycled the whole way, fully loaded with all my equipment, despite a car with my guide and driver up ahead. It was a challenging climb, and I was being stubborn – a good trait for getting me to this point in my journey, but completely unnecessary here. Part of me wanted to impress my guide and driver, whilst another part of me wanted to illustrate that I didn't really need such assistance (it is next to impossible to get about Bhutan without a guide, a car, and a driver – as a tourist, it's obligatory). Also, as they were taking photos and filming me, I wanted to have all my equipment with me so that I looked the part.

With hindsight I wish I'd put my bags in the car, because by the time I reached the hotel in Gedu the sun had long set; I was now 2,000 metres up into the sky, and it was cold and dark. I felt happy and satisfied, but I had been exposed to the elements for a long time that day – first the heat, then the cold. Yet, we feasted well, and I began to get to know my guide and driver. Although I tried to get some good sleep that night, I was too excited, and I ended up being on social media for too long and too late. I was trying to make the most of my arrival in Bhutan and share some thoughts with the world.

The next day was the most spectacular I have ever experienced on a bicycle – weaving through the Himalayas – touching the divine inside and out, all day long. There was a lot of bliss on that day. But again, the day was too long, and there was about as much climbing to do as on the first: yet more ups and downs. I was also still fully loaded with all my equipment. Caught up in my excited mind, I chose to ignore how my body was feeling. Plus, I had to be in Paro, because that was where I was supposed to stay for the night. It seems old habits (that we may think we have relinquished long ago – back in Panama for me) do indeed die hard.

By the time I arrived at a very beautiful homestay in Paro, I was again feeling the cold. That evening I took a Bhutanese hot stone bath, which was exquisite. However, again with hindsight, messing around with my body temperature in this way was not a good idea. I then ate a lot and talked for a long while with my hosts, who, it later turned out, refused pay for my stay because they were fascinated by my journey and wanted to contribute to it. Afterwards, there was so much I wanted to do online in preparation for the big day ahead that I did not relax and get much sleep. I was again caught up in the moment. To be honest I was feeling very high, very happy, and I wanted to prolong that state. Grasping. Old habits, again dying hard.

So, when it came to getting up out of bed the next day on International Day of Happiness, I knew I'd suffer physically in the days that followed if I didn't stay exactly where I was. I was certain that I had some sort of illness coming on, yet how could I stay in bed? This was my blaze of glory! (Or so my mind kept telling me.) Despite all the work I'd begun doing back in the Andes at what it means to succeed at something in life, I was not resolute enough in my own notions of success that day to stay in bed. Still a bloody human – I just can't shake it.

At least I didn't cycle the eight miles to the base of the trek up to Bhutan's Tiger's Nest monastery on the morning of the International Day of Happiness as planned. Instead, after giving an interview for the UK's TalkRADIO about my arrival, I let go of my stubbornness and we drove there. Yet there was still the 900-metre hike up to the Himalayan Buddhist monastery, breathtakingly set into the mountains. Although we took things nice and slow, I could feel a sickness definitely on its way.

Halfway up, my guides, Sangay and Kunzang, and I stopped for a picnic. No matter where I am in the world, there is nothing that brings me more happiness – in all senses of the word – than sharing local food with local people. There was the outwardly calm and ever-present Sangay, the joyful and radiant Kunzang, and me, the happiness journeyman from afar. The Tiger's Nest monastery lay in the background above us. We shared simple stories about our lives – recognising all the important elements of each other within ourselves – and we laughed. We laughed a lot. These are the moments.

A little further on, we arrived at the Tiger's Nest, built where Guru Padmasambhava (the 'second Buddha', according to adherents of Tibetan Buddhism) is said to have meditated for three years, three months, three weeks, three days and three hours, back in the 8th century. Words can't describe it. Pictures don't do it justice. I was overcome with a calm and a feeling of awe. I had arrived. And whilst there was something like a happiness, I think in the end it was more like a profound relief. My journey for happiness was complete.

Can there be much happiness on the International Day of Happiness?

As I sat in one of the temples in the Tiger's Nest monastery, I wondered about the significance of my journey for the International Day of Happiness. As I described earlier in the book, I'm sceptical about the purpose of the day. Undoubtedly, I think it is important to draw attention to happiness, yet I am dubious as to how much this day benefits our happiness. The International Day of Happiness has been similar every year since its inception in 2013; on the whole it's a superficial affair. We will read the happiness league tables, based on a lop-sided notion of what happiness is, plus innumerable simplistic media articles about how to find happiness as individuals, with no allusion to a wider societal context that prevents those choices from being made. That may inspire a few people, but is the International Day of Happiness actually asking us to celebrate happiness in an unhelpful way?[1]

I worry that the International Day of Happiness does more

to remind most people that they're not lucky enough to live in one of the 'happiest countries' in the world, nor are they doing all the things they know they should be doing for more happiness in their lives. It's difficult to do those things when the central aim of society is a bigger economy, and support for choices to greater happiness is not available to most people. My sense is that people roll their eyes at the International Day of Happiness, and dismiss it for its triviality. I mean, I know I do. I wonder if people perhaps feel sadder – recognising that they aren't anywhere near as happy as they'd like to be, and that they have little hope of making the changes to their lives that they'd really like.

I think a better use of the day would be to get beyond the narrow definition of happiness and our individual pursuits of it, and question instead how we can construct societies where people support one another and find happiness collectively. As I sat in the temple, I wondered whether my journey might offer a different story for the happiness news agenda that day.

By the time we had descended from the Tiger's Nest monastery, I had three interviews lined up for the next day with Bhutanese journalists. That was exciting and promising, but I didn't really want to do it. I needed a day in bed. Nevertheless, I wrapped up warm and got on with the job in hand – it may not have made me feel good, but it seemed meaningful and purposeful at the time. And then the day after, I had a meeting arranged with the Gross National Happiness Centre. Again, I honoured that commitment. After all, I wanted to learn as much as I could about Bhutanese happiness whilst I was there. I was still flying fairly high on purpose.

And what about the happiness of the Bhutanese – has something been lost in translation?

Not many people that I encountered on my journey had heard of Bhutan. However, those that have, often believe it to be the happiest country on Earth. Whilst Bhutan leads the way when it comes to an integrated approach to happiness policy, this doesn't automatically mean they are the happiest. According to the happiness ranking of countries, Bhutan ranked 95th out of 156 countries in 2019. Their average score on the evaluative happiness was only 5.1 out of 10. This doesn't make for much of a compelling case for happiness policy.[2]

However, having now journeyed to Bhutan on a bicycle, and met those working in policy there, I have a far richer understanding of what they are doing. Firstly, Bhutan is largely a subsistence economy, and so is unlikely to do well when citizens are asked about evaluative happiness. This kind of happiness tends to depend on the achievement of goals and expectations around what one supposedly *ought* to have achieved in life, particularly in the economic domain, and it does not necessarily mean that other kinds of happiness are high. Unfortunately, there is no internationally publicly available comparable data for the moment-to-moment happiness to compare with other countries, as I did in Chapter 7. However, if it were available, it wouldn't surprise me if moment-to-moment happiness was not very high in Bhutan either. People's interactions with one another didn't exude as much warmth compared to those I saw in Latin America, for example.

One important thing that I did learn upon arrival in Bhutan was that the word for happiness in Dzongkha, the Bhutanese language, is '*dekyid*' (commonly translated into English simply as 'happiness'). However, *dekyid* means something much more than happiness as English-speaking people might understand it, i.e., it goes beyond smiling and laughing or achieving certain goals. A more accurate translation would be peace or tranquillity. The Bhutanese conception of happiness is steeped in the country's cultural and spiritual values, rather than how it is understood in the English language. Discussions as to what constitutes happiness to the Bhutanese have taken place within the country over decades (though not necessarily across the whole society), to refine what exactly they are trying to improve. As such, happiness – as the Bhutanese conceive it – is neither the evaluative happiness nor the moment-to-moment hedonic happiness.

Dekyid is happiness as understood by the Bhutanese themselves, rather than through the lens of western academics, as I once was. As I found out from the Gross National Happiness Centre, the Bhutanese notion of happiness is underpinned by four contributing pillars: sustainable and equitable socio-economic development, environmental conservation, preservation and promotion of culture, and good governance. Whether a policy is enacted in Bhutan or not depends on how it is considered to influence each of these four pillars. A policy that only benefits the economy, without considering repercussions to the environment, culture, or governance, will not be enacted. A new policy initiative must consider all four pillars, and sufficiently balance costs and benefits in a broader sense, not just the financial sense.

There is also the Gross National Happiness Index, which seeks to track happiness across Bhutanese society. To do this, the Bhutanese set goals and measures against nine different agreed-upon outcomes. These include living standards, education, health, environment, community vitality, time-use, psychological wellbeing, good governance, and cultural resilience and promotion. These are similar outcomes to the ones in the wellbeing frameworks from Chapter 14, such as the OECD's Better Life Index, the Canadian Index of Wellbeing, or Scotland's National Performance Framework. I'm sure few would disagree that these aspects of life are all important contributors to happiness, however it is conceived. With this index, the Bhutanese track national happiness levels, as well as how different regions compare, and importantly highlight where policy could be directed to improve the Bhutanese kind of happiness – *dekyid* – the most.

One particularly curious element of Bhutan's index is that they discern sufficiency levels. Someone is deemed 'happy' (to have *dekyid*) if they attain sufficiency in at least six of the nine Gross National Happiness outcomes. Denoting sufficiency levels is important, because it asks us to ponder what is sufficient to live well. It also means that policy is directed towards ensuring all can live well, rather than aiming for continued improvement in areas of life that exceed sufficiency levels, to the detriment of other areas of human happiness. I think many people would agree that having some concept of material sufficiency is desperately needed in the world today.

What is important about Bhutan is that happiness is addressed at the societal level, and has been discussed, defined, and implemented into society in a way that makes sense to the Bhutanese. It is not an individualistic pursuit of happiness. They have defined their collective journey for happiness, and it is unique to them and their culture. It is their own sense of happiness that matters more to them than where they stand according to a narrow definition of happiness. That's not to say we should ignore how they score on a range of internationally comparable metrics. It's a question of balance, and a one-size globalisation agenda of the supposed good life does *not* fit all, nor should it.

Some final thoughts on Bhutan

After my meeting at the Gross National Happiness Centre, I went back to my hotel and sank straight into bed. I spent the whole day there. At some point I wrote in my journal:

> 22nd March 2019: Here it is – The End. I sit in a hotel room overlooking Thimpu Dzong – mountains in the background and sun in the sky. This is Bhutan, this is my final day. I am a bit sad. Mostly because these last few days I have been ill, and my mind tells me I didn't make the most of my time here. But I did my best. And that is always enough.

While the first, second and third day of my time in Bhutan had been spectacular, I over-stretched myself, and on the final three days I suffered for it. Although, perhaps it was worth it, because many months later, when I consulted my happiness scores – how happy, anxious, and worthwhile I felt during each day – it turned out they were on average very high. Overall, Bhutan was the country in which I had my second-highest levels of happiness on my journey: both the laughing and smiling kind (7.7 out of 10) and the purposeful and meaningful kind (9.2 out of 10).

So, it turns out that after my long journey to Bhutan – though, as described above, it is unclear as to whether the Bhutanese are, in truth, happy – I certainly was a happy human upon arriving in Bhutan. But I am pleased that my journey was about more than the happiness I experienced upon arrival at my final destination. If the happiness I personally experienced when I arrived was all this journey had been about, I don't think it would have been worth the journey. I was happy in Bhutan, sure, but I am glad I had a concrete purpose at the core of my journey, that extended far beyond moment-to-moment happiness and feeling satisfied from an achievement.

That being said, I felt very sad upon leaving Bhutan. I had spent over 500 days trying to reach the place, and only six days there. That was how long I had requested for the visa; I didn't know what it would be like in Bhutan, and I hadn't wanted to take advantage of anyone that helped me. Though the US$250 daily visa fee had been waived for me, there were still costs to be covered. I'd have liked to have been completely self-supported, as I had been throughout my journey, and had I been able to do so, my costs would have been minimal. However, that is not how it works in Bhutan, because as a tourist you *must* have a guide and you won't get very far without one. There were the transport costs, guide and driver fees, accommodation, and food to pay for. Sangay, founder of Nobventure, who had helped me obtain the visa, had been willing to bear many of those costs himself, and also took me to places where people were willing to host me for a night or two at no charge. Six days in total seemed to strike a good balance with everyone's needs. It would be enough time to do what was necessary.

It was strange, because in Bhutan, I travelled in a way I

hadn't on any other part of my journey. I was fully supported. Whilst I was a little disappointed at not having the freedom I normally would have, it was also something of a relief not to have to fret about practical matters, such as whether I'd find somewhere peaceful to sleep, or what I was eating. It is telling that, anxiety-wise, my daily score in Bhutan was the second-lowest of any country I travelled through, at 3.0 out of 10. In Bhutan, I had only my social media feed to worry about. My guides had the rest covered, and that enabled me to get on with what I needed to do whilst there.

I am generally sceptical about guided tours, because travelling in that way, it can be difficult to find genuine connection with local people and their culture. Whilst there might be some safety in taking a guided tour (safety that many are willing to pay for), there are always things that get missed out. We may see all of the tourist attractions that are supposed to be seen in a place, but often it will be at a rapid pace, and it is all those bits in between where the real beauty is. It is those unplanned elements that are often more interesting, becoming treasured memories, and bringing the greatest happiness – in the moment and upon recollection. Perhaps in one of these in-between places, an old man might shuffle up, look us in the eyes, and smile. Perhaps he'll offer a tea, as we share a view over some mountains. Maybe a local person will take us under his or her wing for a few days, and treat us as their honoured guest, shown to friends and family around their village with pride.

On account of the visa cost, there are very few tourists in Bhutan. The Bhutanese get on with their daily lives, and therefore, interactions – when they do happen – feel sincere. There is no hidden agenda. They are a welcoming people. People come to the country individually rather than in droves, as is often the case elsewhere in places that were once beautiful – and Bhutanese society as a whole sees some benefit in this protection. Though Bhutan costs a lot to visit, it certainly does not feel commercialised.

What I found there is that the guide and driver take the place of locals, taking a tourist under their wing for a short period of time whilst they journey in the unfamiliar land. They invited me to immerse with them in their culture. This temporary adoption is a rare and special thing when journeying, and something I received a lot throughout my journey, by virtue of how and why I travelled. However, it is in this way that a deeper understanding and respect for the Bhutanese way of life comes. I was curious, and I asked many questions of Sangay and Kunzang. Sometimes we talked quite candidly about our lives, and we became friends.

The best word to describe my time in Bhutan is 'surreal'. On the one hand, there was the sheer intensity of emotion, with me not quite believing I was where I was; on the other, that surreal feeling is just what Bhutan seems to evoke. For six days, it felt as if I had literally stepped into a dream world, something artificially constructed for a movie set, or a photo-shopped scene created entirely on computer. Bhutan is without doubt otherworldly, and when I was dropped off back at the same hotel in Jaigon from which I'd left six days before, staying in the exact same room, I wondered whether I'd been in Bhutan at all.

As I sat in that room, I began pondering the dream I had been living. It wasn't only the last days in Bhutan to consider, but the entire 18 months since I'd handed in my notice at work and embarked on this journey. The main thought that burned away at me, too quickly and too fiercely in that hotel, was, "Well, what next?" What do you do after you've spent a year and a half cycling to Bhutan? Or for that matter, what does anyone do, after any life-defining event? Well, we have to go somewhere we feel safe, somewhere familiar, with people who know us and love us, and start trying to make some sense of what we've just experienced. It was, at last, time to go home.

CHAPTER 20

Returning home with a touch of magic

"I do love this journey, and it has been the making of me. But I do fantasise about being at home and enjoying warm hugs, familiar places, and ease to go into a shop and get what I need – stability, familiar sounds, and a damn good rave up!"
Journal entry, 12th January 2019

Whenever the moon sat high above me, I would feel deeply reassured. I loved the nights when its glow lit up the entire landscape around me, or when I could still see it in the light of day, as I rode out westward in the mornings. Much like the orange-swirly carpet I had in my room as a small boy, I could gaze at the moon for hours at a time. Especially the full moon – when the sun was shining at its fullest onto it from the other side of our planet. The moon would bring a warmth to the small tent of mine, as I lay down to sleep in the many spectacular places I'd call home for a night on the way to Bhutan.

Some of my most beautiful rides as I journeyed were in the middle of the night. There were a few times when it had been so hot in the day that I'd wake up early and head out on my bicycle in the early hours of the morning – perhaps around 4am, but sometimes as early as 3am when I was having difficulty sleeping. However, there were also a few times when there was a full moon in the sky, and I'd ride most of the night just for the hell of it. There is nothing quite like cycling when the moon is shining the way. There is an otherworldliness to things. On my journey it was a bit scary and eerie – some might say risky

– but boy was it exhilarating! There was always magic in the air on such rides.

The first time I rode on a full moon was in Peru. Crazy as it sounds, even to me as I check the dates and write about it here, I did my first full moon ride two weeks after the dog bite. This was me dealing with my fears full and head on. I had descended from the mountains by then, and I was in the jungle for the first time. I was well on my way to catching the boat that would take me along the Amazon to reach the jungle city of Iquitos, where I would rest for nearly a month. More than anything, I'd gotten up early to beat the sweltering heat of the day. However, it just so happened to be a full moon that night. It was thrilling. There was no-one except me – and whatever happened to be lurking in the green jungle either side of me. I tried not to think about the lurking things too much, and just stuck to the middle of the road, letting the moon guide me safely. It did.

Two months later I did a similar ride, this time in Colombia. I had a big climb to do that day up to Medellín (2,000+ metres) and I didn't want the heat to drain me early on. Other than a few trucks passing by, it was just me, the road, and the moon. It was one of the most enchanting rides of my life, and pure ecstasy, when I finally stopped to have breakfast and watch the sun light up the valley below which I'd been riding through. The next time I did another full moon ride was close to a year later, in Laos. It's not often that the night warmth, reasonably safe roads, my courage, and a decent-sized and visible moon combined to make such a ride possible. These rides were few and far between, and that kept them special.

More than anything, though, the moon would make me think of home. There are very few things that a person can look at in this world of ours and have some certainty that at least one other soul will be similarly mesmerised by. The moon sits in the sky shining over all of us – it always has, and always will. It asks for nothing, but takes care to give its reflecting light to beings like you and me, all over the planet. Whenever I sat alone in my tent, I'd watch the moon and start to wonder who else I knew would be looking at it, in that exact same moment. Would the moon be visible to them, at whatever part of the day or night they were in, on the other side of the world? I'd picture them in their maybe-moonlit lands, and imagine how they might be feeling. The moon was a tonic for my aloneness in my temporary tent home, but it also became a representation to me of a deep longing for a real home.

Longing for a home

I wrote this by hand under moonlight, to a fellow moon-lover about home:

> I look at the river before me. Perhaps home is here where I am. Home has become something of a feeling to me – where I can relax into myself and just be. In part, that feeling is about me. I feel this sense of home a lot on the bike and when I'm in the tent. But there is something about the movement element of that feeling of home that I am not satisfied with. I come back to this feeling of home inside of me, when what is outside of me is not supportive, not relaxing, toxic even; much as I feel it has been throughout much of my life. For too long, I have felt it necessary to retreat from places and people, to come back to that home feeling inside, rather than feel it in relation to places or people. Yet, over the years I have found places and people where I have that feeling, and I don't need to be so guarded, where I can relax into who and what I am. Nature helps me to do that. Unconditionally supportive relationships – family, friends, and loves too. And so, returning home after this journey can't only be about that feeling inside – I need to have a life where I am supported by everything around me – the land, the people. I feel that in Scotland, and it feels like home to me in a way nowhere else ever has. My relationship with the land and the people has taken years to develop, and there has been much intention around that

development. It is not perfect, but I must come back. I do not want to keep moving forever.

On a bicycle it got easier and easier to be and do the things essential for happiness that I've described in this book – to let go of expectations, develop resilience in the face of adversity, be more present-focused, confront anxieties, receive people's help, face my life traumas, unconditionally accept all before me, and journey for a purpose beyond myself. It was my everyday life on a bicycle, and I'd sometimes think about staying on my bicycle long after I'd reached Bhutan. It was tempting. Yet, what I wanted more than anything was to feel at home – not just in myself, but in the land under my feet and the people in my arms. That doesn't come from moving around all the time, exciting though it may be. I needed to integrate all the happiness lessons that I'd learnt on this journey to Bhutan into a life for myself in Scotland, the place that I set out from all those months ago. I'd prolonged that return for a life-affirming reason in Canada, but there was no solid reason not to return after I'd made it to Bhutan. I was certain that I would make a home for myself when I returned, and also that I could use my knowledge and skills to make life a little better for others too.

I could have cycled most of the way back. If I had, I'm sure I would have met amazing people, co-created many happy moments, had more adventures, maybe had a better story – Bhutan: there and back with happiness on a bicycle – and no doubt, I would have learnt more about happiness. However, I also realised that it would have been more of the same. Although, like many things, it would have been nice to say I'd done it, I didn't actually *need* to do it. There was no real sense to it. It was in the Americas where all the personal work had taken place. I had continued onto Asia to do the wider work. After Bhutan, I wanted to return and integrate all I'd learnt on my journey into my everyday life.

I did want to give myself a little bit of time on the bicycle back in the UK, though, and so I booked a direct flight from

Delhi to London. From there I would pedal back to Scotland, and begin making a little sense of a unique and special time in my life.

A little bit of Bhutan in Britain

The day before I finally rolled back into Scotland on my bicycle has to be one of the strangest days of my entire life.

It was May, nearly two months after I'd arrived in Bhutan. To make the direct flight back from Delhi it had been all buses and train rides. From London, I cycled back to Scotland which, in times gone by, I would have thought was a really long way to go on a bike. I caught up with some family and friends along the way, and each time, I left with a small part of me wanting to stay with these people forever. I also had a very decent amount of help from strangers. Something had clearly shifted in me while I was away. Much less fear, far more receptive. I think other people were better able to see that in me now.

The last day before I crossed back into Scotland from England was uncanny. Not only did I end the day in desperate need of medical attention, but I also had my worst bicycle accident since I'd left. The two incidences were completely unrelated – the medical attention was not as a result of the bicycle accident. However, before I reveal too much about those incidents, let me recount the story of some strangers I met, before each of these things happened.

First, there was Jim, a retired man in his 70s, who was out for a Sunday ride up the coast. I was with him when I came off the bicycle. It really wasn't a bad fall at all. In my distraction, going through a seaside town not too far north of Newcastle, I didn't get on my brakes quick enough and ran into the back of him. I ended up with a slight graze as I hit the ground at low speed. It was my worst bicycle accident of the entire journey though. Jim and I rode about 15 miles and stopped to take lunch together about halfway through. He insisted on paying for our lunch, and to his delight, I obliged him.

Later that day, I met Dawn, a woman who happened to pop out of her home just as I was passing by. I stopped and asked whether there was anywhere close by I could call in and get a cup of tea, a café or something. It's true that it was unlikely there'd be anything in this tiny village in Northumbria, and I knew that. That's not to say I was contriving anything per se, but after my months on a bicycle, I do know that there are some questions that a curious looking stranger passing through can ask that may invite in a little magic. Dawn took one look at my bicycle, saw my smile, and then, with little hesitation said, "My house."

It is important to say that this happened *before* she had seen the flag of Bhutan, swaying from the back of my bicycle. Most people are unfamiliar with the Bhutanese flag and pay it little heed; Dawn, however, was excited by the flag when she saw it. It is, of course, a beautiful flag, inscribed with the Thunder Dragon. However, Dawn knew exactly what the flag represented. A committed Buddhist, she had, once upon a time, been to Bhutan herself. She had brought back a Bhutanese prayer wheel, now installed by the entrance to her home, and she encouraged me to give that prayer wheel a good spin as I entered. I was exactly where I needed to be. I had that cup of tea and then, when her partner arrived home, there followed an invitation to stay for dinner. I ate dinner, and then came the invitation to stay the night.

It was then that I thought to show them my leg, and get their opinion. The leg had been slowly swelling up for some time, and it was becoming painful. Stubborn and persistent as I am, I kept riding, avoiding medical attention for as long as possible, hoping it would sort itself out, as many things do. It seemed to be a reaction to some sort of bite. There was a grave look from my hosts when I showed them, and they suggested I get medical treatment as soon as possible. Wonderful people that they were, they drove me to an NHS walk-in centre ten miles away, and I was treated there and then. I was fit enough to reach Scotland the next day, but somewhere along the way

– maybe at the walk-in centre, maybe before – I picked up the potentially lethal MRSA infection, and the wound soon turned raw and angry. The following weeks back in Edinburgh were a painful worry, and just like when those Bhutanese mountains came into sight, that triumphant feeling I had long imagined I might have upon my return didn't come. It was another lesson about expectations.

There was also a lesson about how to tell a story. Over the following months, as the wound healed, I would recount this recent bite story, alongside many of the other stories I had begun piecing together from my journey that people enjoyed hearing about. With this bite, however, I found it always made for a better story when I didn't mention anything about where I'd got bitten and by what. The drama would build as I recounted the struggle until at some point someone would have to ask me by what and where. No-one expected me to say that it was the result of a horsefly bite in Lincolnshire. Bloody Lincolnshire! A horsefly!

EPILOGUE

A journey for all journeys

"There was a time when I would have looked at someone like me and just thought I could not do that. And now I am doing it. There is nothing special about me."
Journal entry, December 14th 2017

When I set off for Bhutan on my bicycle, I wasn't as clued-up as this book may imply. At the beginning, and for much of the journey, I was bogged down with anxieties, sadness, and shame. At the time, I didn't really understand just how besieged I was. I thought a lot of what I felt was innately *me* – rather than the way I had learnt to become in this world. It became clearer, as the journey progressed through new lands and cultures, that much of how I experienced the world was my way of coping in the particular culture I was born into. If you like analogies, it was the kind of water I was swimming in. As David Foster Wallace once described: "It is about simple awareness – awareness of what is so real and essential, so hidden in plain sight all around us, that we have to keep reminding ourselves, over and over: This is water, this is water." It took 18 months to grasp the thickness of the water I had been in, and its currents – and that time again to put what I'd learnt into words.

As things were happening during my journey, I often struggled to make sense of them. In fact, when I began, I saw the journey more about having some adventures, rather than a journey that would transform me. Hence my original #AdventuresInHappiness hashtag, which was also the title of my then personal blog on happiness, through which I'd attempted to dispel some of my gloom as an academic. Over time, my cycle adventure to Bhutan evolved. Embarking on the journey may not have made complete sense in my head at the time I set off, but I knew deep within that it was mine to embark upon, and I could not refuse it. What I knew then, as much as I know now, was that it would have been a glaring travesty not to have tried. My instinct as to how to act – whether it be accepting someone's help or staying in a place a little longer – became clearer as I became more present with myself and those around me.

There were key moments of realisation, many of which I have described in this book – such as suddenly recognising that this journey, were I ever to complete it, would take twice as long than initially expected, and I was okay with that. And as the miles clicked by, I began to understand more about the processes that were going on within me, in response to what I was experiencing. Many of these processes I was familiar with, thanks to the research career I had left behind, and I meaningfully mapped my experiences onto them. Other experiences were less familiar, and at times scary. Yet they were all just regular human processes, that will no doubt be taking place somewhere within you, as well as within me.

There was no intention to write a book when I returned. All I came back knowing was that if I wanted to be happy in life, then I would need to see the *water* for what it was, and apply what I'd learnt from my journey to my everyday life. I thought that if I could create a journey centred on happiness, then I might be able to build a life centred on happiness too. At the time, what I knew for sure was that meant leaning into others, being mindful of my own and others' anxieties, and not to rush into anything without first having a clear awareness of what is.[1] Indeed, that is what I did. And not without struggle. It was my father – who for me was the real hero of this journey – who kept telling me I ought to write a book. He doesn't really read that much, and so I didn't take the idea that seriously. Maybe, I thought – but I didn't think it the best use of my energy, and I'm not one for shoulds or ought-tos. I gave a few talks about my journey in the summer of 2019, and people were really curious about what I had to say. Others, whom I didn't know, told me that they'd love to read a book about it. I began to get a better sense of the journey through sharing my experiences with others – a story here and there, a new blog post, and the key ingredient: giving myself time and space. Actually, I mooched about on my bicycle in Scotland for some time, appreciating the land and its people in a way I had not done before.

Somewhere amongst all this I began getting a concrete understanding about my wider purpose in life. The only sense I could make of my academic career when I got back was that it had been a great set up for the curious adventures of an unhappy happiness academic. My journey probably wouldn't have been quite as interesting to others had I just been some random man that cycled to Bhutan. And why would someone cycle to Bhutan anyway? I had a solid back-story, and many people with whom I talked found the irony that had set me off enticing. Yet, I knew that my wider life purpose was to bring more happiness to the world, and what I did next with my life needed to have that at its core. By then, I had a few ideas about what I could do – be it a return to academia, retraining as a mental health care practitioner, volunteering, meditating on a mountain, working in wellbeing policy – but my over-riding question was what would be the most effective way I could serve that wider purpose. What would be the best use of me? I had no attachment as to how I would do that – I was interested in the end, not the means. The calling would come when it was time, and I would be ready.

About six months after returning, it became clear that the next step was to write a book – the book that you've nearly finished reading. It took me another six months to write a first draft. That was a whole different journey – day-in, day-out, largely stationary in front of a screen, rather than on two wheels zipping from town to town. I earnt my keep by pet-sitting whilst people went on holiday – looking after cats and dogs. (I've made my peace with dogs.) However, the really curious thing was that everything I've written about in this book about my journey for happiness to Bhutan also seemed to apply when I was writing this book – letting go of expectations about the outcome, developing resilience to deal with adversity, being more present-focused, confronting my anxieties, receiving people's help, facing personal life trauma, staying aware of societal encouragements to make mistakes, unconditionally accepting all before me, and ensuring my actions were meaningful.

About March 2020, there was a first draft, and I had a meeting with a keen publisher lined up. It was then that the COVID-19 pandemic hit, and then we all collectively embarked on a whole different journey. For me, life pretty much crumpled – I had no home at the time (I got stuck in someone's house with their pets and no idea if and when they'd return) and the little bit of paid work I'd started getting completely dried up. Yet, it was uncanny: the learnings from my book were completely relevant throughout the ordeal. This time it wasn't just me slowing down – more people had the time and space to consider what was really important in their lives. Did our super-fast, busy lives of service to the economy bring us much in the way of health and happiness?

Conversations about what mattered began to shift. In fact, we began to have more heartfelt conversations with one another entirely. Who, when asked how they were, could really answer with honesty that they were doing just fine? Struggles came to the surface, ones that we had long known were there, and some had it far worse than others. It became okay to not be okay. Personally, my writing languished – on account of the international lockdowns, the meeting with that keen publisher was cancelled, and their interest died away. I would often spend my days wondering what the point was. But I kept as true as I could to what I had learnt on my bicycle journey – I stayed present, I allowed my anxieties an outlet, I stayed connected with the people I loved, and I remained in touch with what was most meaningful to me. All the happiness lessons in this book still applied, because these are happiness lessons that transcend time and space; and I guarantee they'll be crucial for your own journey for happiness too. I only wish I'd learnt them a little bit earlier in life, or that someone had given that little five-year-old boy in me a few tricks to help him through. But that wasn't my journey for happiness; what you've read was *my* journey. Now, more importantly, what's yours? Or deeper still, what's ours?

"We are the music-makers
We are the dreamers of dreams"[2]

References

Abdallah, S., Thompson, S., Michaelson, J., Marks, N., & Steuer, N., (2009) *The Happy Planet Index 2.0: Why Good Lives Don't Have to Cost the Earth*, New Economics Foundation.

Abramowitz, J. S., Deacon, B. J., & Whiteside, S. P. (2019). *Exposure Therapy for Anxiety: Principles and Practice*, Guilford Publications.

Agaibi, C. E., & Wilson, J. P., (2005) 'Trauma, PTSD, and resilience: A review of the literature' in *Trauma, Violence, & Abuse*, 6, 195–216.

Andreoni, J., (1990) 'Impure altruism and donations to public goods: A theory of warm-glow giving' in *The Economic Journal*, *100*, 464–477.

Akala, (2019) *Natives: Race and Class in the Ruins of Empire,* Two Roads.

Baumeister, R. F., & Leary, M. R., (1995) 'The need to belong: Desire for interpersonal attachments as a fundamental human motivation' in *Psychological Bulletin*, *117*, 497.

Becker, G. S., & Murphy, K. M., (1988) 'A theory of rational addiction' in *Journal of Political Economy, 96*, 675–700.

Blanchflower, D. G., & Oswald, A. J., (2004) 'Well-being over time in Britain and the USA' in *Journal of Public Economics, 88*, 1,359–1,386.

Bleidorn, W., Kandler, C., Riemann, R., Angleitner, A., & Spinath, F. M., (2009) 'Patterns and sources of adult personality development: Growth curve analyses of the NEO PI-R scales in a longitudinal twin study' in *Journal of Personality and Social Psychology, 97*, 142.

Bonanno, G. A., (2004) 'Loss, trauma, and human resilience: Have we underestimated the human capacity to thrive after extremely aversive events?' in *American Psychologist, 59*, 20.

Boyce, C. J., (2014) 'However you spend it, money isn't the key to happiness' in *The Conversation*. Retrieved on 18th December 2021 http://theconversation.com/however-you-spend-it-money-isnt-the-key-to-happiness-25289

Boyce, C. J., (2018) 'Why I quit my day job researching happiness and started cycling to Bhutan' in *The Conversation*. Retrieved on 18th

December 2021 http://theconversation.com/why-i-quit-my-day-job-researching-happiness-and-started-cycling-to-bhutan-105531

Boyce, C. J., Brown, G. D., & Moore, S. C., (2010) 'Money and happiness: Rank of income, not income, affects life satisfaction' in *Psychological Science, 21*, 471–475.

Boyce, C. J., Daly, M., Hounkpatin, H. O., & Wood, A. M., (2017) 'Money may buy happiness, but often so little that it doesn't matter' in *Psychological Science, 28*, 544–546.

Boyce, C. J., & Oswald, A. J., (2012) 'Do people become healthier after being promoted?' in *Health Economics, 21*, 580–596.

Boyce, C. J., & Wood, A. M., (2010) 'Money or mental health: The cost of alleviating psychological distress with monetary compensation versus psychological therapy' in *Health Economics, Policy & Law, 5*, 509.

Boyce, C. J., & Wood, A. M., (2011a) 'Personality and the marginal utility of income: Personality interacts with increases in household income to determine life satisfaction' in *Journal of Economic Behavior & Organization, 78*, 183–191.

Boyce, C. J., & Wood, A. M., (2011b) 'Personality prior to disability determines adaptation: Agreeable individuals recover lost life satisfaction faster and more completely' in *Psychological Science, 22*, 1,397–1,402.

Boyce, C. J., Wood, A. M., Banks, J., Clark, A. E., & Brown, G. D., (2013) 'Money, well-being, and loss aversion: Does an income loss have a greater effect on well-being than an equivalent income gain?' in *Psychological science, 24*, 2,557–2,562.

Boyce, C. J., Wood, A. M., & Brown, G. D., (2010) 'The dark side of conscientiousness: Conscientious people experience greater drops in life satisfaction following unemployment' in *Journal of Research in Personality, 44*, 535–539.

Boyce, C. J., Wood, A. M., Daly, M., & Sedikides, C., (2015) 'Personality change following unemployment' in *Journal of Applied Psychology, 100*, 991–1,011.

Boyce, C. J., Wood, A. M., Delaney, L., & Ferguson, E., (2017) 'How do personality and social structures interact with each other to predict important life outcomes? The importance of accounting for personality change' in *European Journal of Personality*, *31*, 279–290.

Boyce, C. J., Wood, A. M., & Ferguson, E., (2016a) 'For better or for worse: The moderating effects of personality on the marriage-life satisfaction link' in *Personality and Individual Differences*, 97, 61–66.

Boyce, C. J., Wood, A. M., & Ferguson, E., (2016b) 'Individual differences in loss aversion: Conscientiousness predicts how life satisfaction responds to losses versus gains in income' in *Personality and Social Psychology Bulletin*, 42, 471–484.

Boyce, C. J., Wood, A. M., & Powdthavee, N., (2013) 'Is personality fixed? Personality changes as much as "variable" economic factors and more strongly predicts changes to life satisfaction' in *Social Indicators Research*, 111, 287–305.

Boyle, M., (2010) *The Moneyless Man: A Year of Freeconomic Living*, Simon and Schuster.

Brickman, P., Coates, D., & Janoff-Bulman, R., (1978) 'Lottery winners and accident victims: Is happiness relative?' in *Journal of Personality and Social Psychology*, 36, 917–927.

Brockmann, H., Delhey, J., Welzel, C., & Yuan, H., (2009) 'The China puzzle: Falling happiness in a rising economy' in *Journal of Happiness Studies*, 10, 387–405.

Brown, B., (2017) *Braving the Wilderness: The Quest for True Belonging and the Courage to Stand Alone*, Random House.

Busby, M., (2018) 'Social media copies gambling methods to create psychological cravings' in *The Guardian*. Retrieved on 18th December 2021 http://www.theguardian.com/technology/2018/may/08/social-media-copies-gambling-methods-to-create-psychological-cravings

Buunk, A. P., & Gibbons, F. X., (2007) 'Social comparison: The end of a theory and the emergence of a field' in *Organizational Behavior and Human Decision Processes*, 102, 3–21.

Carnegie, D., (2006) *How to Win Friends and Influence People*, Vermilion.

Campbell, J., (1949) *The Hero with a Thousand Faces*, New World Library.

Capaldi, C. A., Passmore, H.-A., Nisbet, E. K., Zelenski, J. M., & Dopko, R. L., (2015) 'Flourishing in nature: A review of the benefits of connecting with nature and its application as a wellbeing intervention' in *International Journal of Wellbeing*, 5, Article 4.

Christakis, N. A., & Fowler, J. H., (2009) *Connected: The Surprising Power of Our Social Networks and How They Shape Our Lives*,

Little, Brown Spark.

Cialdini, R. B., (2007) *Influence: The Psychology of Persuasion* (Vol. 55), Collins New York.

Clark, A. E., d'Ambrosio, C., & Ghislandi, S., (2016) 'Adaptation to poverty in long-run panel data' in *Review of Economics and Statistics, 98*, 591–600.

Clark, A. E., Diener, E., Georgellis, Y., & Lucas, R. E., (2008) 'Lags and leads in life satisfaction: A test of the baseline hypothesis' in *The Economic Journal, 118*, F222–F243.

Clark, L. A., Watson, D., & Leeka, J., (1989) 'Diurnal variation in the positive affects' in *Motivation and Emotion, 13*, 205–234.

Clarke, J. A., (2018) *Adventures In Happiness: A True Story of Travel, Change, and Adventure*, self-published.

Crawford, J. R., & Henry, J. D., (2004) 'The Positive and Negative Affect Schedule (PANAS): Construct validity, measurement properties and normative data in a large non-clinical sample' in *British Journal of Clinical Psychology*, 43, 245–265.

Crespo, R. F., & Mesurado, B., (2015) 'Happiness economics, eudaimonia and positive psychology: From happiness economics to flourishing economics' in *Journal of Happiness Studies, 16*, 931–946.

Csikszentmihalyi, M., (1990) *Flow: The Psychology of Optimal Experience* (Vol. 1990), Harper & Row New York.

Daly, M., Boyce, C., & Wood, A., (2015) 'A social rank explanation of how money influences health' in *Health Psychology*, 34, 222.

Di Tella, R., Haisken-De New, J., & MacCulloch, R., (2010) 'Happiness adaptation to income and to status in an individual panel' in *Journal of Economic Behavior & Organization, 76*, 834–852.

Diener, E., & Emmons, R. A., (1984) 'The independence of positive and negative affect' in *Journal of Personality and Social Psychology*, 47, 1105.

Diener, E., Inglehart, R., & Tay, L., (2013) 'Theory and validity of life satisfaction scales' in *Social Indicators Research, 112*, 497–527.

Diener, E., Suh, E. M., Lucas, R. E., & Smith, H. L., (1999) 'Subjective well-being: Three decades of progress' in *Psychological Bulletin, 125*, 276–302.

Dijkstra, K., Pieterse, M. E., & Pruyn, A., (2008) 'Stress-reducing effects of indoor plants in the built healthcare environment: The mediating role of perceived attractiveness' in *Preventive Medicine*, 47, 279–283.

Dolan, P., (2014) *Happiness by Design: Finding Pleasure and Purpose in Everyday Life*, Penguin UK.

Dolan, P., (2019) *Happy Ever After: Escaping the Myth of the Perfect Life*. Penguin UK.

Dolan, P., Peasgood, T., & White, M., (2008) 'Do we really know what makes us happy? A review of the economic literature on the factors associated with subjective well-being' in *Journal of Economic Psychology*, 29, 94–122.

Duckworth, A., (2016) *Grit: The Power of Passion and Perseverance* (Vol. 234), Scribner New York.

Dweck, C., (2000) *Self-theories: Their Role in Motivation, Personality, and Development*, Psychology Press.

Dweck, C., (2012) *Mindset: Changing the Way You Think to Fulfil Your Potential*, Hachette UK.

Easterlin, R. A., (1974) 'Does economic growth improve the human lot? Some empirical evidence' in (eds. David, P. A., & Reder, M. W.) *Nations and Households in Economic Growth* (pp. 89–125), Elsevier.

Easterlin, R. A., (2021). *An Economist's Lessons on Happiness: Farewell Dismal Science!*. Springer Nature.

Eberth, J., & Sedlmeier, P., (2012) 'The effects of mindfulness meditation: A meta-analysis' in *Mindfulness*, *3*, 174–189.

Economist Intelligence Unit., (2020) *Democracy Index 2019. A Year of Democratic Setbacks and Popular Protest*, EIU.

Eddo-Lodge, R., (2020). *Why I'm No Longer Talking to White People About Race*, Bloomsbury Publishing.

Ekman, P., Davidson, R. J., & Friesen, W. V., (1990) 'The Duchenne smile: Emotional expression and brain physiology: II' in *Journal of Personality and Social Psychology*, *58*, 342.

Emmons, R. A., & Mccullough, M. E., (2003) 'Counting blessings versus burdens: An experimental investigation of gratitude and subjective well-being in daily life' in *Journal of Personality and Social Psychology*, *84*, 377–389.

Ferguson, E., Taylor, M., Keatley, D., Flynn, N., & Lawrence, C., (2012) 'Blood donors' helping behavior is driven by warm glow: More evidence for the blood donor benevolence hypothesis' in *Transfusion*, 52, 2,189–2,200.

Fischer, E. F., (2014) *The Good Life: Aspiration, Dignity, and the Anthropology of Wellbeing*, Stanford University Press.

Flèche, S., Clark, A. E., Layard, R., Powdthavee, N., & Ward, G., (2019) *The origins of happiness: The science of well-being over the life course*, Princeton University Press.

Forgas, J. P., (2013) 'Don't worry, be sad! On the cognitive, motivational, and interpersonal benefits of negative mood' in *Current Directions in Psychological Science*, 22, 225–232.

Fowler, J. H., & Christakis, N. A., (2008) 'Dynamic spread of happiness in a large social network: Longitudinal analysis over 20 years in the Framingham Heart Study' in *British Medical Journal*, 337.

Frederick, S., & Loewenstein, G., (1999) 'Hedonic Adaptation' in (eds. Kahneman, D., Diener, E., & Schwarz, N.) *Well-Being: The Foundations of Hedonic Psychology* (pp. 302–329), Russell Sage.

Frey, B. S., & Stutzer, A., (2000) 'Happiness, economy and institutions' in *The Economic Journal*, *110*, 918–938.

Gallup, (2019) Gallup Global Emotions 2019, Gallup Inc.

Gascon, M., Zijlema, W., Vert, C., White, M. P., & Nieuwenhuijsen, M. J., (2017) 'Outdoor blue spaces, human health and well-being: A systematic review of quantitative studies' in *International Journal of Hygiene and Environmental Health*, 220, 1,207–1,221.

George, M. S., Ketter, T. A., Parekh, P. I., Horwitz, B., Herscovitch, P., & Post, R. M., (1995) 'Brain activity during transient sadness and happiness in healthy women' in *American Journal of Psychiatry*, *152*, 341–351.

Gillborn, D., (2008) *Racism and Education: Coincidence or Conspiracy?*, Routledge.

Graham, C., Zhou, S., & Zhang, J., (2017) 'Happiness and health in China: The paradox of progress' in *World Development*, *96*, 231–244.

Greenwald, A. G., Banaji, M. R., & Nosek, B. A., (2015) 'Statistically small effects of the Implicit Association Test can have societally large effects' in *Journal of Personality and Social Psychology*, *108*, 553–561.

Griffiths, J., (2008) *Wild: An Elemental Journey*, Penguin UK.

Gu, J., Strauss, C., Bond, R., & Cavanagh, K., (2015) 'How do mindfulness-based cognitive therapy and mindfulness-based stress reduction improve mental health and wellbeing? A systematic review and meta-analysis of mediation studies' in *Clinical Psychology Review*, 37, 1–12.

Helliwell, J. F., Huang, H., & Wang, S., (2016) 'The distribution of world happiness' in (eds. Helliwell, J., Layard, R., & Sachs, J.) *World Happiness Report 2016* (pp. 8–48), Sustainable Development Solutions Network.

Helliwell, J., Layard, R., & Sachs, J., (2018) *World Happiness Report 2018*, Sustainable Development Solutions Network.

Hickel, J., (2020) 'The sustainable development index: Measuring the ecological efficiency of human development in the Anthropocene' in *Ecological Economics, 167*, 106331.

Hoekstra, R., (2019) *Replacing GDP by 2030: Towards a Common Language for the Well-Being and Sustainability Community*, Cambridge University Press.

Hopwood, M., (2019) *A Human Love Story: Journeys to the Heart*, Birlinn.

Joseph, S., & Linley, P. A., (2006) 'Growth following adversity: Theoretical perspectives and implications for clinical practice' in *Clinical Psychology Review*, 26, 1,041–1,053.

Kahneman, D., & Deaton, A., (2010) 'High income improves evaluation of life but not emotional well-being' in *Proceedings of the National Academy of Sciences, 107*, 16,489–16,493.

Kahneman, D., Krueger, A. B., Schkade, D. A., Schwarz, N., & Stone, A. A., (2004) 'A survey method for characterizing daily life experience: The day reconstruction method' in *Science, 306*, 1,776–1,780.

Kohn, R., Harhay, M. O., Cooney, E., Small, D. S., & Halpern, S. D., (2013) 'Do windows or natural views affect outcomes or costs among patients in ICUs?' in *Critical Care Medicine, 41*, 1,645–1,655.

Kurtz, J., (2017) *The Happy Traveler: Unpacking the Secrets of Better Vacations*,. Oxford University Press.

Lawson, M., Parvez Butt, A., Harvey, R., Sarosi, D., Coffey, C., Piaget, K., & Thekkudah, J., (2020) *Time to Care: Unpaid and Underpaid Care Work and the Global Inequality Crisis*, Oxfam.

Layard, R., (2006) 'The case for psychological treatment centres' in *British Medical Journal, 332*, 1,030–1,032.

Layard, R., (2011) *Happiness: Lessons From a New Science*, Penguin UK.

Layard, R., & Clark, D. M., (2015) *Thrive: The Power of Psychological Therapy*, Penguin UK.

Layard, R., & Ward, G., (2020) *Can We Be Happier?: Evidence and Ethics* (Illustrated Edition), Pelican.

Lindqvist, E., Östling, R., & Cesarini, D., (2020) 'Long-run effects of lottery wealth on psychological well-being' in *The Review of Economic Studies, 87*, 2,703–2,726.

Mackay, G. J., & Neill, J. T., (2010) 'The effect of "green exercise" on state anxiety and the role of exercise duration, intensity, and greenness: A quasi-experimental study' in *Psychology of Sport and Exercise, 11*, 238–245.

Martela, F., (2018) 'Finland is the happiest country in the world, and Finns aren't happy about it' in *Scientific American.* Retrieved on 18th December 2021 https://blogs.scientificamerican.com/observations/finland-is-the-happiest-country-in-the-world-and-finns-arent-happy-about-it/

Martela, F., Greve, B., Rothstein, B., & Saari, J., (2020) 'The Nordic exceptionalism: What explains why the Nordic countries are constantly among the happiest in the world' in (eds. Helliwell, J., Layard, R., Sachs, J., & De Neve, J. -E.) *World Happiness Report 2020* (pp. 129–146), Sustainable Development Solutions Network.

Maslow, A. H., (1943) 'A theory of human motivation' in *Psychological Review, 50*, 370–396.

Matz, S. C., Gladstone, J. J., & Stillwell, D., (2016) 'Money buys happiness when spending fits our personality' in *Psychological Science, 27*, 715–725.

Mauss, I. B., Tamir, M., Anderson, C. L., & Savino, N. S., (2011) 'Can seeking happiness make people unhappy? Paradoxical effects of valuing happiness' in *Emotion, 11*, 807.

Mazzucato, M,. (2018) *The Value of Everything: Making and Taking in the Global Economy,* Hachette UK.

McCrae, R. R., & Costa, P. T., Jr., (2008) 'The five-factor theory of personality' in (eds. John, O. P., Robins, R. W., & Pervin, L. A.) *Handbook of Personality: Theory and Research* (pp. 159–181), The Guilford Press.

Meadows, D. H., Randers, J., & Meadows, D. L., (1972) *The Limits to Growth*, Universe Books.

Millburn, J. F., & Nicodemus, R., (2015) *Minimalism: Live a Meaningful Life*, Asymmetrical Press.

Mishel, L., Gould, E., & Bivens, J., (2015) 'Wage stagnation in nine charts' in *Economic Policy Institute, 6*, 2–13.

Murphy, R. P., Boyce, C. J., Dolan, P., & Wood, A. M., (2020) 'Valuing the Q in QALYs: Does providing patients' ratings affect population values?' in *Health Psychology, 39*, 37.

Nettle, D., (2006) 'The evolution of personality variation in humans and other animals' in *American Psychologist, 61*, 622.

Newall, P. W. S., (2019) 'Dark nudges in gambling' in *Addiction Research & Theory, 27*, 65–67.

Nickerson, R. S., (1998) 'Confirmation bias: A ubiquitous phenomenon in many guises' in *Review of General Psychology, 2*, 175–220.

Oswald, A. J., (1997) 'Happiness and economic performance' in *The Economic Journal, 107*, 1,815–1,831.

Oswald, A. J., & Powdthavee, N., (2008) 'Does happiness adapt? A longitudinal study of disability with implications for economists and judges' in *Journal of Public Economics, 92*, 1,061–1,077.

Ott, J., (2005) 'Level and inequality of happiness in nations: Does greater happiness of a greater number imply greater inequality in happiness?' *Journal of Happiness Studies, 6*, 397–420.

Park, A., (2010) 'Study: Money isn't everything—But status is!' in *Time*. Retrieved 18th December 2021 http://content.time.com/time/health/article/0,8599,1974718,00.html

Powdthavee, N., (2008) 'Putting a price tag on friends, relatives, and neighbours: Using surveys of life satisfaction to value social relationships' in *The Journal of Socio-Economics, 37*, 1,459–1,480.

Przybylski, A. K., Murayama, K., DeHaan, C. R., & Gladwell, V., (2013) 'Motivational, emotional, and behavioral correlates of fear of missing out' in *Computers in Human Behavior, 29*, 1,841–1,848.

Quispe-Torreblanca, E. G., Brown, G. D., Boyce, C. J., Wood, A. M., & De Neve, J.-E., (2020) 'Inequality and social rank: Income increases buy more life satisfaction in more equal countries' in *Personality and Social Psychology Bulletin*. https://doi.org/10.1177/0146167220923853

Quoidbach, J., Dunn, E. W., Petrides, K. V., & Mikolajczak, M., (2010) 'Money giveth, money taketh away: The dual effect of wealth on happiness' in *Psychological science*, 21, 759–763.

Raanaas, R. K., Patil, G. G., & Hartig, T., (2012) 'Health benefits of a view of nature through the window: A quasi-experimental study of patients in a residential rehabilitation center' in *Clinical Rehabilitation*, 26, 21–32.

Raworth, K., (2017) *Doughnut Economics: Seven Ways to Think Like a 21st-Century Economist,* Chelsea Green Publishing.

Roberts, B. W., & Mroczek, D., (2008) 'Personality trait change in adulthood' in *Current Directions in Psychological Science, 17*, 31–35.

Rockström, J., Steffen, W., Noone, K., Persson, Å., Chapin, F. S., Lambin, E. F., Lenton, T. M., Scheffer, M., Folke, C., Schellnhuber, H. J., Nykvist, B., de Wit, C. A., Hughes, T., van der Leeuw, S., Rodhe, H., Sörlin, S., Snyder, P. K., Costanza, R., Svedin, U., … Foley, J. A., (2009) 'A safe operating space for humanity' in *Nature*, *461*, 472–475.

Rodriguez, T., (2013) 'Life satisfaction linked to personality changes' in *Scientific American*. Retrieved on 18th December 2021 https://doi.org/10.1038/scientificamericanmind0713-8

Rogers, C. R., (1967) *On Becoming a Person: A Therapist's View of Psychotherapy*, Constable London.

Rojas, M., (2018) 'Happiness in Latin America has social foundations' in (eds. Helliwell, J., Layard, R., & Sachs, J.) *World Happiness Report 2018* (pp. 114–145), Sustainable Development Solutions Network.

Romans, S., Clarkson, R., Einstein, G., Petrovic, M., & Stewart, D., (2012) 'Mood and the menstrual cycle: A review of prospective data studies' in *Gender Medicine, 9*, 361–384.

Rosenberg, M. B., & Chopra, D., (2015) *Nonviolent Communication: A Language of Life: Life-changing Tools for Healthy Relationships*, PuddleDancer Press.

Schor, J. B., (1998) *The Overspent American: Upscaling, Downshifting, and the New Consumer*, Basic Books.

Schwartz, B., (2004) *The Paradox of Choice: Why More is Less*, Ecco.

Seligman, M. E., (2012) *Flourish: A Visionary New Understanding of Happiness and Well-Being,* Simon and Schuster.

Shaw, M., (2016) *Scatterlings: Getting Claimed in the Age of Amnesia*,

White Cloud Press.

Sirgy, M. J., (1998) 'Materialism and quality of life' in *Social Indicators Research*, 43, 227–260.

Soussignan, R., (2002) 'Duchenne smile, emotional experience, and autonomic reactivity: A test of the facial feedback hypothesis' in *Emotion*, 2, 52.

Specht, J., Egloff, B., & Schmukle, S. C., (2011) 'Stability and change of personality across the life course: The impact of age and major life events on mean-level and rank-order stability of the Big Five' in *Journal of Personality and Social Psychology*, 101, 862–882.

Spicer, A., (2019) 'Camping satisfies our urge to escape. But we take our baggage with us' in *The Guardian*. Retrieved on 18th December 2021 http://www.theguardian.com/commentisfree/2019/sep/10/camping-culture-escape-campsite

Srivastava, S., John, O. P., Gosling, S. D., & Potter, J., (2003) 'Development of personality in early and middle adulthood: Set like plaster or persistent change?' in *Journal of Personality and Social Psychology*, 84, 1,041.

Steger, M. F., Oishi, S., & Kashdan, T. B., (2009) 'Meaning in life across the life span: Levels and correlates of meaning in life from emerging adulthood to older adulthood' in *The Journal of Positive Psychology*, 4, 43–52.

Steinpreis, R. E., Anders, K. A., & Ritzke, D., (1999) 'The impact of gender on the review of the curricula vitae of job applicants and tenure candidates: A national empirical study' in *Sex Roles*, 41, 509–528.

Stevenson, B., & Wolfers, J., (2008) *Economic Growth and Subjective Well-Being: Reassessing the Easterlin Paradox*, National Bureau of Economic Research.

Stiglitz, J. E., Sen, A., & Fitoussi, J. P., (2009) *Report by the Commission on the Measurement of Economic Performance and Social Progress*. Retrieved on 18th December http://citeseerx.ist.psu.edu/viewdoc/download?doi=10.1.1.215.58&rep=rep1&type=pdf

Stutzer, A., (2004) 'The role of income aspirations in individual happiness' in *Journal of Economic Behavior & Organization*, 54, 89–109.

Thaler, R. H., & Sunstein, C. R., (2009) *Nudge: Improving Decisions About Health, Wealth, and Happiness*, Penguin.

Trebeck, K., & Williams, J., (2019). *The Economics of Arrival: Ideas for a Grown-Up Economy*. Policy Press.

Troy, A. S., & Mauss, I. B., (2011) 'Resilience in the face of stress: Emotion regulation as a protective factor' in (eds. Southwick, S. M., Litz, B. T., Charney, D., & Friedman, M. J.) *Resilience and Mental Health: Challenges across the Lifespan* (pp. 30–44), Cambridge University Press.

Turner, V., (1969) 'Liminality and communitas' in (eds. Turner, V., & Abrahams, R. D.) *The Ritual Process: Structure and Anti-Structure* (pp. 94–113), Aldine Publishing.

Tversky, A., & Kahneman, D., (2000) *Choices, Values, and Frames*, Cambridge University Press.

Ulrich, R. S., (1984) 'View through a window may influence recovery from surgery' in *Science,* 224, 420–421.

Ulrich, R. S., Zimring, C., Zhu, X., DuBose, J., Seo, H.-B., Choi, Y.-S., Quan, X., & Joseph, A., (2008) 'A review of the research literature on evidence-based healthcare design' in *HERD: Health Environments Research & Design Journal,* 1, 61–125.

University of Cambridge, (2016) 'Spending for smiles: Money can buy happiness after all' in *Research News at the University of Cambridge*. Retrieved on 18th December 2021 https://www.cam.ac.uk/research/news/spending-for-smiles-money-can-buy-happiness-after-all

Veenhoven, R., (2012) 'Cross-national differences in happiness: Cultural measurement bias or effect of culture?' in *International Journal of Wellbeing,* 2, 333–353

Victor, C. R., & Yang, K., (2012) 'The prevalence of loneliness among adults: A case study of the United Kingdom' in *The Journal of Psychology*, 146, 85–104.

Ware, B., (2012) *The Top Five Regrets of the Dying: A Life Transformed by the Dearly Departing*, Hay House.

Watts, A., (1999) *The Way of Zen,* Vintage.

Wellbeing Economy Alliance, (2021) *Wellbeing Economy Policy Design Guide,* Wellbeing Economy Alliance

White, M. P., Alcock, I., Grellier, J., Wheeler, B. W., Hartig, T., Warber, S. L., Bone, A., Depledge, M. H., & Fleming, L. E., (2019) 'Spending at least 120 minutes a week in nature is associated with good health and wellbeing' in *Scientific Reports,* 9, 1–11.

White, M. P., Alcock, I., Wheeler, B. W., & Depledge, M. H., (2013) 'Would you be happier living in a greener urban area? A fixed-effects analysis of panel data' in *Psychological Science, 24*, 920–928.

White, M. P., Smith, A., Humphryes, K., Pahl, S., Snelling, D., & Depledge, M., (2010) 'Blue space: The importance of water for preference, affect, and restorativeness ratings of natural and built scenes' in *Journal of Environmental Psychology, 30*, 482–493.

Wilkinson, R., & Pickett, K., (2010) *The Spirit Level. Why Equality Is Better for Everyone,* Penguin UK.

Winkelmann, L., & Winkelmann, R., (1998) 'Why are the unemployed so unhappy? Evidence from panel data' in *Economica, 65*, 1–15.

Wood, A. M., & Boyce, C. J., (2017) 'Developing, evaluating, and using subjective scales of personality, preferences, and well-being: A guide to psychometrics for psychologists and economists' in (ed. Raynard, R.) *Economic Psychology* (pp. 88–103), Wiley.

Wood, A. M., Boyce, C. J., Moore, S. C., & Brown, G. D., (2012) 'An evolutionary based social rank explanation of why low income predicts mental distress: A 17 year cohort study of 30,000 people' in *Journal of Affective Disorders, 136*, 882–888.

Worland, J., (2015) 'How being unemployed changes your personality' in *Time*. Retrieved 18th December 2021 https://time.com/3705838/unemployment-personality/

Wunsch, H., Gershengorn, H., Mayer, S. A., & Claassen, J., (2011) 'The effect of window rooms on critically ill patients with subarachnoid hemorrhage admitted to intensive care' in *Critical Care, 15*, 1–10.

Yalom, I. D., (2020). *Existential Psychotherapy,* Hachette UK.

Zschirnt, E., & Ruedin, D., (2016) 'Ethnic discrimination in hiring decisions: a meta-analysis of correspondence tests 1990–2015' in *Journal of Ethnic and Migration Studies* 42, 1,115–1,134.

Notes

Chapter 1: A journey for happiness begins...

1. The first time I walked into Andrew Oswald's office was when I was as a Masters student in 2005. I laid it on the line to him quickly that "I had become increasingly disillusioned with Economics, but that I had found some hope and inspiration in reading his work." One of his research articles "Economic Performance and Happiness" (Oswald, 1997) showed that in industrialised countries, increases in national income had resulted in rises in happiness that were so small as to be almost undetectable. I have long since smiled at the thought that had I known then how famous and influential he was, I wouldn't have had the confidence to say such a thing. I did my Masters dissertation on happiness with him, and later he took me on as his PhD student.
2. The research article "Does Economic Growth Improve the Human Lot? Some Empirical Evidence" (Easterlin, 1974) was ahead of its time, and was mostly ignored by economists until the 90s, when it was resurrected and re-examined by Andrew Oswald and many others. The debate on this question still goes on (more on this question in Chapter 7, in relation to some of the places I cycled through). Though, as an additional side note, I did once meet with Richard Easterlin in a café in Paris, and I suggested to him an alternative explanation for his famous 'Easterlin Paradox', based on research I'd been carrying out (see Boyce et al. 2013). At the time, he didn't go for it. Some years later, though, some of the ideas I talked to him about found their way into his research (see Easterlin, 2021).
3. Bronnie Ware, an Australian nurse, spent years working in palliative care, caring for patients in the final weeks of their lives. She recorded their dying wishes and put her observations into a profoundly moving book, *The Top Five Regrets of the Dying* (Ware, 2012).

Chapter 2: Why Bhutan? Why a bicycle? And why me?

1. There are a number of reviews of the research on happiness that point to the most important factors for happiness (see for example, Diener et al., 1999; Dolan et al., 2008).

2. Our study, Boyce, Wood, Powdthavee (2013) regularly picks up mentions in other academic articles, and was once given decent coverage in *Scientific American* (Rodriguez, 2013). I will talk more about personality change in Chapter 9.
3. In pioneering work, Winkelmann & Winkelmann (1998) explore why the unemployed are so unhappy, showing that resulting unhappiness reaches deeper than simply loss of earnings.
4. Our research article, Boyce, Daly, Hounkpatin, & Wood (2017) was published as a comment to a paper claiming that money buys happiness. I will explore this research article and the circumstance in which it was written in Chapter 9, to illustrate a point about how we use evidence to support our beliefs.
5. The original study by Blanchflower & Oswald (2004) highlighting the marriage effect in monetary terms was carried out in the US and US$100,000 is equivalent to approximately £75,000 based on the currency exchange rate at the time of writing (£1 = US$1.33). In this book, when monetary figures relate to personal costs I've used pounds and provided the equivalent in US$.
6. For a while it became quite common for researchers to put monetary values on life events as a way of conveying their value (see for example, Blanchflower & Oswald, 2004; Oswald & Powdthavee, 2008; Powdthavee, 2008). I did it myself in an article (Boyce, Wood, Powdthavee, 2013), despite pointing out in one of my first published articles (Boyce & Wood, 2010) that this was a misleading thing to do. To assign monetary values, researchers carry out statistical analyses to estimate the effect of different life circumstances, including income, on happiness. It is then possible to calculate how much income someone would need to get an equivalent happiness-effect for various life circumstances.
7. As Richard Layard discusses in *Happiness: Lessons From a New Science* (Layard, 2011), generosity, compassion, and gratitude are all personality characteristics that foster deeper relationships, and are the most strongly associated with happiness and wellbeing.
8. I'll overview some of the research into the effects of environment on health and happiness in Chapter 11. However, Mathew White and colleagues have shown wide-ranging effects on personal happiness from being close to green and blue spaces (White et al., 2010, 2013).

9. I first met Matthew Hopwood in Edinburgh during his walk to the outer Hebrides in which he collected love stories for his first book *A Human Love Story* (2019). He and his partner (plus their little dog) stayed with me to rest and recuperate for a few days before journeying onwards.
10. In mythological texts, it is well known that refusing a call to an adventure can have severe psychological consequences (see *The Hero with a Thousand Faces* by Joseph Campbell, New World Library, 1949).
11. In the UK, those ethnically-white are less happy than those of Asian ethnicity, have about the same happiness as those that are Black, and are happier than those that are mixed-race or Arabic. The gap in happiness between Black and white people has diminished over the last ten years (see, for example, https://www.ethnicity-facts-figures.service.gov.uk/health/wellbeing/well-being-happiness-yesterday/latest).
12. The state of flow has been extensively examined by Hungarian psychologist Mihaly Csikszentmihalyi. He has many books on the topic, his most celebrated being *Flow: The Psychology of Optimal Experience* (Csikszentmihalyi, 1990).
13. Everyone will face some sort of challenge throughout life – some grow from it, others will not. Whether we grow depends on a lot of different factors, including our circumstances to begin with, and whether we have the support needed to embrace the challenge. There has been a healthy amount of research exploring growth from adversity (see for example, Bonanno, 2004; Joseph & Linley, 2006) and I'll examine some of it in Chapter 6 when a severe challenge came along on this journey.
14. In the book *The Happy Traveler* (Kurtz, 2017), Jamie Kurtz examines the overlooked importance of embracing challenge when travelling, and how it can bring greater fulfilment. Her book also has a multitude of tips and advice on finding happiness through travel, based on research findings from positive psychology.

Chapter 3: Out beyond the front door

1. As a person's income increases they adapt to that higher amount, such that after a relatively short period a higher income has little effect on happiness (Di Tella et al., 2010). Adaptation to pleasurable and unpleasurable experiences is common – from bereavement and disability to food and

incarceration (see, for example, Boyce & Wood, 2011b; Clark et al., 2008; Frederick & Loewenstein, 1999; Oswald & Powdthavee, 2008). However, there are other life experiences that people don't adapt to, including poverty (Clark et al., 2016) and unemployment (Clark et al., 2008).

2. People have a strong need for frequent and caring interactions; we form social attachments readily under most conditions and resist the dissolution of existing bonds. Lack of social attachments is linked to a variety of ill effects on health, adjustment, and wellbeing (Baumeister & Leary, 1995).
3. Maya Angelou's expression on freedom and belonging is beautifully examined by Brene Brown in her book *Braving the Wilderness* (2018).
4. I'll speak more about the importance of unconditional acceptance in our relationships in Chapter 15, drawing on the work of Carl Rogers (Rogers, 1967).
5. There is an abundance of research exploring social comparison: why we do it, and how it influences our behaviour, health, and happiness (Buunk & Gibbons, 2007).
6. One of my earliest and most influential pieces of work showed that when it comes to how much a person earns, it is not the amount of income that matters for happiness, but how it compares to others (Boyce et al., 2010). We also showed a similar effect on mental and physical health (Daly et al., 2015; Wood et al., 2012).

Chapter 4: Paying with freedom

1. I was at a university in the UK and the £12,000 I got paid was exempt from tax. This made the sum equivalent to an annual salary of £13,000 to £14,000. Given this, as well as the fluctuating exchange rate at the time, it would approximate to around US$20,000.
2. *The Paradox of Choice: Why More Is Less* (2004) by Barry Schwartz examines why choice is not always a good thing.
3. *Jose Mujica: The World's 'Poorest' President.* Retrieved on 18th December https://www.bbc.co.uk/news/magazine-20243493
4. For example, both Mark Boyle, the legendary Moneyless Man (Boyle, 2010) and *The Minimalists* (Millburn & Nicodemus, 2015) were big influences on guiding my approach to possessions.
5. Racial attitudes and stereotypes have been reliably detected using

Implicit Association Tests and even if prejudices are subtle they can have large societal effects (Greenwald, Banaji, & Nosek, 2015). There are racial biases in education to such an extent that there are strong claims to suggest race inequality is intentional and deliberate (Gilborn, 2008). In the job market equivalently qualified candidates from minority ethnic and racial groups need to send around 50 per cent more applications to be invited for an interview than majority candidates (Zschirnt & Ruedin, 2016). With regard to gender, male job applicants are preferred when curriculum vitae are identical in all but name (Steinpreis, Anders, & Ritzke, 1999).
6. It is well understood that poverty creates misery (Layard & Ward, 2020), and that it is not something a person gets used to (Clark et al., 2016). Poverty hurts, and it hurts badly.
7. In line with this, money has been shown to impair people's ability to savour everyday positive emotions and experiences (Quoidbach et al., 2010).

Chapter 5: Letting go of Bhutan

1. There is a whole bunch of research supporting the use of self-reported scales to measure happiness (see e.g., Diener et al., 2013; Ekman et al., 1990; George et al., 1995; Soussignan, 2002; Wood & Boyce, 2017).
2. This was stated by Nobel Prize Winner Joseph Stiglitz, as part of an influential report he and other influential economists wrote critiquing the size of the economy as an indicator of progress (Stiglitz et al., 2009).
3. In its annual population survey, the UK's Office for National Statistics asks people the life satisfaction question "Overall, how satisfied are you with your life nowadays?" – more details can be found here https://www.ons.gov.uk/visualisations/dvc490/dashboard/index.html
4. It has been shown that aspiring to ever higher levels of income is detrimental to happiness (Stutzer, 2004).
5. In *Happy Ever After: Escaping the Myth of the Perfect Life* (2019), Paul Dolan examines how subscribing to social narratives doesn't bring as much happiness as people expect, and can sometimes be detrimental. He also suggests that many of the social narratives championed by the powerful are crafted to protect the interests of the powerful.

6. Those that pursue materialist objectives typically experience greater dissatisfaction with their standard of living than those that aren't materialist-minded. The dissatisfaction arises because materialists set standard-of-living goals that are inflated and unrealistically high, and this dissatisfaction with standards of living spills over to life satisfaction more generally (Sirgy, 1998).
7. I came across a newspaper article exploring how camping satisfies our need to escape day to day life (Spicer, 2019), and in it Victor Turner's concept of liminal spaces was discussed (Turner, 1969).

Chapter 6: Along comes a crisis

1. Confrontations with our own mortality can give our lives a renewed vigour (Yalom, 2020).
2. One classic technique to improve gratitude is to keep a gratitude diary. Regularly listing things we're grateful for can improve gratitude and happiness (Emmons & Mccullough, 2003).
3. We often underestimate the human capacity to thrive after extremely adverse events (see Bonanno, 2004).
4. As Agaibi and Wilson describe (2005), resilience is a complex phenomenon, dependent upon general behavioural tendencies.
5. Troy and Mauss (2011) examine the importance of a person's ability to emotionally regulate (being able to adapt our emotions to the moment) for resilience.
6. In her book *Grit: The Power of Passion and Perseverance* (2016), Angela Duckworth explores the benefits of having and developing grit. Whilst grit can keep us going when we need to, it does also keep us going when we *don't* really need to. Having too much of a particular personality trait can be detrimental to our happiness (Nettle, 2006).

Chapter 7: The happiest people on earth

1. The 2018 Gallup World Poll data on emotions were originally available at the website that follows (retrieved 1st February 2020). However, they have since been replaced with findings from 2020 data: https://news.gallup.com/interactives/248240/global-emotions.aspx

2. The Gallup World Poll asks five questions relating to a person's positive experiences the previous day, including whether a person (i) experienced a lot of enjoyment, (ii) smiled or laughed a lot, (iii) felt well-rested, (iv) was treated with respect all day, and (v) learnt or did something interesting. It is the average response to all five questions from citizens living in the country that make up the scores in Table 1. Taken from Gallup Global Emotions (2019).
3. The cultural element of how people answer these types of questions has been widely explored. The conclusion is that, whilst there are some issues with comparability, this doesn't prevent happiness scores being meaningfully compared across nations and cultures (Veenhoven, 2012).
4. It comes up time and time again in the news that Nordic countries are among the happiest. See for example this BBC article "Happiness report: Finland is world's 'happiest country' – UN" – https://www.bbc.co.uk/news/world-43414145
5. Here is the link to the 2018 World Happiness Report – https://worldhappiness.report/ed/2018/
6. See 'Finland Is the Happiest Country in the World, and Finns Aren't Happy about It' by Frank Martela (2018) in the *Scientific American* – https://blogs.scientificamerican.com/observations/finland-is-the-happiest-country-in-the-world-and-finns-arent-happy-about-it/
7. *In Happy Ever After: Escaping the Myth of the Perfect Life* (2019), Paul Dolan compares and contrasts how achieving different life objectives influences our life satisfaction and happiness in the moment, with some striking conclusions.
8. Curiously, the results linking inequality and happiness are mixed. Some studies indicate that inequality is linked to more happiness, others less happiness (see Quispe-Torreblanca et al., 2020, for an overview). However, in *The Spirit Level* (Wilkinson & Pickett, 2010), the authors show that inequality affects a range of other important quality-of-life indicators negatively. In addition, it has been demonstrated that inequality in happiness scores, as opposed to income inequality, consistently predicts lower levels of happiness in a country (Ott, 2005).
9. In *The Good Life: Aspiration, Dignity, and the Anthropology of Wellbeing* (Fischer, 2014), Edward Fischer examines what constitutes the 'good life' in very different cultural contexts, and how best to achieve it.
10. The economists' notion of happiness is notoriously limited in scope and it

hasn't helped people take the subject seriously (see, for example, Crespo & Mesurado, 2015, who appeal to a richer type of happiness that I'll speak to in Chapter 16). My hunch is that economists want to appear as if they're not too serious, when this is far from the truth.

11. There are some economists who don't conform to the mainstream notion that there is nothing more important than a growing economy as I'll describe in Chapter 14.
12. In the 2018 'World Happiness Report' there is a chapter dedicated to understanding why Latin American countries are happier than might be expected given material living standards (Rojas, 2018).
13. Some put the point at which individual income has no more benefit to wellbeing at US$35,000 (Schor 2011); others claim there is no satiation point for Cantril's ladder question at the individual level (Kahneman and Deaton, 2010). Satiation level or not, the effects are still small relative to other things.
14. In the 2020 'World Happiness Report', there is a chapter dedicated to understanding why Nordic countries are so happy (Martela et al., 2020).
15. The debate around whether economic growth increases happiness has gone back and forth over the years, beginning with Richard Easterlin's 1974 paper showing that it did not. For evidence that there is a link between economic growth and happiness, people always point to Stevenson and Wolfers (2008). However, Blanchflower and Oswald (2004) show that happiness has not risen in the USA, despite high economic growth, and Brockmann and colleagues (2009) point to the same for China. In addition, there is often little discussion as to how large the link is. Often, beyond the level of meeting basic needs, the effects of economic growth are marginal (see Boyce et al., 2017, for a discussion of this issue in money and happiness research). This issue is often side-stepped in discussion. There may be statistical significance (i.e., there is an effect), but that doesn't mean it is of a meaningful magnitude – an issue that some scientists, and many economists, just don't seem to want to understand.
16. Scales used to determine happiness and wellbeing will typically undergo extensive evaluation before they can be meaningfully used to answer research questions (see Wood & Boyce, 2017 for how this is carried out).
17. Psychologists have examined how people feel doing a whole range of day-to-day activities (see Kahneman et al., 2004).

18. In its annual population survey the UK's Office for National Statistics asks people the life satisfaction question, "Overall, how happy did you feel yesterday?" https://www.ons.gov.uk/visualisations/dvc490/dashboard/index.html
19. On average, happiness tends to rise sharply from early morning until noon, and then remains relatively constant until 9 pm, at which point it falls rapidly. There is, however, individual variation, particularly in the afternoon, and there are distinct differences between morning and evening types (Clark et al., 1989).
20. Whilst there are many studies showing that the menstrual cycle affects mood, other studies suggest there is no clear link (see Romans et al., 2012, who highlight the dangers of perpetuating links between female reproduction with negative emotionality).
21. Valuing happiness can leave people feeling disappointed when they don't achieve it (Mauss et al., 2011).
22. *Buen vivir* itself is the Spanish translation of *Sumak Kawsay*, a concept originating from the Quechuan people of the Andes.
23. Researchers have shown that people are typically happier in their day-to-day activities when other people are involved (Kahneman et al., 2004).
24. Those that see friends and family often are markedly happier than those that don't (Powdthavee, 2008).
25. We get happier when those in our social network get happier (Fowler & Christakis, 2008). Such social contagion has been shown to influence our ideas, emotions, health, relationships, behaviour, and politics (Christakis & Fowler, 2009).

Chapter 8: Life in the here and now

1. An overview of 39 studies by Eberth & Sedlmeier (2012) showed that courses in either mindfulness based stress reduction or meditation resulted in more positive emotions, fewer negative emotions, and greater wellbeing. There was an effect of between 0.5 to 0.6, which is an effect that is at least as large as being in a committed relationship (e.g., being married). That's considered a large effect.
2. Gu and colleagues (2015) examine the main mechanisms by which mindfulness helps in daily life.
3. Have a look at the newly re-launched Happy Planet Index, which shows a

country's happiness accounting for life expectancy and ecological impact. Costa Rica leads the way. Go to https://happyplanetindex.org/ or see Abdallah et al., (2009) for more.

4. Frey and Stutzer (2000) highlight the importance of institutional factors, such as direct democracy and local autonomy, for happiness.
5. See 'Our World in Data' https://ourworldindata.org/life-expectancy
6. See *Democracy Index 2019. A Year of Democratic Setbacks and Popular Protest* by the Economist Intelligence Unit (2020).

Chapter 9: Beyond belief

1. A popular way of assessing whether money buys happiness is through studying the effects of lottery wins on people's happiness. One of the most influential pieces of research in this area is from Brickman and colleagues (1978), and their data seemed to suggest that lottery winners were no happier than non-lottery winners. Their conclusions, however, have not held up under later scrutiny, and later research has shown that winning the lottery can bring sustained happiness increases (Lindqvist et al., 2020). However, as is typical with any money-influences-happiness studies, the effect is never very large.
2. The University of Cambridge issued a press release claiming that, after all, money could buy happiness (University of Cambridge, 2016) based on research carried out by Sandra Matz and colleagues (2016).
3. Our comment to the 'money buys happiness if it fits your personality' article (Boyce et al., 2017) showed that their research had a questionable methodology, and their key effect was vastly overstated.
4. Confirmation bias shows up nearly everywhere in beliefs and expectations about the world (Nickerson, 1998).
5. Carol Dweck outlines how intelligence forms in her classic book *Self-Theories: Their Role in Motivation, Personality, and Development* (Dweck, 2000). These ideas have since been reformulated within positive psychology as the 'growth mindset' (Dweck, 2012), which is considered an essential ingredient to overcoming challenge (i.e., resilience as discussed in Chapter 6, in relation to the dog bite I experienced).
6. McCrae and Costa (2008) were the main proponents of the so-called 'set like plaster' hypothesis of personality change.

7. For evidence that personality develops throughout life, see Roberts & Mroczek (2008) and Srivastava and colleagues (2003). For evidence that changes in personality are linked to sizeable changes in happiness, see my own research (Boyce et al., 2013), and for evidence that personality change takes place in response to things that commonly happen in our lives, see some of my own work (Boyce et al., 2015), and the work of Specht and colleagues (2011).
8. The 50/50 contribution of biology and experiences to personality is based on studies of identical twins (Bleidorn et al., 2009).
9. In 2019, the average wealth per adult was US$77,309. Yet, half of humanity is living on less than US$5.50 a day, nowhere near close to having that sort of wealth (Wellbeing Economy Alliance, 2020).

Chapter 10: Gifts: the worst and the best

1. Some say (economists mostly) that purely selfless giving doesn't exist, and that often humans act out of the joy they experience from doing their bit to help others. The 'warm glow' represents a selfish pleasure from the act of giving, rather than a purely altruistic action that is motivated by the sheer desire to help others (Andreoni, 1990). It has been shown, for example, that blood donation is motivated by donors feeling good about themselves after giving blood (Ferguson et al., 2012).
2. Negative emotional states can have evolutionary adaptive benefits. Mild and temporary mood states should therefore be welcomed. This stands in contrast to the emphasis placed on experiencing positive emotional states in popular culture (Forgas, 2013).
3. In a given moment when people are experiencing highly emotional situations, there is a clear negative link between pleasant and unpleasant emotions – more/less happiness, less/more sadness etc. However, over longer time spans this link diminishes, with the extent to which people feel pleasant and unpleasant emotions being largely independent (Diener & Emmons, 1984).
4. The Positive and Negative Affect Schedule asks people about their experiences of 20 different emotional states for a given moment (Crawford & Henry, 2004).
5. I published six of these 'environment interacts with personality to predict happiness' research articles (Boyce & Wood, 2011a, 2011b; Boyce, Wood,

& Brown, 2010, Boyce, Wood, & Ferguson, 2016a, 2016b, Boyce, Wood, Delaney, et al., 2017). We showed, for example, that personality predicts the happiness and wellbeing response to income changes (Boyce, Wood, & Ferguson, 2016b; Boyce & Wood, 2011a), unemployment (Boyce, Wood, & Brown, 2010), marriage (Boyce, Wood, & Ferguson, 2016a), and disability (Boyce & Wood, 2011b). In other research, we showed that personality changes (e.g., Boyce, Wood, & Powdthavee, 2013; Boyce, Wood, Daly, et al., 2015).

6. The Fear of Missing Out (or FoMO) is associated with lower need satisfaction, mood and life satisfaction, and higher use of social media (Przybylski et al., 2013).
7. More exposure to the thing we fear has been shown to reduce fear (Abramowitz et al., 2019).

Chapter 11: A wilder space

1. It was Roger Ulrich (1984) that first demonstrated that following a gallbladder removal, patients with 'a view through a window' had shorter hospital stays, fewer negative evaluative comments in nurses' notes, and took fewer potent painkillers. Although benefits have been shown to vary across patient type (Raanaas et al., 2012), and some studies find no effects (Kohn et al., 2013; Wunsch et al., 2011), the overall evidence is fairly conclusive that the presence of nature in healthcare is important (Ulrich et al., 2008).
2. The evidence that nature is beneficial is abundant. There are benefits to mental health and wellbeing of living near to green and blue spaces in both urban and non-urban areas (Gascon et al., 2017; White, Smith et al., 2010; White, Alcock, Wheeler et al., 2013); exercising in nature is particularly beneficial (Mackay & Neill, 2010; White, Alcock, Grellier et al., 2019).
3. Capaldi and colleagues (2015) highlight the reasons as to why nature is so beneficial for our health, happiness, and wellbeing.
4. A classic effect in psychology is that 'losses loom large than gains'. The experience of a loss has a stronger psychological impact than an equivalent gain. We were the first to show that this applied to the income and happiness relationship, showing that an income loss reduces a person's happiness by twice as much as that gained from an equivalent income increase (see Boyce, Wood, Banks, Clark, Brown, 2013).

5. Jay Griffiths *Wild: An Elemental Journey* (2008) is a fascinating account of the author's exploration of the wild through the lens of her time spent with indigenous people.
6. Martin Shaw spent several years walking the land and unearthing local stories in Dartmoor. I didn't read *Scatterlings* (2016) until I returned from my journey to Bhutan.
7. The video in which I pronounced myself a 'happy man' in the Arizonian desert just before the man with the firing a gun showed up can be found here https://www.youtube.com/watch?v=n3I5qG4V07w

Chapter 12: Manufacturing misery

1. It was through reading *Choice, Values and Frames* (Tversky & Kahneman, 2000) that I first started learning about how psychology applied to economic decisions. I started to learn about the routine decision errors that humans make.
2. Economists generally use the word utility in their modelling. This equates to the hedonic kind of happiness seen in Chapter 7. Interestingly of all the kinds of happiness, hedonic happiness is the one with the weakest link to income both within and across countries (Kahneman & Deaton, 2010).
3. Gary Becker and Kevin Murphy (Becker & Murphy, 1988) set out a theoretical model to suggest that addiction is a person's rational plan to maximise their utility/happiness over time.
4. *Nudge* (Thaler & Sunstein, 2009) has had a major influence on policy in recent years. The UK's Behavioural Science Unit – aka The Nudge Unit – was set up in 2010 by David Cameron to apply behavioural science to public policy.
5. Here are some more mental health statistics https://mhfaengland.org/mhfa-centre/research-and-evaluation/mental-health-statistics/
6. Richard Layard and his co-authors have illustrated that mental health in childhood is the single biggest cause of later-life unhappiness (Flèche et al., 2019) and that psychological therapy can be hugely effective (Layard & Clark, 2015). Layard has also made an economic case for psychological therapy by demonstrating that the cost of mental illness to the economy far outweighs the cost of psychological therapy to treat it (Layard, 2006). My own research has shown that from a happiness and wellbeing perspective, psychological therapy is one of the best ways a person can spend their money (Boyce & Wood, 2010) and that one reason mental health is

chronically underfunded relative to physical health is because people underestimate how debilitating a mental health struggle can be for their wellbeing (Murphy et al. 2020).

7. There are countless books illustrating various techniques as to how people can be persuaded to act in the interests of the persuader rather than their own interests. One classic is *Influence: The Psychology of Persuasion* (Cialdini, 2007). Another, and one of my favourites, because it helped my younger self who wanted to understand people is *How to Win Friends and Influence People* (Carnegie, 2006). I won at least three friends from reading that book – possibly more to my own delight than theirs.
8. Dark nudges are designed to exploit peoples' biases. This has been demonstrated to be particularly pervasive in gambling (see Newall, 2019).
9. The documentary *The Social Dilemma* highlights how social media platforms contrive to keep people engaging for longer. This is depicted by Mattha Busby (2018) in the article "Social Media Copies Gambling Methods to Create Psychological Cravings".
10. I always think that if something has to be put in a bright and shiny wrapper, or advertised in order to influence me to purchase it, then it probably isn't going to be that good for me.

Chapter 13: Happiness havens

1. Volunteer opportunities like this are abundant throughout the world, and they are a great way to explore new places and different cultures, learn new ideas, get beyond money, and discover what matters the most in life. Take a look at World Wide Organisation for Organic Farming (WWOOF), help-x, or Workaway, for opportunities.
2. The book *Nonviolent Communication: A Language of Life – Life-Changing Tools for Healthy Relationships* (Rosenberg & Chopra, 2015) revolutionised my life.
3. Here is a link to the short news clip from when I was in Mexico - https://www.youtube.com/watch?v=ie1YZW-44FQ
4. Abraham Maslow proposed the idea that there is a hierarchy of needs in his 1943 research article "A theory of human motivation" (Maslow, 1943). Though it is a dated model, it has been widely influential, and can help a person think about whether and how they are meeting important needs.

Chapter 14: Towards a wellbeing economy

1. You can become a Wellbeing Economy Alliance Citizen today https://citizens.weall.org/signup
2. *The Limits of Growth* (Meadows et al., 1972) ignited debate around infinite growth in a finite world, and offered dire warnings if we did not change course. There are now numerous books arguing that we need to entirely repurpose our societal objectives and get beyond growth. Some of my favourite more recent reads include: *The Economics of Arrival* (Trebeck & Williams, 2019), *Doughnut Economics* (Raworth, 2017), *The Value of Everything* (Mazzucato, 2018).
3. In 2019, the world's 2,153 billionaires had more wealth than 4.6 billion people (Lawson et al., 2020) and those at the top of the income distribution have gained much more than those lower down in recent decades (Mishel et al., 2015).
4. This TED Talk on "Why Governments Should Prioritise Wellbeing" by Scotland's First Minister Nicola Sturgeon is worth a watch – https://www.ted.com/talks/nicola_sturgeon_why_governments_should_prioritize_well_being?language=en
5. Rockström (2009) set out nine interlinked planetary boundaries, three of which had already been overstepped upon publication of their study.
6. The Human Development Index, first compiled in 1990, compares and evaluates a country's development progress with respect to health, education, and income – these are three components considered essential for development in the traditional sense. Recently, however, it was proposed that the Human Development Index ought to also incorporate a country's ecological impact, including average per person of both CO_2 emissions and material footprint, to give a Sustainable Development Index (Hickel, 2020).
7. In their book, *The Economics of Arrival* (2019), Katherine Trebeck and Jeremy Williams, illustrate that growth shouldn't be the goal, highlighting that most growth doesn't benefit our lives, and is often the result of failure demand (fixing harm), defensive expenditures (minimising damage) and consolation goods (making us feel better because of how terrible the economy makes us feel). They advocate that many economies are big enough and should concentrate on 'making themselves at home' – that is, meeting needs without putting undue pressure on other people or the ecosystem.

8. There are countless indicators of societal progress (see Hoekstra, 2019 for an overview and why these need to be synthesised for progress), but the Genuine Progress Indicator is worth highlighting here, to emphasise this point about progress over time. The Genuine Progress Indicator incorporates environmental and social costs in its calculation of economic activity. What is striking is that in many 'developed' countries, the Genuine Progress Indicator has stagnated since the 1970s.
9. The Office for National Statistics asks these questions routinely. Sometimes their reporting is questionable. They tend to focus on the proportion of people scoring above a certain threshold, for example, the proportion scoring 8 or more. If the proportion of those experiencing misery also increases, then this doesn't show up when those scoring higher than 8 is reported. It can mask inequalities, which may be a political choice. Is it more important to reduce misery, or to increase the happiness of the already-quite-happy?

Chapter 15: Alone and broken

1. Loneliness is prevalent across all age groups, and is associated with depression and poor physical health. For those in mid and later life, the quality of social engagement is protective against loneliness, while for young adults it is the quantity of social engagement (Victor & Yang, 2012).
2. Many of Carl Rogers' ideas are embodied in his book *On Becoming a Person* (Rogers, 1967) – not always the easiest of reads, but containing some wonderful insights about the human condition. For example, "The degree to which I can create relationships, which facilitate the growth of others as separate persons, is a measure of the growth I have achieved in myself."
3. One of my most influential pieces of research was to show that money's ability to bring happiness depends to a large extent on how our income ranks in comparison to others (Boyce et al., 2010). And even then, the happiness improvement isn't very large at all (Boyce et al., 2017).

Chapter 16: A life on purpose

1. Quote by Mooji is (c) Mooji Media Ltd (2010), www.mooji.org.
2. Somewhere on the west coast of the USA, some people took a photo of me cycling along, and then searched my hashtag to try and get in contact.

Their search revealed that it was not only me who was having Adventures In Happiness. Though I'd been writing a blog under this title for years, someone had written a book with the same title (Clarke, 2018). With hindsight I wished I'd used a Journey for Happiness hashtag all along. I suppose when I started, it was more a case of smaller adventures rather than a wider journey, so it made sense at the time.

3. One of my more popular articles, 'However you spend it, money isn't the key to happiness' (Boyce, 2014) had over 20,000 views in less than a week when it was first written, and still gets several thousand views a year.
4. The article I wrote called 'Why I quit my day job researching happiness and started cycling to Bhutan' (Boyce, 2018) has to date received over 50,000 views.
5. There are many books in Psychology describing flourishing. Martin Seligman, the pioneer of positive psychology, has written one of the most influential books on the topic, *Flourish: A Visionary New Understanding of Happiness and Well-Being* (Seligman, 2012).
6. This was the second research article I began working on as a PhD student (Boyce & Oswald, 2012), and the research was picked up in newspapers all over the world, from the *Daily Mail* and the *Times Education Supplement* to the *Japan Times* and *African Voice*. I also did some radio in the UK.
7. Each time I published an interesting piece of research, I issued a press release. Some of them would attract wider attention, others not. Some of the most notable media mentions of my research have been in *Time* ('Money isn't everything – but status is!', Park, 2010; 'How being unemployed changes your personality', Worland, 2015) and *Scientific American* ('Life satisfaction linked to personality changes', Rodriguez, 2013).
8. The high relationship between meaning in life and aspects of happiness is consistent across age groups (Steger et al., 2009).
9. As Paul Dolan explains in his book *Happiness by Design* (Dolan, 2014), we need both pleasure and purpose in our daily lives. Often the amount of pleasure and purpose a person has can be out of balance, and re-balancing would bring more overall happiness.
10. In Chapter 13: Happiness Havens, I showed that my hedonic happiness when I stayed in hotels was lower than when I camped or stayed with people I met (6.5 versus 7.5/7.7); this was also the case for this eudaimonic kind of happiness (8.1 versus 8.8/9.0).

Chapter 17: The end in sight

1. I didn't do many personal videos on my journey as I prefer words but here are a couple from around this time. "Day 419 – somewhere in China with Christmas approaching" – https://www.youtube.com/watch?v=oX3NSMu2gCQ&t=84s "The end in sight" – https://www.youtube.com/watch?v=N4y9R6nXbdw
2. Thích Nhat Hanh was exiled from his native Vietnam for almost four decades. He spent most of his life at Plumb Village in France.
3. I started reading *The Way of Zen* (Watts, 1999) when I was in Canada – the book has influenced my journey profoundly.
4. I've never got my head around the morals of visiting countries with appalling human rights records. I'd journeyed through the US and China, but Myanmar seemed a stretch too far for me.
5. There are a number of studies highlighting that economic growth has been accompanied by declining happiness (Brockmann et al., 2009; Graham et al., 2017).
6. One of my most influential papers, questioning the fixed nature of personality, was written with Nattavudh Powdthavee (Boyce, Wood, Powdthavee, 2013).
7. Both *Natives: Race and Class in the Ruins of Empire* (Akala, 2019) and *Why I've Stopped Talking to White People About Race* (Eddo-Lodge, 2020) are excellent reads about race in the UK.
8. An RCT is an acronym for a Randomised Control Trial. An RCT is a scientific experiment where people are randomly selected into a control or treatment group, and the difference in outcomes observed.

Chapter 18: One final challenge

1. There is a video kicking about of me, freshly shaved, mid-ascent of the mountain to that blissful spot – https://www.youtube.com/watch?v=bFediFf-47c

Chapter 19: A happy human? On a happy day? In a happy place?

1. As alluded to elsewhere in the book, valuing happiness can leave people feeling disappointed when they don't achieve it (Mauss et al., 2011).

2. Curiously, however, Bhutan does have a very low happiness inequality – in the 2016 World Happiness Report, it was the lowest in the world. This means they have lower overall happiness variation (less extremes). It has also been shown that happiness inequality is a better predictor of overall happiness than income inequality (Helliwell et al., 2016).

Epilogue: A journey for all journeys

1. I shared an article on my blog soon after returning about the three most important things I learnt about happiness from cycling to Bhutan https://adventuresinhappinessblog.wordpress.com/2019/06/05/the-3-most-important-things-i-learnt-about-happiness-from-cycling-to-bhutan/
2. From 'Ode' by Arthur O'Shaughnessy.

Acknowledgements

Where to begin with acknowledging those that made this journey and the book that came from it possible? I mean, everyone played their part in some way, simply because we are all connected and interdependent. Our journeys necessarily intertwine, and it has been the forgetting of that which has taken me further away from happiness. That being said, there were a fair number of people that had a profound influence on this journey – whether it be starting it off, taking it in new and inspiring directions, or helping me turn it into a book.

There were those that were integral to me embarking on the journey in the first place. Matt Hopwood is at the top of that list. There were times I would shake my fist at an imagined version of him by the side of the road, for planting within me the seed of what would often seemed like too ridiculous an idea. Yet, he gave unerring support along the way and has continued to do so ever since. I'd also like to give special thanks to Mike Hogan, a faithful friend and academic, who never thought what I was doing was absurd. He was supportive and honest the whole way through; from the day I set out, until the writing and publication of this book. No doubt he'll invite me to dinner in Galway at some point, to commemorate the publication of this book and then give a talk to his Psychology students. I can't wait.

Then there were those that helped and supported unconditionally along the way. Thanks, in particular, go to Christos, Amy, Mark, Till, JaeAnn, Lee, Maria and Mike, for taking care of the few possessions I left behind when I set out, and their support ever since. This was more than just looking after a few material things – it was an emotional and spiritual holding, for which I am eternally grateful. There are countless friends too that were present, often there with an ear to support a troubled boy when he needed them – Susanna, Nadine, Clare, Gavin, Kat, and Jennifer. Thank you – even if we no longer speak, I won't forget your love. There were also two of the dearest souls, Saule and Géraldine, with whom I sat on beaches, on boats, and by rivers, unencumbered by modern technologies, sharing my heart through hand-written letters. One of those souls was key to resurrecting this journey at all the crucial points when it was in serious threat of going under. The life we share goes beyond words.

There were all those that I met along the way, who brought real joy to my life, and thoughts of them still does. There is my Dalkhola friend Bholu, and all those he introduced me to; Francine, Sara, Mati, Eva, and the entire Lampa crew; Martha, Alejandra, part of the sweetest Mexican family in the world; Anando and his family, Judd, Juan, Lisa, Peter, Alisoun, Tom, Kathy, all my Warmshowers hosts along the way, and the countless unnamed. There are simply too many of you to mention. Thanks to those that offered a passing smile and a twinkle of the eye that helped remind me of the magic and wonder of being alive. And thanks to Clément Mas for the use of TravelMap throughout my journey. In Bhutan, I had invaluable help and guidance from Sangay Thsering, founder of Nobventure, and Kunzang Namgyel. They are amazing guides, and I'd recommend journeying with them, if you ever find yourself in Bhutan.

There are my brothers – my blood brother, Nick, who will always be journeying with me in my heart – as well as the sacred hoop brothers – Asa, Atif, James, John, Rory, and Matt, who have never wavered in their support for me. I love these men.

As for getting this book to print, that has been the toughest journey of all, but it's been kept on course by some wise ones. Amy Wade helped give me early confidence in my prose, and helped me hone the relatability of my story. Her critical feedback on early chapters was crucial. My editor, Is Andrews has also been invaluable in getting this book out to the world. She has made it look like I write far better than I do. Thanks also go to Jennie Renton and Madeleine Mankey for guiding me through the printing process, typesetting, and proofing: it all went rather smoothly! For advice at various stages of the process I thank John Clarke, Robbie Sage, and Nick Tipple. Thanks also to Darren Hilliard for the final glance over, as well as everybody who read a chapter and whose comments pulled me out of a mid-way slump.

A beyond-words thank you to Katie Sykes for the cover design. Worth judging this book by it; it would be fair to say that without it we would have struggled to have made the crowdfund target, and this book wouldn't be in the hands that are holding it now.

Similarly, for help with the crowdfund and her enduring support at all levels of 'the journey', Saule Zukaityte (aka the sugar-tight soul), who not only helped me get all the videos edited, but gave my photos a little more respectability.

Thanks again to everyone who supported the crowdfund, and helped me find enthusiasm for sharing this journey wider, despite a time of setbacks. Particular thanks for getting this book to print via the crowdfund go to Pyramid Cycle Design, a small business in Coventry, UK, owned by long-time triathlon friends Anna Wordsworth and Mark Pharaoh. Pyramid Cycle Design (PCD) were big sponsors of this book and vital in giving the book its initial impetus. PCD designs & manufactures chainrings & other bespoke cycle parts for road, track, time trialling and cyclocross. PCD supplies products to cyclists and triathletes at every level of the sport, from recreational participants to Olympic and Paralympic medallists and national, European and World Champions (www.pyramidcycledesign.co.uk). Special thanks, with some names repeated, go to Nadine Ansorg, Mark Baugh, Graeme Blackett, Nick Boyce, David Comerford, Nikita Goud, Michael Hogan, JaeAnn Huh, Nikki Kenn, The Kennedys, Till Kroeber, Jan-Emmanuel De Neve, Bernardo Nunes, Florian Sturm, and Wellington College, for their generous contributions to the crowdfund. Thanks also to friends Emilia, Gwen, and Silke for their continued encouragement and helping me to reach new audiences.

Thanks also go to friends at the Wellbeing Economy Alliance, particularly Katherine Trebeck, Amanda Janoo, and Claire Sommer, for their continued encouragement and support. And, not least, thank you to Charlie, Freyja, Scally, Minouche, Freddie, Hector, and Mabel for sleeping by my feet and only asking for food, biscuits, strokes, and regular walks, as I typed away most of this manuscript on cold and dark lonely days in the winter of 2019/2020, while their owners were off on holiday. Then there is my father; oh, my father. This book is one long letter to him, to finally thank him for bringing me into this world. He might not see it that way himself, but hey, I love him, and that's always enough. And lastly thank you, the reader. For if there were no reader, then there would be no-one with whom to share either my gratitude, or my happiness.

About the author

Christopher Boyce is a happiness and wellbeing expert. He trained as an economist (BSc, MSc) and went on to explore the links between the economy and wellbeing, completing a PhD in Psychology in 2009. He has worked at various academic institutions, including the University of Warwick, Paris School of Economics, the University of Manchester, and the University of Stirling, where he still has an honorary position. He has published more than 25 peer-reviewed academic papers on happiness and wellbeing, and has written numerous media articles on the topic. He is involved in local, national, and international wellbeing policy discussions, and both a Wellbeing Economy Alliance Research Fellow and a member of the World Wellbeing Panel. He is interested in contributing to the creation of conditions that foster individual & societal wellbeing. He currently lives in the Scottish Borders, where he works supporting community mental health. When he isn't working or cycling he can sometimes be found on Twitter.

Twitter: @drhappyboyce #JourneyForHappiness
Website: https://journeyforhappiness.co.uk/